Reproductive Epidemiology
Principles and Methods

Ray M. Merrill, PhD, MPH, MS
Professor
Department of Health Science
Brigham Young University
Provo, Utah

JONES AND BARTLETT PUBLISHERS
Sudbury, Massachusetts
BOSTON   TORONTO   LONDON   SINGAPORE

World Headquarters

Jones and Bartlett Publishers
40 Tall Pine Drive
Sudbury, MA 01776
978-443-5000
info@jbpub.com
www.jbpub.com

Jones and Bartlett Publishers
Canada
6339 Ormindale Way
Mississauga, Ontario L5V 1J2
Canada

Jones and Bartlett Publishers
International
Barb House, Barb Mews
London W6 7PA
United Kingdom

Jones and Bartlett's books and products are available through most bookstores and online booksellers. To contact Jones and Bartlett Publishers directly, call 800-832-0034, fax 978-443-8000, or visit our website, www.jbpub.com.

Production Credits
Publisher: Michael Brown
Editorial Assistant: Catie Heverling
Editorial Assistant: Teresa Reilly
Senior Production Editor: Tracey Chapman
Associate Production Editor: Kate Stein
Senior Marketing Manager: Sophie Fleck
Manufacturing and Inventory Control Supervisor: Amy Bacus
Composition: Achorn International
Art: diacriTech
Cover Design: Scott Moden
Cover Image: © Sebastian Kaulitzki/ShutterStock, Inc.
Printing and Binding: Malloy, Inc.
Cover Printing: Malloy, Inc.

Library of Congress Cataloging-in-Publication Data
Merrill, Ray.
    Reproductive epidemiology : principles and methods / Ray Merrill.
        p. ; cm.
    Includes bibliographical references and index.
    ISBN-13: 978-0-7637-5869-1 (pbk.)
    ISBN-10: 0-7637-5869-8 (pbk.)
    1. Reproductive health. 2. Epidemiology. 3. Generative organs—Diseases—Epidemiology. I. Title.
    [DNLM: 1. Genital Diseases, Female—epidemiology—Problems and Exercises. 2. Epidemiologic Methods—Problems and Exercises. 3. Pregnancy Complications—epidemiology—Problems and Exercises.
WP 140 M571r 2010]
    RA652.M47 2010
    614.4—dc22   2009019491

6048

Printed in the United States of America
13 12 11 10 09   10 9 8 7 6 5 4 3 2 1

In Memory of Rose and Martell Hodson

TABLE OF CONTENTS

CHAPTER 5
Descriptive Reproductive Health Indicators   111

CHAPTER 6
Study Designs in Reproductive Epidemiology   133

SECTION II
Applications of Reproductive Epidemiology

CHAPTER 8
Nutrition and Reproductive Health   163

CHAPTER 9
Contraception and Reproductive Health   179

CHAPTER 10
Mercury, Lead, Environmental Estrogens, and Reproductive Health   199

CHAPTER 13

Cancer Risk Associated With Early and Late Maternal Age at First Birth   263

APPENDIX I

Classification of Selected Measures of Association and Statistical Tests According to Variable Type   279

ABOUT THE AUTHOR

Ray M. Merrill, PhD, MPH, MS has been actively involved in epidemiology since his professional career began in 1995. As a Cancer Prevention Fellow at the National Cancer Institute, he worked with leading researchers in the area of cancer epidemiology. In 1998, he joined the faculty in the Department of Health Science at Brigham Young University, Provo, Utah, where he continued his research in epidemiology. Since 1999, he has also held an adjunct faculty position in the Department of Family and Preventive Medicine at the University of Utah. In 2001, he spent a sabbatical working in the Unit of Epidemiology for Cancer Prevention at the International Agency for Research on Cancer Administration, Lyon, France. He has won various awards for his research in epidemiology and is currently a Fellow of the American College of Epidemiology. He teaches various classes in epidemiology and biostatistics and is the author of over 150 peer-reviewed publications. Dr. Merrill is currently a full professor of epidemiology and biostatistics at Brigham Young University.

PREFACE

The branch of epidemiology that involves reproduction is called reproductive epidemiology. The primary aim of reproductive epidemiology is to describe and provide information about the distribution and determinants of reproductive-related health states or events in human populations. The application of this study is intended to promote complete physical, mental, social, spiritual, emotional, and environmental health as they relate to the reproductive health system and its functions and processes.

This book introduces epidemiology students and health practitioners to a range of methods used to collect data and conduct analysis in reproductive epidemiology. The focus is to provide a guide on the use of methods appropriate for challenging and sensitive research topics, which include sexual behavior, abortion, illicit drug use, and sexual abuse. The latter part of the book involves application of these methods to specific conditions associated with reproduction.

This book was written as an introductory text for the student who has minimal training in the biomedical sciences and statistics. Epidemiology is unique from biostatistics and in that emphasis is placed on completing the causal picture. Identifying causal factors and modes of transmission, with the assistance of statistical tools and biomedical information, reflects a primary focus in this book.

This book is divided into two sections: Section I, "Foundations and Methods in Reproductive Epidemiology," and Section II, "Applications of Reproductive Epidemiology." Section I consists of Chapters 1 through 7. Chapter 1 presents the foundations of reproductive epidemiology, including definitions, concepts, and applications of the field. How reproductive epidemiology contributes to public health is addressed. Chapter 2 considers the full range of existing environments as they relate to reproduction: the physical, chemical, biological, and psychosocial environments; the inner versus outer environment; the personal versus ambient environment; and the solid, liquid, and gaseous environments. Chapter 3 presents the different phases of the research process in the context of reproductive health. Chapter 4 develops public health surveillance for monitoring birth defects and other reproductive disorders. Chapter 5 presents a number of health indicators commonly used for characterizing various dimensions of reproductive health. Chapter 6 presents several design strategies and statistical measures for investigating reproductive health problems. Selected challenges sometimes encountered in applying these study designs in human reproduction are considered. Chapter 7 presents selected concepts in causal theory and criteria for establishing cause–effect associations. Section II consists of Chapters 8 through 13. Chapter 8 focuses on the association between malnutrition (overnutrition and undernutrition) during pregnancy and reproductive health problems. Chapter 9 addresses issues associated with contraception in selected regions throughout the world. Chapter 10 provides an in-depth assessment of the influence mercury, lead, and environmental estrogen exposure has on reproductive health. Chapter 11 examines associations between marriage and health, clinical abortions and health, and female circumcision practices and health. Chapter 12 presents maternal health, social, and economic consequences associated with early age at first birth. Chapter 13 addresses the risk of selected cancers in the mother associated with early and late maternal age at first birth.

ONE

Foundations and Methods in Reproductive Epidemiology

ONE

Foundations of Reproductive Epidemiology

Learning Objectives

After completing this chapter, you should be able to:

1. Define and describe reproductive epidemiology.
2. Discuss the scientific method as it relates to reproductive epidemiology.
3. Discuss ways reproductive epidemiology contributes to public health.

Human health is complex and involves multiple factors. In 1948, the World Health Organization defined **health** as "a state of complete physical, mental and social well-being and not merely the absence of disease or infirmity."[1] This definition identified physical, social, and mental dimensions of health as indicators of the functionality of an individual. Later, emotional, spiritual, and environmental dimensions of health were added to the definition. The six dimensions of health are described as follows:

Physical—The ability of the human body structure to function properly
Social—The ability to interact with other individuals

Mental—The ability to process information and act properly

Emotional—The ability to cope, adjust, and adapt

Spiritual—A belief in some force or dynamic other than humans

Environmental—External conditions and influences affecting life and development

A number of health surveys and health indicators have been developed to monitor and assess these various dimensions of health. These are addressed in later chapters.

Public health is concerned with the overall health of a community. The mission of public health is to ensure conditions that promote the dimensions of health in the community as a whole. In order to fulfill this mission, three core public health functions have been established, which are:

1. Assessing and monitoring the health of populations at risk and identifying health problems and priorities.
2. Formulating of policies and priorities designed to solve identified health problems.
3. Assuring that all populations have access to appropriate and cost-effective care, including prevention, protection, and health promotion services.[2]

Epidemiology is the basic science of public health, providing the tools for monitoring and evaluating the facts that enable public health officials to identify public health problems and plan and evaluate intervention control measures.

Reproductive health is an important area of public health that is related to each of the six dimensions of health. In 1994, the International Conference on Population Development and the World Conference on Women defined **reproductive health** as a "state of complete physical, mental and social well-being in all matters relating to the reproductive system and to its functions and processes."[3] In other words, reproductive health is a primary component of general health, influencing physical and mental health, human development, and personal relationships at all stages of life. It may also influence emotional, spiritual, and environmental aspects of our lives. Implicit in the definition of reproductive health is the right of men and women to receive effective and affordable family planning, skilled attendance at delivery, and timely emergency obstetric care when complications arise. Reproductive health care also includes sexual health, the purpose of which is the enhancement of life and personal relationships.

Although men may experience reproductive health problems, women bear a far greater burden of such problems, including complications from pregnancy and childbirth, risks associated with birth control, complications from unsafe abortions, contraception use, reproductive tract infections, sexually transmitted diseases, and complications from treatments for maternal and infant complications.

In this book we explore the role of epidemiology in reproductive health. The purpose of this first chapter is to define reproductive epidemiology and present how it contributes to public health.

What Is Epidemiology?

Epidemiology has a long history, with many key individuals contributing to its development. Hippocrates (460–377 BC), a Greek physician who became known as the father of medicine, attempted to explain how diseases affect people and how they spread. He observed that diseases were related to time, season, place, and environmental conditions. He referred to the condition in which disease occurred more frequently than expected as an **epidemic** and the ongoing, expected frequency of disease as **endemic**.[4–7] Thomas Sydenham (1624–1689), an English physician, described and distinguished different diseases, including some psychological maladies. He also promoted useful treatments and remedies, including exercise, fresh air, and a healthy diet, which physicians rejected at the time.[7] James Lind (1716–1794), an English physician, pioneered naval hygiene in the Royal Navy and advanced the idea that citrus fruit was protective against scurvy, on the basis of experimental investigation.[8] Finally, John Snow (1813–1858) became known as the father of epidemiology because of his observational investigative studies of cholera. He used both descriptive and analytic epidemiologic methods to identify contaminated water as the source of cholera outbreaks in London in the mid-1800s.[9]

The word epidemiology is based on the Greek words *epi*, a prefix meaning "on, upon, or befall"; *demos*, a root meaning "the people"; and *logos*, a suffix meaning "the study of." In medical terminology, the suffix is read first, and the prefix is followed by the root. Hence, epidemiology literally means the study of that which befalls the people. The modern definition of **epidemiology** is the study of the distribution and determinants of health-related states or events in specified populations, and the application of this study to control for health problems.[10] Thus, epidemiology is the process of defining, classifying, or categorizing health-related states or events and their connections with potential causes, identifying causal associations and providing a basis for predicting the effects of certain exposures, and using this information to improve the health and social conditions of people.

To better understand the definition of epidemiology, consider the word **study**, which implies the use of sound methods of scientific investigation, where **methods** are rules or procedures employed in order to accomplish a task. A number of study designs and statistical methods are used to this end. The word **distribution** refers to the frequency and pattern of health-related states or events. **Frequency** refers to the number of cases or events. This number is often divided by the population at risk of becoming a case in order to obtain a rate, which is a more appropriate measure of risk. **Pattern** is a description of the reproductive health-related states or events by *who* is experiencing the problem (person), *where* the problem occurs most or least (place), and *when* the problem occurs most or least (time). The term **health-related state or event** refers to the fact that epidemiology involves more than just the study of disease states (e.g., influenza, human immunodeficiency syndrome, and cancer), but also includes the study of events (e.g., injury, homicide, drug abuse), behaviors, and conditions associated with health (e.g., diet, contraceptive use, nutrition, physical activity). Finally, **application** refers to the fact that the information obtained through epidemiology is then applied to better prevent and control health problems in human populations.

Like public health, epidemiology has a population focus. Epidemiologic investigations are directed toward populations, not individuals. For example, is there an excess of infant deaths above what is expected in Zambia (epidemic)? Or is the frequency of infant death what is normally expected (endemic)? If an epidemic in infant deaths is established, the epidemiologic investigation then seeks to characterize the problem according to person, place, and time factors, which may provide important clues as to the cause of the public health problem.

Like the word epidemic, **outbreak** also means an excess of the health-related state or event above what is expected; however, the word outbreak is typically used when a more limited geographic area is involved. In addition, the word outbreak may be less alarming to the public than epidemic.

What Is the Scientific Method?

Epidemiology uses the scientific method to describe and analyze reproductive health-related states or events. The **scientific method** refers to the techniques used for investigating an observable occurrence and acquiring new knowledge. It involves collecting data through observation or experiment, identifying a problem, formulating hypotheses that attempt to characterize some phenomena, and testing the hypotheses. Study designs and statistical methods are selected and employed to test research hypotheses. In hypothesis testing, information is used in a sample of observations, and the results either support or fail to support the research hypothesis.

The presence of a reproductive health problem is established through descriptive epidemiologic methods, which involve observation, definitions, measurements, interpretations, and dissemination. Once the research problem is established, hypotheses are then formulated to explain observed and measured associations with the population of interest. Hypotheses are tested using appropriate analytic epidemiologic study designs and statistical methods. Statistical analyses are then followed by interpretation and dissemination of the health findings.

What Is Reproductive Epidemiology?

Reproductive epidemiology is simply the area of epidemiology concerned with reproduction. **Reproduction**, which is fundamental to all known life, is the biological process by which organisms produce offspring.[11] Thus, **reproductive epidemiology** is the study of the distribution and determinants of health-related states or events in human populations and the application of this study to promote complete physical, mental, and social well-being as they relate to the reproductive system and to its functions and processes.

Reproductive Epidemiology in Public Health

Providing epidemiologic information useful for improving reproductive health may be considered a basic human right that is essential for empowering women. Such information plays a vital role in reducing poverty, increasing economic growth and female productivity, lowering infertility, and improving maternal health and child survival. Both public health and individual decision making rely on epidemiologic information for making informed choices. Information useful for public health and individual decision making is obtained by:

- Identifying risk factors for reproductive health-related states or events.
- Identifying individuals and populations at greatest risk for reproductive health-related states or events.
- Providing an understanding of the critical window of vulnerability.
- Identifying where the public health problem is greatest.
- Monitoring the extent of the reproductive health-related states or events over time.
- Identifying the urgency with which the reproductive health-related states or events need to be addressed.
- Evaluating the efficacy and effectiveness of prevention and treatment programs.
- Providing information useful for improving reproductive health.
  - Family planning to reduce unintended pregnancies
  - Contraceptive safety and efficacy
  - Maternal morbidity and mortality
  - Perinatal and infant health
  - Sexually transmitted diseases
  - Resource allocation

The means by which this information is obtained is through application of an epidemiologic study design. An epidemiologic study design is a plan or detailed approach for obtaining information. Epidemiologic study designs are classified as descriptive and analytic. The descriptive epidemiologic study design is used to describe the public health problem according to person, place, and time. In reproductive epidemiology, for example, it is the means by which we identify individuals and populations at greatest risk for unwanted fertility, high maternal morbidity and mortality, poor sexual health, and inadequate access to and utilization of prenatal care and birth-planning methods. It is also a means for identifying where the health problem is greatest and whether the problem is changing over time. In contrast, the analytic epidemiologic study design provides the tools for determining risk factors and the efficacy and effectiveness of prevention and treatment programs. Specific types of descriptive and analytic study designs used in reproductive epidemiology are presented in Chapter 6, "Study Designs in Reproductive Epidemiology."

Selected examples of what we know about reproductive health because of epidemiology are as follows:

- Approximately 250 million years of productive life are lost each year because of reproductive health problems.

- Over 500,000 women die annually from pregnancy-related causes, whereas millions suffer related disabilities.[12]

- Maternal mortality is the leading cause of death for women ages 15–44 years.

- For every one of these women who die, 15 to 30 experience debilitating injury.

- About 75 million unplanned pregnancies occur each year, with roughly a third resulting in an unsafe abortion.

- All women, both rich and poor, face about a 15% risk of complications at delivery.[13]

- Babies born to adolescent girls compared with older women are 50% more likely to die within a year from birth. Adolescent girls have a greater risk of premature delivery and obstructed labor, which are both primary causes of infant death.[14]

- Women in developing countries bear a disproportionately greater burden of reproductive health problems (see **Table 1-1**). For example, in the developed world, there are approximately 14 maternal deaths per 100,000 live births compared with 472 in Cambodia, 130 in Vietnam, and 44 in Thailand.[15,16] Approximately 99% of all maternal deaths occur in developing countries.[17,18]

- The comparatively high maternal mortality rates in developing countries are primarily the result of poor access to family planning to reduce unintended pregnancies, unskilled attendance at delivery, and a lack of timely emergency obstetric care when complications arise.[16,19]

- Poor access to family planning is a primary reason for about 76 million unintended pregnancies each year in developing countries.[20]

TABLE 1-1   **Maternal Mortality Ratio and Lifetime Risk of Maternal Death, 2000**

Region	Maternal Deaths Per 100,000 Live Births	Lifetime Risk of Maternal Death, 1 in
World	400	74
Developed regions	14	3,800
Commonwealth of independent states	68	820
Developing regions	450	60
Northern Africa	130	210
Sub-Saharan Africa	920	16
Latin America and the Caribbean	190	160
Eastern Asia	55	840
Southern Asia	540	44
Southeastern Asia	210	140
Western Asia	190	110
Oceania	240	83

Source: World Health Organization/United Nations Children's Fund, Maternal Mortality in 2000: Estimates developed by WHO, UNICEF, UNFPA. Available at http://www.unfpa.org/publications/detail.cfm?ID=160&filterLisType=4. Accessed December 29, 2008.

- Roughly 19 to 20 million unsafe abortions are performed annually, causing 68,000 deaths each year.[21]

- Approximately one in 10 pregnancies will result in an unsafe abortion, with the highest numbers in Asia, Africa, and Latin America.[21]

- Because up to 15% of all births are complicated by problems that can be fatal, availability of skilled attendance at all births is a critical intervention in order to recognize problems early, and to control, manage, or stabilize problems.[22]

- A mother's death can be devastating for a surviving child who faces a greater chance of poor health, poverty, and exploitation without the mother's protection and love. If the mother survives but is disabled, her contribution to the family and economy diminishes, and the struggle against poverty is weakened. For every woman who dies in childbirth, roughly 20 women suffer from serious injury or disability because of complications related to pregnancy and childbirth.[13]

- Some success has been observed in lowering maternal mortality in developing countries over past decades. For example, in Matlab, Bangladesh, improved access to surgical obstetric care and other maternal health services led to a significant decline from 600 maternal deaths per 100,000 live births in 1976 to 200 in 2001.[12] Bangladesh and Thailand also stand as examples of developing countries that have met and even exceeded the Millennium Development Goal to reduce maternal mortality by 75% between 1990 and 2015.[12]

Conclusion

The area of epidemiology that involves reproduction is called reproductive epidemiology. Reproductive epidemiology provides useful information about the distribution and determinants of reproductive-related health states or events in human populations. The application of this study is intended to promote complete physical, mental, social, spiritual, emotional, and environmental health as they relate to the reproductive health system and to its functions and processes.

Key Issues

1. This chapter provides a foundation for exploring how reproductive epidemiology contributes to public health.
2. Reproductive epidemiology is the study of the distribution and determinants of health-related states or events in human populations and the application of this study to promote complete physical, mental, and social well-being as they relate to the reproductive system and to its functions and processes.
3. Reproductive epidemiologic studies contribute to public health by (1) identifying risk factors, (2) identifying individuals and populations at greatest risk, (3) providing an understanding of the critical window of vulnerability, (4) identifying where the public health problem is greatest, (5) monitoring the extent of the public health problem, (6) identifying the urgency with which the problem needs to be addressed, (7) evaluating the efficacy and effectiveness of prevention and treatment programs, and (8) providing information useful in family planning and healthcare management.

Exercises

Key Terms

Define the following terms.

Application

Distribution

Epidemiology

Endemic

Epidemic

Frequency

Health

Health-related state or event

Methods

Outbreak

Pattern

Public health

Reproduction

Reproductive epidemiology

Reproductive health

Scientific method

Study

Study Questions

1.1   How does epidemiology enable the fulfillment of the three core public health functions presented in the outset of this chapter?

1.2   Describe the primary purpose of reproductive epidemiology.

1.3   In this chapter, we noted that epidemiology uses the scientific method. Explain.

1.4   How does reproductive epidemiology contribute to public health?

References

1. World Health Organization. National mental health policy 2001–2005. Available at: http://www.searo.who.int/LinkFiles/On-going_projects_Indo_MHP-2001.pdf. Accessed March 2001.
2. MedicineNet.com. The definition of public health page. Available at: http://www.medterms.com/script/main/art.asp?articlekey=5120. Accessed November 13, 2008.
3. Association of Reproductive Health Professionals. Position statements. Available at: http://www.arhp.org/aboutarhp/positionstatements.cfm?ID=30. Accessed January 2, 2008.
4. Hippocrates. Airs, waters, places. In: Buck C, Llopis A, Najera E, Terris M, eds. *The Challenge of Epidemiology: Issues and Selected Readings*. Washington, DC: World Health Organization; 1988:18–19.
5. *Dorland's Illustrated Medical Dictionary*, 25th ed. Philadelphia, PA: Saunders; 1974.
6. Cumston CG. *An Introduction to the History of Medicine*. New York, NY: Alfred A. Knopf; 1926.
7. Garrison FH. *History of Medicine*. Philadelphia, PA: Saunders; 1926.

8. Lilienfeld AM, Lilienfeld DE. *Foundations of Epidemiology*, 2nd ed. New York, NY: Oxford; 1980:30–31.
9. Snow J. *On the Mode of Communication of Cholera*, 2nd ed. 1855. Reprinted by Commonwealth Fund, New York; 1936. Snow J. On the mode of communication of cholera. In: Buck C, Llopis A, Najera E, Terris M, eds. *The Challenge of Epidemiology: Issues and Selected Readings*. Washington, DC: World Health Organization; 1988:42–45.
10. Last JM, ed. *A Dictionary of Epidemiology*, 3rd ed. New York, NY: Oxford University Press; 1995.
11. Stedman TL. *Stedman's Medical Dictionary for the Health Professions and Nursing*, 5th ed. New York, NY: Lippincott, Williams & Wilkins; 2005.
12. Ronsmans C, Graham W. Maternal mortality: Who, when, where, and why. *The Lancet*. 2006;368:1189–1200.
13. United Nations Population Fund. Reproductive fact sheet, 2005. Available at: http://www.unfpa.org/swp/2005/presskit/factsheets/facts_rh.htm. Accessed November 14, 2008.
14. United Nations. *The Millennium Development Goals Report, 2005*. New York, NY: United Nations; 2005.
15. National Institute of Public Health, National Institute of Statistics [Cambodia] and ORC Macro. *Cambodia Demographic and Health Survey 2005*. Phnom Penh, Cambodia and Calverton, MD: National Institute of Public Health, National Institute of Statistics and ORC Macro; 2006.
16. Nanda G, Switlick K, Lule E. Accelerating progress towards achieving the MDG to improve maternal health: a collection of promising approaches. Health, Nutrition, and Population: The World Bank; 2005. Available at: http://siteresources.worldbank.org/HEALTHNUTRITIONANDPOPULATION/Resources/281627-1095698140167/NandaAcceleratingProgresswithCover.pdf. Accessed November 14, 2008.
17. AbouZahr C, Wardlaw T. *Maternal Mortality in 2000: Estimates Developed by WHO, UNICEF, and UNFPA in 2000*. Geneva, Switzerland: World Health Organization; 2004.
18. World Health Organization/United Nations Children's Fund. Maternal mortality in 2000: Estimates developed by WHO, UNICEF, UNFPA. Available at: http://www.unfpa.org/publications/detail.cfm?ID=160&filterListType=4. Accessed December 29, 2008.
19. Yanagisawa S, Oum S, Wakai S. Determinants of skilled birth attendance in rural Cambodia. *Trop Med Int Health*. 2006;2:238–225.
20. Singh S, Darroch JE, Vlassoff M, Nadeau J. *Adding it Up: The Benefits of Investing in Sexual and Reproductive Health Care*. Washington, DC and New York, NY: The Alan Guttmacher Institute and UNFPA; 2004.
21. World Health Organization. *Unsafe Abortion: Global and Regional Estimates of Unsafe Abortion and Associated Mortality in 2003*, 4th ed. Geneva, Switzerland: World Health Organization; 2004.
22. United Nations Population Fund. Skilled attendance at birth page. Available at: http://www.unfpa.org/mothers/skilled_att.htm. Accessed November 14, 2008.

TWO

Environments in Reproductive Epidemiology

Learning Objectives

After completing this chapter, you should be able to:

1. Describe how physical, chemical, biological, and psychosocial environments relate to reproductive epidemiology.
2. Describe how the inner versus the outer environments relate to reproductive epidemiology.
3. Describe how personal versus ambient environments relate to reproductive epidemiology.
4. Describe how the solid, liquid, and gaseous environments relate to reproductive epidemiology.
5. Define "systems approach," and describe why it is useful in reproductive epidemiology.
6. Be familiar with selected environmentally related reproductive health problems.

One of the six dimensions of health presented in the previous chapter involves the environment. In a medical sense, the **environment** reflects the aggregate of those external conditions and influences affecting the life and development of an organism.[1] It has also been defined as all that is external to the human host.[2] Epidemiologic research has identified several environments associated with reproductive health. Identifying how selected environments adversely affect reproductive fitness, including sexual behavior, fertility, menstruation, pregnancy outcomes, lactating ability, and sperm count, can enhance strategic thinking and efforts toward mitigating reproductive health problems.

The purpose of this chapter is to consider the full range of existing environments as they relate to reproduction: the physical, chemical, biological, and psychosocial environments; the inner versus outer environment; the personal versus ambient environment; and the solid, liquid, and gaseous environments.

The Physical, Chemical, Biological, and Psychosocial Environments

Exposure to reproductive risk factors before conception may cause reduced fertility, unsuccessful fertilization or implantation, an abnormal fetus, reduced libido, or menstrual dysfunction. Maternal exposure after conception may cause prenatal death, low birth weight, birth defects, developmental or behavioral disabilities, and cancer. A woman may spread a harmful chemical to her child by it crossing the placenta into the growing fetus or by its presence in the fatty breast milk excreted through nursing. For example, alcohol can circulate in the mother's blood, pass through the placenta, and affect the developing fetus. Some reproductive hazards may more directly affect the mother or the fetus such as radiation, which can directly harm a mother's eggs or the fetus.

A number of **physical**, **chemical**, **biological**, and **psychosocial environments** have been associated with adverse reproductive health outcomes (see **Table 2-1**). For example, ionizing radiation can directly harm the developing fetus; some viruses, drugs, and chemicals can influence the health of the mother, which in turn may reduce the supply of nutrients and oxygen to the developing fetus or have a direct influence on the fetus through the mother's blood, and some psychosocial factors such as maternal stress can cause spontaneous abortion or preterm birth.

TABLE 2-1	Environmental Factors That Affect Human Health and Social Well-Being
Physical stresses	Excessive heat, cold, and noise; radiation; vehicular collisions; workplace injuries; and so on
Chemical	Drugs, acids, alkali, heavy metals (lead and mercury), poisons (arsenic), and some enzymes
Biological	Disease-causing infectious agents, pathogens (viruses, bacteria, fungi, parasites)
Psychosocial milieu	Families and households, socioeconomic status, social networks and social support, neighborhoods and communities, formal institutions, and public health policy

Physical

Physical stresses can increase the risk of many reproductive health problems. Physical stresses that increase the risk of spontaneous abortion, for example, include ionizing radiation, noise (>90 dB), heavy physical work, frequent heavy lifting, and prolonged standing. Reduced sperm count is associated with heat and ionizing radiation. Finally, low birth weight is associated with noise (>90 dB), heavy physical work and prolonged standing, and ionizing radiation. Physical factors that can adversely affect paternal and maternal fertility include ionizing radiation and heat.

Noise is a physical stressor that can cause birth defects. In one study involving 132 women working in the metal industry at Valjevo, Serbia, 82 were identified as being exposed to increased noise, while 50 were not in noisy locations. Those working in the noisy environment were significantly more likely to have a miscarriage, low birth weight, and preterm babies.[3] In a case-control study conducted in 29 hospitals in Shanghai, China, with 1,875 perinatal deaths and newborns with birth defects and 1,875 controls, exposure to occupational noise during pregnancy was significantly associated with increased risk of antepartum (predelivery) fetal death.[4] In a prospective study comparing 111 pregnant women exposed to occupational noise with 181 pregnant women with similar work conditions but no noise exposure, researchers discovered that when the noise exposure was at least 90 dB, a decline in birth weight and gestational age resulted.[5]

Different types of radiation create important environments in reproductive health. Ionizing radiation is a physical environment that has sufficient energy to strip away electrons from atoms or to break certain chemical bonds. The fetus is very sensitive to ionizing radiation. Ionizing radiation exposure has been associated with reduced head or brain size, slowed growth, blindness, spina bifida, cleft palate, and mental retardation.[6] Maternal thyroid exposure to diagnostic radiation is associated with a slight reduction in birth weight.[7] Embryo exposure to radio frequency—an extremely low frequency—and intermediate frequency electromagnetic fields has not shown an adverse affect on childhood development.[8]

Scientists estimate that 4 per 1,000 fetuses between 8 and 15 weeks old exposed to 1 REM (a measure of ionizing radiation) will become mentally retarded. Genetic mutation where a parent passes on a genetic error to their child is estimated to occur in about 50 children per million live births when both parents were exposed to 1 REM (Environmental Protection Agency).[9]

Chemical

Some chemicals can adversely influence reproductive fitness, including sexual behavior, fertility, menstruation, pregnancy outcomes, lactating ability, and sperm count. For example, certain cancer treatment drugs can increase the risk of infertility, miscarriage, birth defects, and low birth weight. Certain ethylene glycol ethers such as 2-ethoxyethanol and 2-methoxyethanol can increase the risk of miscarriages. Carbon disulfide can influence menstrual changes, and lead can increase the risk of infertility, miscarriage, low birth weight, and developmental disorders.[10]

The study of adverse effects of chemicals on living organisms is called **toxicology**. The toxic severity of a substance that enters the body is influenced by the route of exposure, duration of exposure, concentration of exposure; rate and amount absorbed; distribution and concentrations within the body, efficiency with which the body changes the substance and the metabolites produced; ability of the substance or metabolites to pass through cell membranes and affect cell components; duration and amount of the substance or metabolites in body tissues; and the rate, amount, and site of departure of the substance or metabolites from the body.

Reproductive toxicology is the occurrence of biologically adverse effects on the reproductive systems of males and females that result from exposure to environmental agents.[11] A related term to reproductive toxicity is developmental toxicity. **Developmental toxicology** is the study of adverse health effects on the developing organism that result after exposure to chemicals leading to death of the developing organism, structural abnormality, altered growth, or functional deficiency.[12] Adverse health effects may be detected at any point over a person's life span. Developmental toxicity may arise from exposure before conception (in either parent), during prenatal development, or postnatal prior to sexual maturation.[13]

Dioxin is a name given to a class of extremely toxic chemicals that are persistent in the environment and can cause hormone disruption. Dioxin can bind to a cell's hormone receptor, thereby modifying the functioning and genetic mechanism of the cell. A wide range of adverse effects may result from exposure, including miscarriages, birth defects, inability to maintain pregnancy, decreased fertility, reduced sperm counts, endometriosis, learning disabilities, immune system suppression, lowered testosterone levels, nerve and blood disorders, and cancer.

Dioxin literally alters the production and function of many different hormones, growth factors, and enzymes. By changing gene functions, genetic diseases may appear. Even a single dose at a very low concentration of dioxin may seriously disrupt normal reproduction in humans. Hence, there is no "threshold" dose.[14]

Dioxin is formed as an unintentional by-product of many industrial processes by burning chlorine-based chemical compounds with hydrocarbons. Waste-burning incinerators and backyard garbage burning are major sources of dioxin pollution. Other sources include paper mills, the production of polyvinyl chloride (PVC) plastics, and the production of certain chlorinated chemicals (e.g., many pesticides), insecticides, and herbicides (weed killers).[14]

Few people in the population are exposed to high levels of dioxins. When people are exposed to dioxins, it tends to be through their diet. More than 95% of dioxin exposure comes through dietary intake of animal fats. Only a small amount of exposure occurs by breathing air containing trace amounts of dioxins on particles and in vapor form, by inadvertently ingesting soil containing dioxins, or by absorbing it through the skin.[15]

Biological

A number of viruses and other disease-causing (infectious) agents have been shown to adversely affect reproductive health. For example, measles, mumps, and rubella are associated with adverse pregnancy outcomes and fetus development. Evidence of congenital defects of rubella virus infection in early pregnancy is related to congenital defects and, if in the first trimester, increased fetal loss. In addition, a significant association between maternal mumps in the first trimester and an increased risk of spontaneous abortion has been observed. Measles and rubella (but not mumps) virus infections are linked to an increased premature birth rate. For all three types of infections occurring in late pregnancy, birth of an infected infant can occur.[16]

Infection can be devastating and hard to treat, but risk reduction is possible. Immunity through earlier exposure or vaccinations can generally make a person risk free for diseases such as hepatitis B, human parvovirus B19, rubella, or chicken pox. Pregnant women without prior immunity need to take precautions to avoid exposure to infected individuals. Good hygienic practices are important to reduce the spread of infectious diseases among children in schools and daycare centers and among adults in a myriad of settings. Safe disposal of needles and bodily fluids is also important to protect against infectious agents found in blood and urine.

Psychosocial

Psychosocial factors have also been associated with adverse reproductive outcomes. For example, spontaneous abortion and menstrual disturbances are related to irregular work hours, and spontaneous abortion and preterm birth have been associated with stress. Stress and irregular work hours may also affect fertility and pregnancy in women. For example, preeclampsia is a primary cause of maternal and perinatal morbidity. In a study involving 102 cases of preeclampsia compared with 4,381 controls, physically demanding and stressful occupational conditions were significantly associated with increased risk of preeclampsia. Specifically, women who regularly stood at least 1 hour per day without walking, women who frequently climbed stairs, and women who worked more than 5 consecutive days without a day off experienced significantly higher levels of preeclampsia.[17]

A qualitative summary of the potential effects of selected physical, chemical, biological, and psychosocial environments on the female and male reproductive systems is shown in **Table 2-2** and on paternal and maternal fertility in **Table 2-3**. The information in the tables is taken from three review articles,[18–20] combined by Burdolf and colleagues.[21]

Although the results summarized by the review articles represent well-established exposures and reproductive health outcomes, uncertainties remain. First, much of the exposure assessment involved self-reported questionnaire data. Hence, the accuracy of the magnitude and duration of exposure data may be

TABLE 2-2   **Adverse Reproductive Health Outcomes and Their Accompanying Risk Factors**

Risk Factor	Pregnancy Outcomes (Maternal Exposure)	Birth Defects (Fetal Exposure)	Semen Quality (Paternal Exposure)
Physical factors			
Ionizing radiation	Spontaneous abortion	Congenital defects	Reduced sperm count (Azoospermia)
Noise (>90 dBA)	Spontaneous abortion, low birth weight, preterm birth		
Heat			Reduced sperm count
Chemical agents			
Lead	Low birth weight	Neural tube defects	Reduced sperm count
Mercury	Spontaneous abortion		
Organic solvents	Spontaneous abortion		
Tetrachloroethylene	Spontaneous abortion	Cleft lip/palate	
Glycol ethers	Spontaneous abortion		Reduced semen quality
Dibromopropane	Menstrual disturbances, spontaneous abortion	Neural tube defects	Reduced semen quality
Ethylene oxide	Preterm birth, spontaneous abortion	Cleft lip/palate	
Anesthetic gases	Spontaneous abortion		
Antineoplastic drugs	Spontaneous abortion		
Pesticides			Reduced sperm count
Ethylenedibromide		Neural tube defects, cleft lip/palate	Reduced quantity and quality
Carbon sulfide			Reduced quantity and quality
Specific types of welding			Reduced quantity and quality

(continues)

TABLE 2-2   *(Continued)*

Risk Factor	Pregnancy Outcomes (Maternal Exposure)	Birth Defects (Fetal Exposure)	Semen Quality (Paternal Exposure)
Psychosocial factors			
Irregular work hours	Spontaneous abortion, menstrual disturbances		
Stress	Spontaneous abortion, preterm birth		
Physical load			
Heavy physical work (high energy expenditure)	Spontaneous abortion, low birth weight		
Frequent heavy lifting	Preterm birth, spontaneous abortion		
Prolonged standing	Low birth weight, preterm birth, spontaneous abortion		

Source: Burdolf A, Figa-Talamanca I, Jensen TK, Thulstrup AM. Effects of occupational exposure on the reproductive system: core evidence and practical implications. *Occup Med* 2006;56(8):516–520.

biased. In addition, because many of the individuals in these studies were exposed to a mixture of exposures, it is difficult to differentiate the risk of specific chemical compounds. Second, whether the appropriate time window was used for exposure assessment may be questioned. For many occupational hazards, the appropriate time window for greatest susceptibility is not well known. Third, changes in chemical exposures over time complicate determination of the dose. Finally, it is difficult to attribute paternal exposure to an adverse health outcome when there is overlapping exposure between partners.[21]

Observed health effects associated with selected pathological agents are presented in **Table 2-4**. The table also shows potentially high-risk occupations and prevention measures. Adverse reproductive effects in pregnant women may also occur from infectious agents. For example, human cytomegalovirus (CMV) is the leading cause of congenital viral infections in the United States, involving 1% to 3% of live births.[22] Congenital CMV infection is as common as neural tube

TABLE 2-3   **Fertility Outcomes and Their Accompanying Risk Factors**

Occupational Risk Factor	Maternal Exposure	Paternal Exposure
Physical factors		
Ionizing radiation	+	+
Heat	+	+
Chemical agents		
Lead	+	+
Mercury	+	
Toluene	+	
Aliphatic hydrocarbons	+	
Aromatic hydrocarbons	+	
Tetrachloroethylene	+	
Glycol ethers	+	+
Ethylene oxide	+	
Anesthetic gases	+	
Pesticides	+	+
Psychosocial factors		
Irregular work hours	+	
Stress	+	

Source: Burdolf A, Figa-Talamanca I, Jensen TK, Thulstrup AM. Effects of occupational exposure on the reproductive system: core evidence and practical implications. *Occup Med* 2006;56(8):516–520.

defects, fetal alcohol syndrome, and Down syndrome.[23] In the United States, about 40,000 infants are born each year with CMV, of which 8,000 will have neurological disabilities, including mental retardation, neuromotor abnormalities, hearing loss, and chorioretinitis.[24] Maternal CMV infection during gestation is related to a 40% risk of intrauterine transmission, with roughly a quarter of these infants symptomatic.[25,26] One study showed that women treated with hyperimmunoglobulin who have primary maternal CMV infection and whose fetuses were infected gave birth to significantly fewer symptomatic infants than did women who were not treated.[27]

As for birth defects, research has linked them with rubella (German measles), cytomegalovirus, and herpes simplex; untreated syphilis in the mother; and the parasite *Toxoplasma gondii* that can be contracted through undercooked meat, dirt, or feces of infected cats.

TABLE 2-4 **Disease-Causing Agents That Are Reproductive Hazards for Women**

Agent	Observed Effects	Potentially Exposed Workers	Preventive Measures
Cytomegalovirus	Birth defects, low birth weight, developmental disorders	Healthcare workers, workers in contact with infants and children	Good hygienic practices such as hand washing
Hepatitis B virus	Low birth weight	Healthcare workers	Vaccination
HIV	Low birth weight, childhood cancer	Healthcare workers	Practice universal precautions
Human parvovirus B19	Spontaneous abortion	Healthcare workers, workers in contact with infants and children	Good hygienic practices such as hand washing
Rubella (German measles)	Birth defects, low birth weight	Healthcare workers, workers in contact with infants and children	Vaccination before pregnancy if no prior immunity
Toxoplasmosis	Spontaneous abortion, birth defects, developmental disorders	Animal care workers, veterinarians	Good hygiene practices such as hand washing
Varicella-zoster virus (chicken pox)	Birth defects, low birth weight	Healthcare workers, workers in contact with infants and children	Vaccination before pregnancy if no prior immunity

Source: National Institute for Occupational Safety and Health. The effects of workplace hazards on female reproductive health. DHHS (NIOSH) Publication No. 99-104, 1999.

The Inner Versus Outer Environment

The inner environment with respect to the body is compared with the outer environment; that is, harmful substances in the outer environment enter the body through various routes, for example, breathing in (inhalation), swallowing (ingestion), contact with skin, and intravenous. The body has protective mechanisms for contaminants that penetrate these barriers, such as vomiting, diarrhea, detoxification in the liver, excretion through the kidneys, and coughing. A substance is considered to be outside the body until it crosses cellular barriers in the gastrointestinal tract or lungs. Cell membranes (cell walls) are designed to prevent forcing invaders or substances from entering bodily tissue. If a toxic substance is absorbed in the body, it can be distributed to other sites through blood and lymph circulation, liver, kidneys, and lungs.

Once a toxicant passes the lining of the skin, lungs, or gastrointestinal tract, it enters fluid surrounding the cells of that organ (interstitial fluid). Interstitial fluid represents about 15% of body weight. Fluid inside the cells is called intracellular fluid and represents about 40% of body weight. A toxicant in the interstitial fluid can enter cells of local tissue, blood capillaries and the body's circulatory system, or the lymphatic system. A toxicant can then be excreted (through feces, urine, or expired air), stored, or biotransformed into metabolites.

Biotransformation is transformation of a substance into new chemicals (metabolites) by the body. Biotransformation is essential for survival. For example, it involves transforming absorbed nutrients (food, oxygen, etc.) into substances required by the body for normal function. In addition, the body is efficient at biotransforming body wastes or chemicals that are not normally produced or expected in the body. Water-soluble metabolites, which are excreted into bile and passed from the body, may result. Metabolizing a substance to a lower toxicity is called detoxification; however, metabolites may become more toxic (bioactivation). An interaction of metabolites with cellular macromolecules such as DNA can cause serious health effects such as birth defects.

A highly toxic substance that is poorly absorbed into the body may be less dangerous than a substance with low toxicity but which is readily absorbed in the body.

A mutation may arise if genes that govern cell division and cell suicide (apoptosis) are damaged and cannot be repaired. Although the body may fail to repair damaged genes, the process of trying to repair genes may also create mutations. In some cases, the body can repair damaged tissue, but sometimes the damage cannot be repaired, or it may be too widespread and severe to be repaired.

When a gene is damaged, it will no longer properly guide how the body forms and functions. Genes control all aspects of the human body. They are influenced by both radiation and chemicals. Sometimes genes mutate at random, without any explanation. We inherit tens of thousands of genes from each parent, which are arranged on 46 chromosomes. Half of our genes come from our mother and half come from our father. For each pair of genes, one will dominate, while the other is recessive, thereby determining each characteristic. Several birth defects result from dominant inheritance (e.g., high cholesterol, Huntington's disease, nervous system disorders, and some forms of glaucoma).

If both the mother and father have the same recessive gene, the child has a 25% chance of inheriting the disease. Some recessive diseases include sickle cell anemia, cystic fibrosis, and phenylketonuria (PKU), a metabolic disorder. If only one parent passes on genes for the disorder, a normal gene received from the other parent will prevent the disease; however, the child will be a carrier.

Some disorders, like hemophilia and Duchenne muscular dystrophy, occur when defective sex-determining chromosomes carried on the X chromosome are passed on by the parent. A defective egg or sperm can also result in genetic defects (e.g., Down syndrome).

The complicated interaction of genes from either or both parents with environmental factors is thought to explain a host of defects: cleft lip and palate, clubfoot, spina bifida, water on the brain (hydrocephalus), diabetes mellitus, heart defects, and some cancers.

Birth defects have also been linked to diseases in the mother. For example, children of diabetic mothers are significantly more likely to experience cardiovascular malformations.[29] In one study, maternal obesity was significantly associated with spina bifida.[30] The study also found a significant positive association between infants of obese women and omphalocele (a type of hernia), heart defects, and multiple anomalies, and heart defects and multiple anomalies in overweight women prior to pregnancy. Neural tube defects (i.e., defects of the fetal brain or spine) have also been associated with maternal obesity prior to pregnancy;[31] however, another study did not find a significant association between maternal obesity and spina bifida.[32]

The Personal Versus Ambient Environment

The **personal environment** where an individual has control (e.g., diet, smoking, and sexual behavior) may be contrasted with the **ambient environment** where a person has little or no control (e.g., food additives, pollution, and industrial products). Many events and environments in reproductive health may be classified as personal in some situations and ambient in others. For example, we may or may not have control over family planning, skilled attendance at delivery, and timely emergency obstetric care when complications arise, which are important ways to avoid reproductive health problems.

Both personal and ambient environments may cause mutations. Congenital malformations can be genetic or teratogenic. Environmental agents may disrupt the reproductive process by affecting genetic material (DNA or chromosomes) or by directly disturbing the developing embryo or fetus.

If an environmental agent changes DNA, it is **mutagenic**. Relevant exposures should be studied before pregnancy, when the gametes are formed or, more specifically, during the formation of the meiotic divisions. Meiotic divisions leading to the development of sperm cells in men occur 3 months before conception. Eggs enter their first meiotic division during fetal life in women. Eggs remain at this stage until the menstrual cycle, decades later. At that time, it matures and may get fertilized;[33] however, there are many difficulties in identifying environmental agents that increase mutagenic events in gametes. In the study of environmental agents that may cause birth defects and other reproductive problems, environmental exposures affecting both parents in the years or decades before conception should be considered.

When a developing embryo or fetus is exposed to an environmental agent, it is very unlikely that a birth defect will result. Rather, somatic cell mutations (any cell in the body that is not a sperm or egg cell) in developing tissue are more likely to result in congenital, childhood, or adolescent cancers.

A **teratogen** is any environmental exposure that may cause disturbances of the growth and development of an embryo or fetus, causing birth defects. Thus, exposures to pregnant women are of interest. Exposures to men are only of interest when they secondarily affect women (e.g., passive smoke, occupational chemicals carried home, or biological agents). **Teratology** is the study of the frequency, causation, and development of congenital malformations such as morphological abnormalities (e.g., cleft lip and/or palate, anencephaly, or ventricular septal defect) and other phenomena (e.g., increased risk of cancer). The American College of Occupational and Environmental Medicine recognizes the following teratogens:

- Ionizing radiation: atomic weapons, radioiodine, radiation therapy
- Infections: cytomegalovirus, herpes virus hominis I and II, parvovirus B-19, rubella virus (German measles), syphilis, toxoplasmosis, Venezuelan equine encephalitis virus

- Metabolic imbalance: alcoholism, endemic cretinism, diabetes, folic acid deficiency, hyperthermia, phenylketonuria, rheumatic disease and congenital heart block, virilizing tumors

- Drugs and environmental chemicals: 13-cis-retinoic acid (isotretinoin, Accutane), aminopterin and methylaminopterin, androgenic hormones, busulfan, captopril and enalapril (ACE inhibitors), chlorobiphenyls (PCBs), cocaine, coumarin anticoagulants, cyclophosphamide, diethylstilbestrol, diphenylhydantoin (Phenytoin, Dilantin, Epanutin), etretinate, lithium, methimazole, organic mercury compounds, penicillamine, tetracyclines, thalidomide, trimethadione, and valproic acid[34]

Teratogenesis causing specific malformations may occur in limited periods of development, depending on the specific teratogenic process. If a malformation results, the teratogenic period corresponds to when the structure in question is developing. Embryonic timetables may provide very crude estimates of periods of sensitivity.

Although some of these teratogens cannot be controlled, many can. Some infections are sexually transmitted. Some sexually transmitted diseases (STDs) include chlamydia, gonorrhea, hepatitis B, and syphilis. STDs may cause cervical and other cancers, chronic hepatitis, pelvic inflammatory disease, infertility, and other complications, as well as pregnancy complications (e.g., premature labor and uterine infection after delivery).[35] Chlamydia has been linked with male reproductive tract complications such as prostatitis, infertility, and urethral stricture.[36] STDs can also cause problems and be passed to the baby both while in the womb or during birth. The effects of STDs on the baby include stillbirth, neurological damage, meningitis, low birth weight, and possible lifelong STD complications.[35]

Another STD and condition strongly related to reproductive health is HIV/AIDS. This is in itself a reproductive health problem as well as a major contributor to other reproductive health problems. The primary mode of transmission is through sexual contact and from mother to child during childbirth, thus making it a reproductive issue. HIV/AIDS also causes other reproductive problems such as erectile dysfunction,[37] ectopic pregnancy, bacterial pneumonia, urinary tract infections, and other infections in HIV-positive as compared with HIV-negative pregnant women.[38] HIV-positive women also experience lower fertility rate ratios, more postpartum hemorrhaging, a higher risk of major and minor complications after caesarean sections, and a higher risk of both major and minor complications with laparotomy, caesarean section, and induced abortion.[38]

Pregnant women also have control over whether they drink during pregnancy, take illicit drugs, or abuse prescription drugs. If large amounts of alcohol are consumed during pregnancy, a cluster of defects called fetal alcohol syndrome may arise, such as mental retardation, attention-deficit hyperactivity disorder, language deficits, deficits in spatial processing and memory, slow reaction times, decision-making problems, heart problems, and growth deficiency.[39] Binge drinking in early pregnancy has also been shown to be dangerous, even if the woman quits drinking later. There is no safe time during pregnancy to drink. An estimated 1% of all births in the United States are estimated to have some form of fetal alcohol syndrome.[39]

Recreational drug use and abuse of prescription drugs is also a choice. Some drugs like d-lysergic acid diethylamide (LSD) can cause arm and leg abnormalities and central nervous system problems in infants. Crack cocaine also has been associated with birth defects. In the United States in 2002, 3% of pregnant women aged 15 to 44 years used illicit drugs in the past month, and 3% reported binge alcohol drinking. Pregnant women aged 15 to 25 years were more likely to use illicit drugs and binge drink than older pregnant women.[40] Several drugs prescribed for anxiety and mental illness are known to cause specific defects. In the United States in 2002–2004 among women aged 15–44, 6% of pregnant women reported nonmedical use of any prescription drug, pain relievers, stimulants, methamphetamine, and sedatives in the past year.[41]

Drugs taken to treat other health problems may cause damage to a developing fetus as well. For example, certain antibiotics can harm bone growth. Drugs used to treat tuberculosis can cause hearing problems and cranial damage. Drugs given to prevent seizures can cause mental retardation and slow growth. Drugs given to treat cancer can cause congenital malformations, especially central nervous system defects, and male hormones may cause masculinization of a female fetus.[42]

The Solid, Liquid, and Gaseous Environments

Routes of human exposure to contaminants that may cause reproductive health problems are becoming better understood. Transmission of chemical (e.g., carbon monoxide, ozone, and lead) and biological agents (viruses, bacteria, funguses, and parasites) often occurs through air, water, soil, and food. An understanding of how chemical and biological agents can be transmitted is important in avoiding exposure.

On the basis of understanding selected routes of transmission, the National Institute for Occupational Safety and Health recommends the following measures for avoiding hazardous chemical exposure in the workplace:

- Store chemicals in sealed containers when they are not in use.

- Wash hands after contact with hazardous substances and before eating, drinking, or smoking.

- Avoid skin contact with chemicals.

- If chemicals contact the skin, follow the directions for washing in the material safety data sheet (MSDS). Employers are required to have copies of MSDSs for all hazardous materials used in their workplaces and to provide them to workers upon request.

- Review all MSDSs to become familiar with any reproductive hazards used in your workplace. If you are concerned about reproductive hazards in the workplace, consult your doctor or healthcare provider.

- Participate in all safety and health education, training, and monitoring programs offered by your employer.

- Learn about proper work practices and engineering controls (such as improved ventilation).

- Use personal protective equipment (gloves, respirators, and personal protective clothing) to reduce exposures to workplace hazards.

- Follow your employer's safety and health work practices and procedures to prevent exposures to reproductive hazards.

- Prevent home contamination with the following steps:
  - Change out of contaminated clothing and wash with soap and water before going home.
  - Store street clothes in a separate area of the workplace to prevent contamination.
  - Wash work clothing separately from other laundry (at work if possible).
  - Avoid bringing contaminated clothing or other objects home. If work clothes must be brought home, transport them in a sealed plastic bag.[28]

In order to avoid viruses and other infectious agents, follow precautionary practices such as those indicated in Table 2-4. These include good hygienic practices such as hand washing, vaccination before pregnancy if there is no prior immunity, and precautions against HIV.

Certain activities are associated with increased exposure to the chemical and physical agents that cause reproductive problems. For example, healthcare workers and pharmacists are more likely to be exposed to cancer treatment drugs; electronic and semiconductor workers are more likely exposed to certain ethylene glycol ethers; battery makers, solderers, welders, radiator repairers, bridge repainters, firing range workers, and home remodelers are more likely to be exposed to lead; healthcare workers, dental personnel, and atomic workers are more likely exposed to ionizing radiation; and many types of workers experience strenuous physical labor.

Broadly speaking, the study of reproductive epidemiology requires consideration of all of these types of environments and their interrelationships. That is, environmental factors that adversely affect reproductive health should be recognized and understood in terms of how they may become internalized, whether they can be controlled, and the routes of human exposure they might take. The study of the environment may be restricted by person (e.g., adolescent girls), place (e.g., workplace), or time (e.g., summer) and environments that can be modified. Reproductive health interventions may modify physical, biological, chemical, and psychosocial environments and corresponding behaviors (e.g., exercise, diet, sexual practices).

The Systems Approach

A **systems approach** is a comprehensive assessment in which the health problem is related to the complexity of environmental exposures, with consideration given to the interrelated, interacting, or interdependent constituents forming a complex whole. Consideration is given to the fact that environmental exposures may derive from multiple sources, enter the body through multiple routes, and change over time because of constant interaction, altering the degree to which they are harmful. The essence of the systems approach is to understand the source and nature of an environmental contaminant or stress capable of influencing reproductive behavior, assessing how and in what form it influences people, measuring the reproductive health effects, and applying controls when and where appropriate.

This approach often requires the combined efforts of epidemiologists, biologists, toxicologists, respiratory physiologists, and public health officials.

In the context of reproductive health, a systems approach is a comprehensive assessment in which the reproductive health problem is related to the complexity of environmental exposures, with consideration given to the interrelated, interacting, or interdependent constituents forming a complex whole. Consideration of all the definitions of environment presented above is important in the study, prevention, and control of reproductive health problems.

Selected Reproductive Health Outcomes

Menstrual Cycle Effects

Physical or emotional stress or chemical exposure may disrupt the balance between the brain, pituitary glands, and ovaries. Consequently, an imbalance of estrogen and progesterone may result, leading to changes in menstrual cycle length and regularity and ovulation. Overall female health is associated with severe or long-lasting hormone imbalances. Carbon disulfide (CS_2) has been shown to cause menstrual cycle changes among viscose rayon workers.

Infertility and Subfertility

The capability to conceive is sometimes called **fecundity**. The capability to produce live children is termed **fertility**. Environmental hazards to reproduction as well as problems with either the male or female reproductive systems can affect fecundity and fertility. Lack of fertility is referred to as **infertility**, and permanent infertility is termed **sterility**. **Subfertile** is a level of fertility below the normal range, but not infertile. Many factors influence human fecundity and fertility, including genetics, nutrition, physical activity, sexual behavior, endocrinology, timing, culture, and instinct.

Various factors can affect fertility and may involve one or both partners. For example, smoking and alcohol use in males are associated with fewer sperm and poor semen quality.[43] Long-term cigarette smoking has been associated with increased risk of erectile dysfunction.[44] Excessive weight has been associated with lower sperm concentration, total sperm count, and fewer normal forms.[45] Obesity increases the risk of infertility and abnormal or irregular anovulation and reduced response to fertility treatment in women,[46] and cancer, independent of treatment, has been shown to disrupt spermatogenesis.[47]

Between 10% and 15% of all couples cannot conceive a child after 1 year of attempting to become pregnant. Factors that can cause problems with fertility include damage to a man's sperm, damage to a woman's eggs, or a change in the hormones that regulate the normal menstrual cycle. Certain cancer treatment drugs (e.g., methotrexate), lead, and ionizing radiation (e.g., X-rays and gamma rays) are examples of risk factors for infertility/subfertility.[48]

Miscarriage and Stillbirths

Miscarriage (also called spontaneous abortion) is the death and expulsion of an embryo or a fetus; it is an unplanned termination of a pregnancy. It may occur any time after conception and before 20 weeks of gestation.[49,50] Studies reveal that anywhere from 10% to 25% of all clinically recognized pregnancies will end in miscarriage.[51] A **stillbirth** occurs when the fetus, which died in the uterus or during labor or delivery, exits the woman's body. Some of the reasons why miscarriages and stillbirths occur are as follows:

- Damage to the egg or sperm such that the egg cannot be fertilized or that it cannot survive after fertilization.
- The hormone system may not work properly to maintain the pregnancy.
- The fetus may develop abnormally.
- The uterus or cervix may have physical problems.

The cause of miscarriage is often difficult to identify; nevertheless, during the first trimester, the majority of miscarriages have gross chromosomal anomalies.[52] Examples of known risk factors for miscarriage include hormonal problems, infections or maternal health problems, obesity, lifestyle (e.g., drug use, malnutrition, and smoking, maternal age, cancer treatment drugs), certain ethylene glycol ethers, lead, ionizing radiation, and strenuous physical labor (e.g., prolonged standing, heavy lifting). In addition, embryonic development may be normal, but is rejected by the maternal organism.

Birth Defects

In the United States, about 150,000 babies (i.e., approximately 3%, or 1 in 30) are born with a birth defect, with the cause of 60% to 70% of birth defects unknown.[53] A **birth defect** is a structural, functional, or developmental abnormality present at birth or later in life. In the previous chapter, mutagenic effects and teratogenic effects were identified as environmental causes of birth defects. The fetus is most susceptible to adverse effects during the first 3 months of the pregnancy when the internal organs and limbs are formed. Cancer treatment drugs, lead, and ionizing radiation are examples of risk factors for birth defects.

Birth defects develop from both genetic and environmental factors. A single abnormal gene is sufficient to cause birth defects. Humans have at least 30,000 to 35,000 genes that direct the development of our physical and biochemical systems. A chromosome is a single piece of DNA that contains many genes. The average human cell has 46 chromosomes. Because each child gets half of its genes from each parent, an infant may inherit a genetic disease when either parent passes on a single faulty gene, which is called **dominant inheritance**. Achondroplasia (a form of dwarfism) and Marfan syndrome (a connective tissue disease) are examples of dominant inheritance. Other genetic diseases can only be passed on to a child if both parents carry the same abnormal gene, which is called **recessive inheritance**. An example is cystic fibrosis, which is a fatal disorder of lungs and other organs. This disease tends to affect mainly Caucasians. In addition, there is a form of inheritance (X-linked) in which a mother who carries a gene can pass it to her son. This form of inherited disease includes hemophilia (a blood-clotting disorder) and Duchenne muscular dystrophy (progressive muscle weakness).[54]

Numerous birth defects are possible. Error in the development of an egg or sperm cell may cause a baby to be born with too many or too few chromosomes. One or more chromosomes may be broken or rearranged. An extra chromosome 21 (Down syndrome) is a more common chromosomal abnormality. Infants born with extra copies of chromosome 13 or 18 have multiple birth defects. These children do not usually live beyond the first month of life. Extra or missing sex chromosomes can affect sexual development and cause infertility, growth abnormalities, and learning and behavioral problems, but most affected people have normal lives.[54]

Although the association between maternal age and the risk of birth defects has been extensively studied, research has also examined the relationship between paternal age and risk of birth defects. Infants born to younger or older fathers have a slightly increased risk of birth defects; nevertheless, compared with mothers, paternal age plays a smaller role in the etiology of birth defects.[55]

Environmental factors can also result in birth defects, including biological and chemical agents. Although the causes of most birth defects are currently unknown, some teratogens a pregnant women may put into her system that may affect the fetus include *alcohol*, associated with mental retardation, low birth weight, heart defects, poor coordination, and selected malformations; *tobacco*, associated with reduced oxygen available to the fetus, premature rupture of the membranes, hemorrhage before or early in labor, hemorrhage after delivery, congenital abnormality, miscarriage, stillbirth, premature birth, and low birth weight; *caffeine*, which is a stimulant that acts on the nervous system, creating changes in fetal heartbeat and other functions; *aspirin*, which may increase the risk of anemia, excessive bleeding before and after birth, longer pregnancies, and higher frequency of complicated deliveries; *barbiturates*, which can cause the baby to experience tremors, restlessness, and irritability; *amphetamines*, which can cause birth defects; *antibiotics*, which may affect the growth of the baby's bones or yellow mottling and staining of the baby's first teeth and deafness in the infant; *narcotics*, which result in fetal addiction to the drug and an increased risk of premature birth, breach birth, toxemia, and premature separation of the placenta; and hallucinogens, which can affect the central nervous system of the fetus. If a birth defect is caused by a combination of one or more genes and environmental factors, it is called multifactorial inheritance. Examples are cleft lip or palate, clubfoot, and some forms of heart defects.

Just as defects may arise in any organ or part of the body, the severity of the disturbance can vary considerably. Consider a neural tube defect, which occurs in human embryos if there is an interference with the closure of the neural tube around the 28th day after fertilization. Researchers have identified some causes for this condition, including medication for epilepsy taken during pregnancy, folic acid deficiencies, folate antimetabolites, maternal diabetes, maternal obesity, mycotoxins in contaminated cornmeal, arsenic, and hyperthermia during early development.[56] The types of neural tube defects range from spina bifida (incompletely formed spinal cord), encephalocele (sac-like protrusions of the brain and the membranes that cover it through openings in the skull), and anencephaly (absence of a major portion of the brain, skull, and scalp).

In the United States, birth defects surveillance systems historically have collected data on major structural birth defects and birth defects arising from chromosomal abnormalities. Major structural birth defects are conditions that (1) result from a malformation, deformation, or disruption in one or more parts of the body; (2) are present at birth; and (3) have a serious, adverse effect on health, development, or functional ability. The most common type of structural birth defect involves the heart, which affects one in every 125 babies. About 1 in 2,000 babies will experience spinal bifida, which results in varying degrees of paralysis and bladder and bowel problems. Genetic and nutritional factors appear to affect this defect. Metabolic disorders affect 1 in 3,500 babies. Affected infants are missing an enzyme necessary to break down certain fatty substances in brain cells. As these substances build up, brain cells are destroyed. Consequences of this defect are blindness, paralysis, and death by age 5. In addition, roughly 1 in 135 infants will have a structural defect involving the genitals or urinary tract, varying in severity and form.

Congenital infections are also causes of birth defects. For example, if rubella (German measles) infects a pregnant woman during the first trimester, the child has a one in four chance of an outcome of congenital rubella syndrome (deafness, mental retardation, heart defects, or blindness). Vaccination for rubella has now made congenital rubella syndrome rare. Cytomegalovirus is the most common congenital viral infection. In the United States, although roughly 1% of infants are infected, only about 10% of them experience adverse health outcomes such as mental retardation and low vision or hearing. Finally, sexually transmitted infections can endanger the fetus and newborn. For example, if syphilis is untreated it can cause stillbirth, newborn death, or bone defects. Sexually transmitted infections affect about 1 in 2,000 babies.[54]

Fetal alcohol syndrome (mental and physical birth defects) affects 1 in 1,000 babies in the United States. It is common in mothers who drink heavily during pregnancy; however, even moderate or light drinking can be dangerous to the developing fetus.[54]

Rhesus incompatibility disease (Rh disease) in an infant is caused by incompatibility between a mother's blood and that of her fetus, which can cause jaundice, anemia, brain damage, and death in the infant. Prevention of Rh disease is possible by injection of immunoglobulin at 28 weeks of pregnancy after the delivery of an Rh-positive infant.[54]

Low Birth Weight and Premature Birth

Low birth weight is when the birth weight is less than 2,500 grams (about 5 pounds, 5 ounces). Premature birth (also called preterm birth) is when childbirth occurs earlier than 37 completed weeks of gestation. In the United States, approximately 7% of babies are born underweight or prematurely. Most of these cases are believed to be because of poor maternal nutrition, smoking, and alcohol use during pregnancy. For example, in the United States, cigarette smoking during pregnancy explains 20% to 30% of low birth weight babies, about 14% of preterm deliveries, and 10% of infant deaths. Cigarette smoking causes these problems by depriving the fetus of up to 25% of necessary oxygen.[57]

Underweight or premature babies have a greater risk of illness and death during the first year of life. They also have an increased risk of long-term disabilities, such as mental retardation, chronic respiratory problems, cerebral palsy, childhood psychiatric disorders, autism, and hearing and vision impairments. Cancer treatment drugs, lead, ionizing radiation, and strenuous physical labor are examples of risk factors for low birth weight and premature delivery.

In 2004, 12.5% of all births in the United States occurred before 37 weeks gestation (preterm). Premature births are on the rise, increasing 30% since 1981.[58] Roughly two thirds of the increase in premature births are late preterm (born within 34 and 36 weeks of gestation).[59] Mortality rates for late preterm infants are also higher than those born at term.[60–68] All preterm infants have higher morbidity compared with term neonates.[69]

Young and old maternal age at pregnancy has been shown to increase the risk of preterm delivery, low birth weight, and subsequent risk of death and developmental problems.[70–73] Low birth weight infants have greater than six times the risk of infant mortality and are at increased risk of long-term disabilities. **Table 2-5** shows the relationship between low birth weight and maternal age at pregnancy for California in 2006.[74]

TABLE 2-5　**Maternal Age at Pregnancy and Low Birth Weight (<2,500 Grams)**

Maternal Age Group (Years)	Percentage
Under 15	8.9
15–19	7.4
20–24	6.2
25–29	6.1
30–34	6.7
35–39	7.9
40–44	10.2
45 and older	24.4

Data Source: California Department of Public Health. Center for Health Statistics, Vital Statistics Query System. Available at: http://www.applications.dhs.ca.gov/vsq/default.asp. Accessed December 30, 2008.

Developmental Disorders

Sometimes prenatal and postnatal events occur to disrupt cognitive, language, motor, or social skills. Developmental disorder involves one of many disorders that interrupt development in children. A single area of development may be affected or developmental disorders may be pervasive. In the United States, roughly 10% of children have some form of developmental disability (e.g., mental retardation or intellectual disability, autistic disorder, learning disorder, attention deficit hyperactivity disorder, cerebral palsy, vision impairment, and hearing loss). Such problems may not be noticeable at birth, can be difficult to measure, may be temporary, and can reflect a wide range of severity. Lead and ionizing radiation are examples of risk factors for developmental disorders.[75]

Maternal tobacco use during pregnancy has also been shown to have an association with later conduct disorders.[76]

Childhood Cancer

A number of studies are examining suspected or possible risk factors for childhood cancers. These include parental, fetal, or childhood exposures to environmental toxins such as pesticides, solvents, or other household chemicals; parental occupational exposures to radiation or chemicals; parental medical conditions during pregnancy or before conception; maternal diet during pregnancy; and maternal reproductive history. For example, diethylstilbestrol diphosphate is a synthetic (manufactured) form of the female hormone estrogen. In the 1950s and 1960s, it was prescribed to millions of women to prevent miscarriage and premature birth. Its use was discontinued in the 1970s because reproductive abnormalities were found in some of the children of women who took the drug. Prenatal exposure to diethylstilbestrol has also been associated with shown increased risk for cervical and vaginal cancers in female offspring, most often detected in the age range of 14 to 25 years.[77]

The most likely explanation connecting prenatal exposure and cancer is the occurrence of somatic mutations in the fetal cells. This is the mechanism that explains mutations because of prenatal X-rays and possibly chemical carcinogenesis. X-rays and specific genetic syndromes have been associated with leukemia Studies have also associated childhood leukemia with paternal exposure to solvents and paints, and employment in motor vehicle–related jobs, and cancer of the childhood nervous system was associated with paternal exposure to paints.[78] In a large study conducted in the United Kingdom, small but statistically increased risks of leukemia and acute lymphoblastic leukemia were observed in children whose fathers were exposed to exhaust fumes, driving, and/or inhaled particulate hydrocarbons.[79,80]

Genetic susceptibility may be a risk factor for Hodgkin's disease. Similarly, a retinoblastoma gene has been identified, with each child of a parent with familial bilateral retinoblastoma having a 50% risk of inheriting the gene.

In a study involving hospitals in the United States and Canada, maternal exposures to selected chemicals were not associated with neuroblastoma. On the other hand, paternal exposures to selected chemicals (i.e., diesel fuel, lacquer thinner, turpentine, wood dust, and solders) showed evidence of increased risk of neuroblastoma.[81]

Conclusion

This chapter presented how various environments affect reproductive health. Focus was given to how physical, chemical, biological, and psychosocial environments influence reproductive health; how exposures can penetrate protective mechanisms in the body to adversely affect reproductive health; how a large portion of environmental exposures that influence human reproduction may harm reproductive health; and how an understanding of the routes of exposure to environmental influences can help prevent and control reproductive health problems. By understanding the full range that environments can have on reproductive health, health and social conditions of people may improve.

Key Issues

1. An important part of reproductive epidemiology involves identifying whether the cause of a health-related state or event is the physical, chemical, biological, or psychosocial environment; how a substance can penetrate protective mechanisms in the body; whether a person has control over the environmental exposure; and the routes of human exposure.

2. Reproductive health–related states or events can be caused by substances from the outer environment that enter through inhalation, ingestion, skin contact, or intravenous means or from the inner environment found already within the body (e.g., damaged genes).

3. Reproductive health–related states of events can be caused by factors in the personal environment (within a person's control) and in the ambient environment (where a person has little or no control).
4. Pathologic agents can be transmitted to humans in solid, liquid, and gaseous environments. Understanding how agents can be transmitted is important in avoiding exposure.
5. The systems approach in reproductive epidemiology considers the fact that environmental exposures may derive from multiple sources, enter the body through multiple routes, and that elements in the environment can change over time because of constant interaction, altering the degree to which they are harmful.

Exercises

Key Terms

Define the following terms.

Ambient environment

Biological environment

Biotransformation

Birth defect

Chemical environment

Developmental toxicology

Dioxin

Dominant inheritance

Environment

Fecundity

Fertility

Infertile

Miscarriage

Personal environment

Physical environment

Psychosocial environment

Recessive inheritance

Reproductive toxicology

Sterility

Stillbirth

Subfertile

Systems approach

Teratogen

Teratology

Toxicology

Study Questions

2.1　Identify and discuss routes of human exposure in the environment.

2.2　Give an example of each of the following environments and how each can affect reproductive health outcomes: physical, chemical, biological, and psychosocial.

2.3 Discuss the difference between the inner environment and the outer environment.

2.4 Discuss the difference between a teratogen and a genetic factor. Why would it be important to know the difference?

2.5 Describe the difference between the personal and the ambient environment, and give examples of both.

2.6 Identify some of the high–risk occupations for environmental exposures, and discuss some of the precautions that can be taken to reduce risk.

2.7 Define and discuss three reproductive problems and identify a risk factor for each.

References

1. Stedman TL. *Stedman's Medical Dictionary for the Health Professions and Nursing*, 5th ed. New York, NY: Lippincott, Williams & Wilkins; 2005.
2. Last JM, ed. *A Dictionary of Epidemiology*, 3rd ed. New York, NY: Oxford University Press; 1995.
3. Knezevic M. Effect of noise on birth capability. *Srpski Arhiv Za Celokupno Lekarstvo*. 1995;123(5–6):120–122.
4. Zhang J, Cai WW, Lee DJ. Occupational hazards and pregnancy outcomes. *Am J Ind Med*. 1992;21(3):397–408.
5. Hartikainen AL, Sorri M, Anttonen H, Tuimala R, Läärä E. Effect of occupational noise on the course and outcome of pregnancy. *Scand J Work Environ Health*. 1994;20(6): 444–450.
6. Personal Health Center. Birth defects. Available at: http://www.healthatoz.com/healthatoz/ Atoz/common/standard/transform.jsp?requestURI=/healthatoz/Atoz/ency/birth_defects.jsp. Accessed February 28, 2009.
7. De Santis M, Di Gianantonio E, Straface G, et al. Ionizing radiations in pregnancy and teratogenesis: a review of literature. *Reprod Toxicol*. 2005;20(3):323–329.
8. Juutilainen J. Developmental effects of electromagnetic fields. *Bioelectromagnetics*. 2005; (7):S107–S115.
9. Environmental Protection Agency. Health effects. Available at: http://www.epa.gov/ radiation/understand/index.html. Accessed October 1, 2008.
10. National Institute for Occupational Safety and Health. The effects of workplace hazards on female reproductive health [online]. Publication No. 99-104, Feb 1999. Available from: NIOSH, Cincinnati, Oh. at http://www.cdc.gov/NIOSH/99-104.html. Accessed November 21, 2008.
11. Schrager TF. What is toxicology. Available at: http://www.toxicologysource.com/ whatis-toxicology.html. Accessed November 21, 2008.
12. Environmental Protection Agency. Guidelines for the health assessment of suspect developmental toxicants. *Fed Reg*. 1986;51(185):34029.
13. Environmental Protection Agency. Guidelines for developmental toxicity risk assessment. *Fed Reg*. 1996;61(212):56274–56322. Available at: http://www.epa.gov/ncea/raf/pdfs/ repro51.pdf. Accessed November 21, 2008.

14. EJnet.org. Dioxin homepage. Available at: http://www.ejnet.org/dioxin/. Accessed November 21, 2008.
15. Environmental Protection Agency. Questions and answers about dioxins. July 2000. Available at: http://www.epa.gov/ncea/pdfs/dioxin/dioxin%20questions%20and%20answers .pdf. Accessed November 21, 2008.
16. Enders M, Biber M, Exler S. Measles, mumps and rubella virus infection in pregnancy: possible adverse effects on pregnant women, pregnancy outcome and the fetus. *Bundesgesundheitsblatt Gesundheitsforschung Gesundheitsschutz.* 2007;50(11):1393–1398.
17. Haelterman E, Marcoux S, Croteau A, Dramaix M. Population-based study on occupational risk factors for preeclampsia and gestational hypertension. *Scand J Work Environ Health.* 2007;33(4):304–317.
18. Figà-Talamanca I. Occupational risk factors and reproductive health of women. *Occup Med (Lond).* 2006;56:521–531.
19. Thulstrup AM, Bonde JP. Maternal occupational exposure and risk of specific birth defects. *Occup Med (Lond).* 2006;56:532–543.
20. Jensen TK, Bonde JP, Joffe M. The influence of occupational exposure on male reproductive function. *Occup Med (Lond).* 2006;56:544–553.
21. Burdolf A, Figa-Talamanca I, Jensen TK, Thulstrup AM. Effects of occupational exposure on the reproductive system: core evidence and practical implications. *Occup Med.* 2006;56(8):516–520. Available at: http://occmed.oxfordjournals.org/cgi/content/full/56/8/ 516. Accessed November 21, 2008.
22. Fowler KB, Stagno S, Pass RF, Britt WJ, Boll TJ, Alford CA. The outcome of congenital cytomegalovirus infection in relation to maternal antibody status. *N Engl J Med.* 1992;326:663–667.
23. Colugnati FA, Staras SA, Dollard SC, Cannon MJ. Incidence of cytomegalovirus infection among the general population and pregnant women in the United States. *BMC Infect Dis.* 2007;7:71.
24. Demmler GJ. Congenital cytomegalovirus infection and disease. *Adv Pediatr Infect Dis* 1996;11:135–162.
25. Britt WJ. Congenital cytomegalovirus infection. In Hitchcock PJ, MacKay JT, Wasserheit JN, ed. *Sexually Transmitted Diseases and Adverse Outcomes of Pregnancy.* Washington, DC: ASM Press; 1999: 269–281
26. Fowler KB, Stagno S, Pass RF. Maternal immunity and prevention of congenital cytomegalovirus infection. *JAMA.* 2003;289:1008–1011.
27. Nigro G, Adler SP, La Torre R, Best AM. Passive immunization during pregnancy for congenital cytomegalovirus infection. *N Engl J Med.* 2005;353:1350–1362.
28. National Institute for Occupational Safety and Health. The effects of workplace hazards on female reproductive health. DHHS (NIOSH) Publication No. 99-104, 1999. Available at: http://www.cdc.gov/NIOSH/99-104.html. Accessed February 28, 2009.
29. Wren C, Birrell G, Hawthorne G. Cardiovascular malformations in infants of diabetic mothers. *Heart* [serial online]. 2003;89:1217–1220. Available from: BMJ Publishing Group & British Cardiac Society http://heart.bmj.com. Accessed November 21, 2008.
30. Watkins ML, Rasmussen SA, Honein MA, Botto LD, Moore CA. Maternal obesity and risk for birth defects. *Pediatrics.* 2003;111(5 Pt 2):1152–1158.
31. Shaw GM, Todoroff K, Schaffer DM, Selvin S. Maternal height and prepregnancy body mass index as risk factors for selected congenital anomalies. *Paediatr Perinat Epidemiol.* 2000;14(3):234–239.

32. Shaw GM, Carmichael SL. Pre-pregnant obesity and risks of selected birth defects in offspring. *Epidemiology.* 2008;19(4):616–620.

33. Kallen B. *Epidemiology of Human Reproduction.* Boca Raton, FL: CRC Press; 2000.

34. Teratogen.net. Teratogenesis. Available at: http://www.teratogen.net/. Accessed November 21, 2008.

35. Centers for Disease Control and Prevention. STDs and pregnancy. Available at: http://www.cdc.gov/std/STDFact-STDs&Pregnancy.htm#affect. Retrieved February 28, 2009.

36. Trei JS, Canas LC, Gould PL. Reproductive tract complications associated with chlamydia trachomatis infection in US Air Force males within 4 years of testing. *Sex Transm Dis.* 2008;35(9):827–833.

37. Fakoya A, Lamba H, Mackie N, et al. British HIV Association, BASHH and FSRH guidelines for the management of the sexual and reproductive health of people living with HIV infection 2008. *HIV Med.* 2008;9(9):681–720.

38. Berer M. HIV/AIDS, pregnancy and maternal mortality and morbidity: implications for care. In: Berer M, Ravindran TK, eds. *Safe Motherhood Initiatives: Critical Issues.* Oxford: Blackwell Science; 1999:198–210.

39. Riley EP, McGee CL. Fetal alcohol spectrum disorders: an overview with emphasis on changes in brain and behavior. *Exp Biol Med.* 2005;230(6):357–365.

40. National Survey on Drug Use and Health. The NSDUH Report: Pregnancy and substance use. Available at: http://www.oas.samhsa.gov/2k3/pregnancy/pregnancy.pdf. Accessed February 28, 2009.

41. U.S. Department of Health and Human Services. Prevalence and recent trends in misuse of prescription drugs, 2008. Available at: http://www.oas.samhsa.gov/prescription/Ch2.htm#2.4.7. Accessed February 28, 2009.

42. HealthAtoZ. Birth defects. Available at: http://www.healthatoz.com/healthatoz/Atoz/common/standard/transform.jsp?requestURI=/healthatoz/Atoz/ency/birth_defects.jsp. Accessed November 21, 2008.

43. Kalyani R, Kumar ML. Factors influencing quality of semen: a two year prospective study. *Indian J Pathol Microbiol.* 2007;50(4):890–895.

44. McKay A. Sexuality and substance use: the impact of tobacco, alcohol, and selected recreational drugs on sexual function. *Can J Hum Sex.* 2005;14(1):47–56.

45. Jensen TK, Andersson AM, Jørgensen N, et al. Body mass index in relation to semen quality and reproductive hormones among 1,558 Danish men. *Fertil Steril.* 2004;82(4):863–870.

46. Zain MM, Norman RJ. Impact of obesity on female fertility and fertility treatment *Womens Health (Lond Engl).* 2008;4(2):183–194.

47. Agarwal A, Allamaneni SS. Disruption of spermatogenesis by the cancer disease process. *J Natl Cancer Inst Monogr.* 2005;34:9–12.

48. Duffy C, Allen S, Clark M. Discussions regarding reproductive health for young women with breast cancer undergoing chemotherapy. *J Clin Oncol.* 2005;23(4):766–773.

49. Petrozza, JC. Early pregnancy loss. eMedicine by WebMD. August 29, 2006. Available at: http://www.emedicine.com/med/topic3241.htm. Accessed July 20, 2007.

50. Pregnancy-bliss.co.uk. Early pregnancy loss (miscarriage). Available at: http://www.pregnancy-bliss.co.uk/miscarriage.html. Accessed July 20, 2007.

51. The American College of Obstetricians and Gynecologists. *Planning Your Pregnancy and Birth*, 3rd ed. Washington, DC: The American College of Obstetricians and Gynecologists; December 31, 2000.

52. Ljunger E, Cnattingius S, Lundin C, Anneren G. Chromosomal anomalies in first-trimester miscarriages. *Acta Obstet Gynecol Scand.* 2005;84(11):1103–1107.
53. Centers for Disease Control and Prevention. Improved national prevalence estimates for 18 selected major birth defects—United States, 1999–2001. *MMWR Weekly* [serial online]. 2006;54 (51&52):1301–1305. Available at: http://www.cdc.gov/mmWR/preview/mmwrhtml/mm5451a2.htm#tab. Accessed November 21, 2008.
54. Georgia Department of Human Resources. Birth defects fact sheet. Available at: http://health.state.ga.us/pdfs/epi/mch/gbdris/birthdefects.fs.04.pdf. Accessed November 21, 2008.
55. Yang Q, Wen SW, Leader A, Chen XK, Lipson J, Walker M. Paternal age and birth defects: how strong is the association. *Hum Reprod.* 2006;1–6.
56. Jallo G, Becske, T. Neural Tube Defects. eMedicine by WebMD. Jan 10, 2007. Available at: http://www.emedicine.com/NEURO/topic244.htm. Accessed July 20, 2007.
57. U.S. Department of Health and Human Services. *Women and Smoking: A Report of the Surgeon General.* Washington, DC: U.S. Department of Health and Human Services; 2001.
58. Behrman RE, Butler AS, eds. *Preterm Births: Causes, Consequences, and Prevention.* Washington, DC: The National Academies Press; 2007.
59. Davidoff MJ, Dias T, Damus K, et al. Changes in the gestational age distribution among U.S. singleton births: impact on rates of late preterm birth, 1992 to 2002. *Semin Perinatol.* 2006;20(1):8–15.
60. Escobar GJ, Clark RH, Greene JD. Short-term outcomes of infants born at 35 and 36 weeks gestation: we need to ask more questions. *Semin Perinatol.* 2006;30(1):28–33.
61. Escobar GJ, Gonzales VM, Armstrong MA, Folck BE, Xiong B, Newman TB. Rehospitalization for neonatal dehydration: a nested case-control study. *Arch Pediatr Adolesc Med.* 2002;156(2):155–161.
62. Shapiro-Mendoza CK, Tomashek KM, Kotelchuck M, Barfield W, Weiss J, Evans S. Risk factors for neonatal morbidity and mortality among "healthy," late preterm newborns. *Semin Perinatol.* 2006;30(2):54–60.
63. Tomashek KM, Shapiro-Mendoza CK, Weiss J, et al. Early discharge among late preterm and term newborns and risk of neonatal morbidity. *Semin Perinatol.* 2006;30(2):61–68.
64. Watchko JF, Maisels MJ. Jaundice in low birth weight infants: pathobiology and outcome. *Arch Dis Childhood.* 2003;88(6):F455–F458.
65. Wight NE. Breastfeeding the borderline (near-term) preterm infant. *Pediatr Ann.* 2003; 32(5):329–336.
66. Wang ML, Dorer DJ, Fleming MP, Catlin EA. Clinical outcomes of near-term infants. *Pediatrics.* 2004;114(2):372–376.
67. Kramer MS, Demissie K, Yang H, Platt RW, Sauve R, Liston R. The contribution of mild and moderate preterm birth to infant mortality: Fetal and Infant Health Study Group of the Canadian Perinatal Surveillance System. *JAMA.* 2000;284(7):843–849.
68. Tomashek KM, Shapiro-Mendoza CK, Davidoff MJ, Petrini, JR. Differences in mortality between late-preterm and term singleton infants in the United States, 1995–2002. *J Pediatr.* 2007;151(5):450–456, 456e1.
69. Raju TN, Higgins RD, Stark AR, Leveno KJ. Optimizing care and outcome for late-preterm (near-term) infants: a summary of the workshop sponsored by the National Institute of Child Health and Human Development. *Pediatrics.* 2006;118(3):1207–1214.

70. Aldous MB, Edmonson MB. Maternal age at first childbirth and risk of low birth weight and preterm delivery in Washington State. *JAMA.* 1993;270(21):2574–2577.

71. Khoshnood B, Wall S, Kwang-sun L. Risk of low birth weight associated with advanced maternal age among four ethnic groups in the United States. *Matern Child Health J.* 2005;9(1):3–9.

72. Friede A, Baldwin W, Rhodes PH, et al. Young maternal age and infant mortality: the role of low birth weight. *Public Health Rep.* 1987;102(2):192–199.

73. Reichman NE, Teitler JO. Paternal age as a risk factor for low birth weight. *Am J Public Health.* 2006;96(5):862–866.

74. California Department of Public Health. Center for Health Statistics, Vital Statistics Query System. Available at: http://www.applications.dhs.ca.gov/vsq/default.asp. Accessed December 30, 2008.

75. Centers for Disease Control and Prevention. National Center on Birth Defects and Developmental Disabilities page. Available at: http://www.cdc.gov/ncbddd/. Accessed December 4, 2008.

76. Brennan PA, Grekin ER. Maternal smoking during pregnancy and adult male criminal outcomes. *Arch Gen Psychiatry.* 1999;56(3):215–219.

77. Mills DH. Prenatal diethylstilbestrol and vaginal cancer in offspring. *JAMA.* 1974;229 (4):471–472.

78. Colt JS, Blair A. Parental occupational exposures and risk of childhood cancer. *Environ Health Perspect.* 1998;106(Suppl 3):909–925.

79. McKinney PA, Fear NT, Stockton D, UK Childhood Cancer Study Investigators. Parental occupation at periconception: findings from the United Kingdom Childhood Cancer Study. *Occup Environ Med.* 2003;60(12):901–909.

80. Bernstein L, Linet M, Smith MA, Olshan AF. Renal tumors. In: Ries LAG, Smith MA, Gurney JG, et al., eds. *Cancer Incidence and Survival Among Children and Adolescents: United States SEER Program 1975–1995.* Bethesda, MD: National Cancer Institute, SEER Program, NIH Pub NO. 99-4649; 1999.

81. De Roos AJ, Olshan AF, Teschke K, et al. Parental occupational exposures to chemicals and incidence of neuroblastoma in offspring. *Am J Epidemiol* 2001;154(2):106–114.

THREE

Research Process in Reproductive Epidemiology

Learning Objectives

After completing this chapter, you should be able to:

1. Describe the research process in reproductive epidemiology.
2. Be familiar with methods for measuring, describing, and testing hypotheses about the distribution of a single sample.
3. Be familiar with common reproductive epidemiologic outcome measures.
4. Define surveillance and understand its role in determining reproductive health problems and identifying changes in them over time.
5. Be familiar with methods for measuring and testing associations between exposure and outcome variables.

Research is a scientific or scholarly investigation that aims to advance human knowledge. The research process in reproductive epidemiology involves a health problem, questions about why the problem exists, how it can be prevented and controlled, formulation of hypotheses, and an appropriate study design and statistical methods for assessing the hypotheses. The **study design** is a plan for data collection, analysis, and interpretation. The data collection phase should consider the possibility of **random error** (a wrong result caused by chance) and **systematic error** (a wrong result caused by bias). Each of these influences can produce results that do not represent the truth.

Internal validity is the degree to which the study results represent the truth. The plan for collecting data should minimize threats to internal validity. Several ways to improve the internal validity of a study are addressed in this book. For example, when a study is based on sampled data, it is possible that a statistical association between a purported exposure and disease outcome may be the result of chance—the luck of the draw. To minimize the role of chance, a representative sample of the population is required. Both randomization and a sufficiently large sample size are necessary to minimize chance findings.

Threats to internal validity are best controlled for at the design level of a study. After the data have been collected, it may be impossible to control for the threats to validity. Even with confounding, which may be controlled for at the analysis level of a study, the researchers must have enough foresight at the design phase of the study to collect data on the potential confounder. Various ways to control for threats to internal validity in selected study designs are discussed in this and later chapters.

At the analysis phase of the study, an appropriate statistical test is applied to evaluate the hypotheses. Inferences from the results are then drawn to the general population. **External validity** (also called generalizability) is the degree to which conclusions can be appropriately made to people beyond the study. The process of drawing conclusions from sampled data is called **statistical inference**. A related term is **causal inference**, which is a conclusion about a causal association. A conclusion about causal association is based on the totality of information available, which includes temporality and a valid statistical association. These and other concepts and criteria about causality are addressed in Chapter 7, "Causal Inference in Reproductive Epidemiology." Selected research designs for addressing reproductive health problems are presented in Chapter 6, "Study Designs in Reproductive Epidemiology."

The purpose of this chapter is to present the different phases of the research process in the context of reproductive health.

The Problem

The research process begins with a statement of the problem. A **reproductive health problem** is a disruption to the normal reproductive process. The problem is established through observed or measured phenomena. Data of a reference population provide the basis of the **research problem**; data are the building blocks of epidemiologic research. A **population** is a group sharing some common characteristic of interest. Social, economic, family (marriage and divorce), work and labor force, and geographic factors may characterize populations.

The Case Definition

The research problem is centered on a **health outcome variable**, which is a consequence or an end result. A number of health outcome variables have been identified in reproductive epidemiology, such as menstrual problems, semen quantity and quality, couple infertility or reduced fertility, time to pregnancy, embryonic and fetal death, spontaneous abortion, stillbirth, premature delivery (<37 weeks), infant mortality rate, maternal mortality rate, gender ratio at birth, low birth weight (<2,500 grams), survival and growth, birth defects, developmental disorders, and childhood cancer.

Error in the data collection may result in identification bias, where **bias** is defined as a deviation of the results from the truth. To avoid identification bias, a standard case definition and adequate levels of reporting are required. A **case definition** is a set of standard clinical criteria to determine the presence of a particular health-related state or event. A standard set of clinical criteria will ensure that cases are consistently diagnosed, regardless of where or when they are identified and who diagnoses the case. Whatever the criteria, it should be applied consistently and without bias to all those under investigation.

A case definition may be restricted by person (e.g., women trying to become pregnant), place (e.g., employees at a certain worksite), and time (e.g., when a pregnancy occurs) variables. The clinical criteria may include laboratory confirmation. Clinical criteria may also involve a combination of signs, symptoms, and other findings. Clinicians characterize health-related states or events by examining and analyzing the specific symptoms and performing tests on the patient.

A case definition should be simple, understandable, acceptable, and sufficiently sensitive and specific. A case definition is sufficiently sensitive if it identifies most people with the condition being considered. A case definition is sufficiently specific if it excludes those people without the health-related state or event.

Data

The history of epidemiology involves individuals who sought to understand and explain health-related states and events from an observational scientific perspective. Their intent was to advance the study of disease, injury, and death from a supernatural viewpoint to one based on a rational, scientific foundation. This approach involved the development of systematic methods for summarizing and describing public health problems.

Data are pieces of information and may be thought of as observations or measurements of a phenomenon of interest such as reproductive health problems according to person, place, and time variables or environments that may contribute to the health problem. Data are obtained by observation, measurement, or experiment of variables, where a **variable** is a characteristic that varies from one observation to the next and can be measured or categorized. In a research study, variables are selected that represent the phenomena of interest.

The standard classifications of data are nominal, ordinal, discrete, and continuous. A description of these types of data, along with some of the statistics and graphs that are commonly used to describe these data, is presented in **Table 3-1**.

Nominal data are data that fall into unordered categories. Nominal data may be referred to as qualitative data because they describe the quality of something, with distinct levels differing in quality, not quantity. We typically represent the categories of a nominal variable by numbers. For instance, 1 represents males and 2 represents females; however, the fact that we label these categories with numbers does not mean the order and magnitude of the numbers are important. We could have just as easily assigned females as 1 and males as 2. In contrast, the ordering among categories is important with **ordinal data**. With ordinal data, a natural ordering exists in the data, such as 1 = disagree, 2 = neutral, and 3 = agree. The magnitude of the numbers is not important, but the ordering is. Hence, it is not appropriate to apply many arithmetic operations to nominal or ordinal data.

| TABLE 3-1 | Ways to Present and Test Types of Data | | | |

	Description	*Statistics*	*Graphs*	*Statistical Tests*
Nominal	Categorical— unordered categories	Number of cases Frequency distribution Relative frequency	Bar chart Spot map Area map	Binomial test Multinomial test Runs test χ^2 goodness-of-fit test Test of homogeneity of Poisson rates
Ordinal	Categorical— ordering informative	Number of cases Frequency distribution Relative frequency	Bar chart	χ^2 goodness-of-fit test
Discrete	Quantitative— integers Ordering and magnitude important	Geometric mean Arithmetic mean Median	Bar chart	Kolmogorov-Smirnov test Lilliefors test Shapiro-Wilk test
Continuous	Quantitative— values on a continuum	Mode Range Variance Standard deviation Coefficient of variation Chebychev's inequality	Histogram or frequency polygon Box plot Stem-and-Leaf plot P-P plot Q-Q plot	Kolmogorov-Smirnov test Lilliefors test Shapiro-Wilk test

Discrete data are those where ordering and magnitude are important and the data represent quantities, not labels. A natural order exists in these data. Discrete data are restricted to take on only integer values. In contrast, **continuous data** represent values measurable on a continuum. A decimal place is involved with continuous data, and the difference between two levels of a continuous variable may be arbitrarily small.

The type of data considered is often determined by accessibility, which in turn influences the type of statistics used to describe and analyze the variable.

Methods for Measuring and Describing Data

Descriptive statistics are a means of organizing and summarizing data. There are two methods for describing data: numerical and graphical. Types of descriptive statistics include tables, graphs, numerical summary measures, and proportions. Essentially, descriptive statistics are used to summarize the distribution of data, are a final step in editing, characterize the study participants, and inform choice of analytic statistics.

Numerical methods involve measures of central location and dispersion. A **measure of central location** is used as a single value that best represents a group of people that are described in a distribution. A **measure of dispersion** is used to show how much people described in a distribution vary from one another and from a measure of central location. There are several measures of central location such as the arithmetic **mean**, median, mode, and geometric mean. Likewise, there are several measures of dispersion, including the range, interquartile range, variance, standard deviation, and confidence interval for the mean. Selecting a measure of central location for quantitative data depends on whether the distribution of observations is skewed or not. The **arithmetic mean** is the measure of central location you are most likely familiar with because it has many desirable statistical properties; it is the arithmetic average of a distribution of data. It is an appropriate summary measure for data that are approximately normal.

If the data are not normally distributed but have an exponential pattern (1, 2, 4, 8, 16, etc.) or a logarithmic pattern (1/2, 1/4, 1/8, 1/16, etc.), then the geometric mean is an appropriate measure of central tendency. The **geometric mean** is calculated as the nth root of the product of n observations. It is used when the logarithms of the observations are normally distributed. The geometric mean will always be less than or equal to the arithmetic mean for any given data set. Other measures of central tendency include the **median** (middle) and **mode** (most). The median is less sensitive to outliers than the mean and is commonly reported with the range (highest minus the lowest values). The mean is reported with the standard deviation, which together have nice mathematical properties, making them useful in statistical inference.

The **coefficient of variation** is a measure of relative spread in the data. It is a normalized measure of dispersion of a probability distribution that adjusts the scales of variables so that meaningful comparisons can be made. It is an appropriate measure for noncategorical data. It is the ratio of the standard deviation to the mean.

The **empirical rule** states that approximately 67% of the observations are within 1 standard deviation of the mean; 95% of the observations are within 2 standard deviations of the mean, and almost all the observations are within three standard deviations of the mean. The empirical rule, however, is an approximation that only applies when the data are symmetric and unimodal. Alternatively, **Chebychev's inequality** can be used to summarize the distribution of data. It is less specific than the empirical rule but applies for any set of data, no matter what its distribution. It says that for any number k that is greater than or equal to 1, at least $[1 - (1/k)^2]$ of the measurements in the data set lie within k standard deviations of the mean.[1] If $k = 2$ then $[1 - (1/2)]^2 = 3/4$, or 75% of the values lie within 2 standard deviations of the mean. We can also say that $\bar{x} \pm 2s$ includes at least 75% of the observations. If $k = 3$, then $\bar{x} \pm 3s$ contains at least 88.9% of the observations. It is a conservative statement, more so than the empirical rule.

The simplest table is the frequency distribution of one variable, such as number of cases in each age group. A **frequency distribution** is a complete summary of the frequencies of values or categories of a measurement made on a group of persons. The distribution tells either how many or what proportion of the group was found to have each value (or each range of values) out of all possible values that the quantitative measure can have. To create a frequency distribution, values or categories that the variable may take are listed and the number of persons in the group who are at each value or category are shown. **Relative frequency** is derived by dividing the number of people in each group by the total number of people.

A **contingency table** is when all entries are classified by each of the variables in the table. In epidemiology, the 2×2 table is often used to classify people according to exposed or unexposed; that is, two nominal characteristics are measured on the same set of subjects. If two numerical measures were taken on the same subjects, a scatter plot would be appropriate for displaying the data.

Ratios, proportions, and rates are commonly used methods for describing nominal data. In epidemiology, we are often interested in assessing the presence of a health-related state or event that has a nominal scale. Ratios, proportions, and rates are used in descriptive epidemiology to characterize health-related states or events by person, place, and time.

The general formula for a ratio, proportion, or rate is:

$$\frac{x}{y} \times \text{Rate base}$$

where x represents the number in one group, y represents the number in a second group, and the **rate base** is equal to 1, 100, 1,000, 10,000, 100,000, or 1,000,000. The purpose of the rate base is to express the ratio, proportion, or rate in a more easily interpretable manner.

In a **ratio**, the values of x and y are independent such that x is not contained in y and the rate base is 1. For example, the birthrate of White males to White females in 1970 was 1.055; that is, there were 105.5 males born to every 100 females. In 2001, the ratio was 1.046.[2]

In a **proportion**, x is contained in y. The rate base for a proportion is typically 100, such that the result is expressed as a percentage. For example, 15 of every 100 newly married couples (or 15%) have difficulty conceiving a child.[3]

A **rate** is the number of health-related states or events during a given time period divided by the at-risk population during the same time period. A rate may be calculated using the following equation:

$$\text{Rate} = \frac{\text{Number of health-related states or events occurring during a given time period}}{\text{Population at risk during the same time period}} \times \text{Rate base}$$

The size of the rate base for a rate is somewhat arbitrary, but it is generally selected to remove the decimal place. For example, the rate of babies born in the United States each year that involved assisted reproductive technologies is .01. This rate is multiplied by 100 and interpreted as 1 per 100 births each year, or 1% of births each year involve assisted reproductive technologies.[4]

If the numerator in the rate calculation involves live cases, it is an incidence rate. If it involves deaths, it is a mortality rate. If the denominator in the rate calculation involves the total time people are followed in the study, the rate is referred to as a **person-time rate**.

A useful measure for describing the burden of health-related states or events is **point prevalence proportion**. The numerator is distinct from that in the incidence rate in that it contains the number of all existing cases, events, or behaviors. The denominator is distinct from that in the incidence rate in that it contains the total study population at a point in time. The rate base is typically 100.

$$\text{Rate} = \frac{\text{All existing health-related states or events at a point in time}}{\text{Total study population at a point in time}} \times 100$$

The point prevalence proportion is useful for measuring the magnitude (burden) of a health-related state or event. It is also useful for measuring an outcome where it is difficult to know when an individual became a case.

Several graphical methods are used to display data (see **Table 3-2**). In general, graphs may further help clarify the public health problem. Graphs are used to find patterns, trends, aberrations, similarities, and differences in data; they are useful for effectively describing and communicating health-related states or events according to person, place, and time. Simplicity is an important feature of graphs. Graphs may involve numbers, ratios, proportions, or rates.

TABLE 3-2 **Graph or Chart for Describing Data**

Type of Graph	*When to Use*
Arithmetic-Scale Line Graph	Line graphs are used mostly for data plotted against time. An arithmetic graph has equal quantities along the y-axis. An arithmetic graph shows actual changes in magnitude of the number or rate of a health-related state or event across time.
Semilogarithmic Scale-Line Graph	The y-axis is changed to a logarithmic scale. In other words, the axis is divided into cycles with each being ten times greater than the previous cycle. Focus is on the rate of change. A straight line reflects a constant rate of change.
Histogram	A graphic representation of the frequency distribution of a variable. Rectangles are drawn in such a way that their bases lie on a linear scale representing different intervals, and their heights are proportional to the frequencies of the values within each of the intervals. Epidemic curve: a histogram that shows the course of a disease outbreak or epidemic by plotting the number of cases by time of onset.
Frequency polygon	A graphical display of a frequency table. The intervals are shown on the x-axis and the frequency in each interval is represented by the height of a point located above the middle of the interval. The points are connected in that together with the x-axis they form a polygon.
Cumulative frequency	A running total of frequencies. A cumulative frequency polygon is used to graphically represent it, where straight lines join the points.

(continues)

TABLE 3-2   *(Continued)*

Type of Graph	*When to Use*
Scatter plot	This graph is a useful summary of the association between two numerical variables. It is usually drawn before calculating a linear correlation coefficient or fitting a regression line since these statistics assume a linear relationship in the data. It provides a good visual picture of the relationship between the two variables and aids in the interpretation of the correlation coefficient or regression model.
Simple bar chart	A visual display of the magnitude of the different categories of a single variable, with each category or value of the variable represented by a bar.
Grouped bar chart	Multiple sets of data are displayed as side-by-side bars.
Stacked bar chart	Similar to a grouped bar chart, except each of the segments in which the bar or column is divided belongs to a different data series. It shows how a total entity is subdivided into parts.
Deviation bar chart	Illustrates differences, both positive and negative, from baseline.
100% component bar chart	The bar is divided into proportions that are the same as the proportions of each category of the variable; helps compare how components contribute to the whole in different groups.
Pie chart	Shows components of a whole.
Spot map	A map that indicates the location of each case of a rare health-related state or event by a place that is potentially relevant to the health event being investigated, such as where each cased lived or worked.
Area map	A map that indicates the number or rate of a health-related state or event by place, using different colors or shadings to represent the various levels of the disease, event, or behavior.
Box plot	Also called a box-and-whisker plot, a box plot is a graphical depiction of numerical data through five-number summaries, the smallest observation, the first quartile, the median, the third quartile, and the largest observation. The box represents the middle 50% of the data. The plot is useful for describing the distribution of the data, whether it is skewed, and if outliers are present.

Statistical Tests for Evaluating a Single Variable

The **binomial test** is an exact probability test that is used when there is one nominal variable with only two values. The most common use of the binomial test is in the case where the null hypothesis is that two categories are equally likely to occur. For more than two categories of a variable, the **multinomial test** should be used. The multinomial test is the test of the null hypothesis that the parameters of a multinomial distribution equal specified values. The **runs test** is a nonparametric test that checks a randomness hypothesis for a two-valued data sequence. It tests the hypothesis that the elements of the sequence are mutually independent.

The χ^2 **goodness-of-fit test** is used to test that a set of data come from a hypothesized distribution. That is, how close are the observed values to those that would be expected under the fitted model?

Rare health-related states or events are often modeled using a Poisson distribution. **Poisson regression** is well suited for modeling counts or rates of rare health outcomes. For example, suppose we are interested in estimating the rate of birth defects by place or time. Then a place, time, or place by time variable can be included in the Poisson regression model and the rates tested for homogeneity according to place, time, or place by time.

The **Kolmogorov-Smirnov** test is a goodness-of-fit test that assesses whether a distribution is normally distributed. Samples are standardized and compared with a standard normal distribution, which is equivalent to setting the mean and variance of the reference distribution equal to the sample estimates. The **Lilliefors test** is an adaptation of the Kolmogorov-Smirnov test, which tests the null hypothesis that data come from a normally distributed population, when the null hypothesis does not specify which normal distribution (i.e., the expected value of the variance is not specified). The **Shapiro-Wilk test** examines the null hypothesis that a sample came from a normally distributed population.

Morbidity, Mortality, and Natality Outcome Measures for Understanding the Health Problem

Some common reproductive health measures are presented in **Table 3-3**. These measures are primarily descriptive (i.e., proportions and rates) and are useful for identifying and formulating the research problem. The risk ratio, rate ratio, and **odds ratio** are typically analytic, allowing us to measure the strength of association between exposure and outcome variables.

Frequently used measures of morbidity, mortality, and natality are presented according to the numerator, denominator, and rate base in **Tables 3-4, 3-5, and 3-6**.

TABLE 3-3 Ratios, Proportions, and Rates for Measuring Morbidity, Mortality, and Natality

	Ratios	*Proportions*	*Rates*
Morbidity (incidence)	Risk ratio (relative risk) Rate ratio Odds ratio	Point prevalence Attributable proportion	Incidence rate Person-time rate
Mortality (death)	Maternal mortality ratio	Proportionate mortality	Maternal mortality rate Infant mortality rate Neonatal mortality rate Postneonatal mortality rate Perinatal mortality rate Fetal death rate Abortion rate
Natality (birth)		Low birth weight	Birth rate Fertility rate

TABLE 3-4 Measures of Morbidity

Measure	*Numerator (x)*	*Denominator (y)*	*Expressed Per Number at Risk (Rate Base)*
Incidence rate	Number of new cases of a specified disease reported during a given time interval	Estimated population at midinterval	Varies
Attack rate	Number of new cases of a specified disease reported during an epidemic period	Population at start of the epidemic period	Varies
Secondary attack rate	Number of new cases of a specified disease among contacts of known cases	Size of contact population at risk	Varies
Point prevalence	Number of current cases, new and old, of a specified disease at a given point in time	Estimated population at the same point in time	Varies
Period prevalence	Number of current cases, new and old, of a specified disease identified over a given time interval	Estimated population at midinterval	Varies

TABLE 3-5   Measures of Mortality

Measure	Numerator (x)	Denominator (y)	Expressed Per Number at Risk (Rate Base)
Crude death rate	Total number of deaths reported during a given time interval	Estimated midinterval population	1,000 or 100,000
Cause-specific death rate	Number of deaths assigned to a specific cause during a given time interval	Estimated midinterval population	100,000
Proportional mortality	Number of deaths assigned to a specific cause during a given time interval	Total number of deaths from all causes during the same interval	100 or 1,000
Death-to-case ratio	Number of deaths assigned to a specific disease during a given time interval	Number of new cases of that disease reported during the same time interval	100
Neonatal mortality rate	Number of deaths under 28 days of age during a given time interval	Number of live births during the same time interval	1,000
Postneonatal mortality rate	Number of deaths from 28 days to, but not including, 1 year of age, during a given time interval	Number of live births during the same time interval	1,000
Infant mortality rate	Number of deaths under 1 year of age during a given time interval	Number of live births reported during the same time interval	1,000
Maternal mortality rate	Number of deaths assigned to pregnancy-related causes during a given time interval	Number of live births during the same time interval	100,000
Maternal mortality ratio	Number of deaths of women during or shortly after a pregnancy	100,000 live births	
Infant mortality rate	Number of fetal deaths after at least 20 weeks of gestation	Number of live births plus fetal deaths	1,000
Abortion rate	Number of abortions done during a given time interval	Number of women ages 15–44 during the same time interval	1,000

TABLE 3-6   **Measures of Natality**

Measure	Numerator (x)	Denominator (y)	Expressed Per Number at Risk (Rate Base)
Crude birth rate	Number of live births reported during a given time interval	Estimated total population at midinterval	1,000
Crude fertility rate	Number of live births reported during a given time interval	Estimated number of women ages 15–44 years at midinterval	1,000
Crude rate of natural increase	Number of live births minus the number of deaths during a given time interval	Estimated total population at midinterval	1,000
Low birth weight ratio	Number of live births under 2,500 grams during a given time interval	Number of live births reported during the same time interval	100

Surveillance for Understanding the Health Problem

Public health surveillance is the systematic ongoing collection, analysis, interpretation, and dissemination of health data. We monitor health-related states or events:

1. To detect sudden changes in occurrence and distribution of health-related states or events.
2. To follow long-term trends and patterns in health-related states or events.
3. To identify changes in risk factors.
4. To detect changes in health behaviors.

Determining unusual aggregations of health problems requires knowledge of what is usual based on the distribution of occurrences in the same location at an earlier time period or in other similar locations at the same time period. Surveillance provides a means for determining whether health problems exist and if so whether they are increasing or decreasing over time and by place. For example, surveillance data may identify in a given population a higher than expected number of birth defects, a greater prevalence of low birth weight, a decrease in fertility rates, or a smaller proportion of births attended by skilled health personnel within a specified population. What is usual may also be obtained from local health officials. These officials often know if more disease is occurring than is expected based on ongoing disease surveillance data through local surveys or health data registries.

Many sources of data are available for use in surveillance. Some key sources of surveillance data include the following:

- Mortality reports
- Morbidity reports
- Epidemic reports
- Reports of laboratory utilization (including laboratory test results)
- Reports of individual case investigations
- Reports of epidemic investigations
- Special surveys (e.g., hospital admissions, disease registers, and seriologic surveys)
- Information on animal reservoirs and vectors
- Demographic data
- Environmental data

Geographic information systems can be used to capture, store, analyze, manage, and present surveillance data. They are a means of evaluating counts and rates of health-related states or events by person and place. Geographic information systems make it possible to effectively map health events and corresponding population information, as well as proximity to the suspected source. Geographic information systems have been used to spatially assess adverse reproductive health outcomes.[5,6] The Centers for Disease Control and Prevention (CDC) currently provides an interactive atlas of reproductive health: Geo-dataset selection. The system allows us to evaluate selected reproductive health outcomes (fetal–infant mortality, infant health, maternal intervention, maternal risks, and pregnancy outcomes) according to geographic area.[7] Geographic information systems have also been used to measure associations between birth defects and environmental exposures like hazardous waste sites and air pollution[8,9] and to explore the association between socioeconomic status and neural tube defects.[10]

Research Question and Hypothesis

Thus far we have discussed ways to identify and describe the health problem. Once a research problem is established, a statement of the problem is needed. This statement may be framed as a question, with the aim to understand why and how the problem exists. A **research question** that is formulated to predict the direction of an association is the **research hypothesis**. For example, the research problem may be that there is an elevated rate of low birth weight in a community. The research question could then be, "Is the chemical company located near town associated with low birth weight infants?" The research hypothesis would then predict the direction of association between low birth weight infants and proximity to the chemical plant. The research hypothesis could be that the occurrence of low birth weight infants increases in direct relation to proximity to the chemical plant. We test the hypothesis by further observation or experimentation with the use of a comparison group. The rate of low birth weights can be compared according to distance lived from the chemical plant. Ideally, personal or environmental exposure can be directly estimated. If not, an indirect measure may be used such as proximity to the chemical company.

When a study involves a comparison group, it becomes an analytic study. The research question provides the basis for statistically testing the significance of the finding in an analytic study. Specifying a hypothesis allows us to then calculate the number of participants needed to achieve the expected difference in outcome between study groups with reasonable probability or power.

Hypotheses

Hypotheses may apply to a single variable (e.g., about the distribution) or involve relationships between or among variables. Hypotheses are shown to be consistent or inconsistent with facts. If established facts or information are lacking to substantiate a hypothesis, then more information should be gathered, or we fail to reject the null hypothesis. In contrast to the research hypothesis, the **null hypothesis** usually states the current belief or what is expected or claimed, or has been in the past. We assume that the null hypothesis is correct unless sufficient evidence exists to the contrary.

The research hypothesis is formulated to relate a health outcome with a suspected environmental exposure. Tests of hypothesis are called tests of significance. Investigators generally try to design tests of significance so they have high power. **Power** is the capability of a study to detect a given difference of a given size if the difference really exists. The choice of analysis and the statistical test for evaluating hypotheses depends on the type of exposure and outcome data. Discrete data are often treated as a continuous variable. When the categories of the discrete variable are small, they may also be treated as categorical variables.

The research hypothesis is formulated to identify how change in the health outcome (also called a response or dependent) variable is related to change in an environmental (also called an explanatory or independent) variable. The distinction between these two types of variables relates to the research purpose. In other words, the researcher chooses how to view the variables, basing the decision on the research problem. Variables may also be considered in an analysis to reduce the risk of attributing explanatory power to the suspected exposure variable that in fact may have no association with a disease outcome (i.e., confounding).

Parameters are always used in the formulation of the hypothesis. A **parameter** is a measurement on the population level. It is typically unknown. On the other hand, a **statistic** is a measurement on the sample level. When sample data are under consideration, it is important to consider the role of chance; that is, is a result due to or influenced by chance—the luck of the draw—or is it real? It is possible that a finding based on sample data may not be reflective of the overall population but is unique to the specific sample taken. This may result if the sample is not random or if a random sample involves a small number of participants.

Some physical, chemical, biological, and psychosocial environments capable of producing adverse reproductive health outcomes were presented in Chapter 2, "Environments in Reproductive Epidemiology." An explanatory variable may represent an actual environmental exposure (e.g., radiation, toxic chemical, or microorganism) or a behavior (e.g., where one works or socializes). Individual attributes may also be associated with increased risk for certain health outcomes (e.g., age, gender, and race/ethnicity). In order to establish whether a given environment is capable of harming the reproductive process, an accurate assessment of the outcome is needed, with a clear and consistently applied case definition.

The Research Design

As described in the first chapter of this book, there are both descriptive and analytic aspects of the epidemiologic research process. A **descriptive epidemiologic study** involves using general epidemiologic knowledge and applying it to specific settings. There are generally no predetermined hypotheses about associations. The study design simply describes what exists in a population according to person, place, and time. Descriptive studies are useful for identifying public health problems and providing clues as to why they exist. The research problem, question, and hypotheses are supported by descriptive epidemiology.

On the other hand, an **analytic epidemiologic study** is a type of assessment that goes beyond characterizing the distribution of data but tests one or more predetermined hypotheses about associations between and among variables. The hope is to draw meaningful conclusions from the study; however, in interpreting the study, consideration needs to be given to potential biases and how they have been addressed. Common study designs employed in reproductive epidemiology will be the focus of Chapter 6, "Study Designs in Reproductive Epidemiology."

An analytic study design is used to evaluate a research hypothesis of association between an environmental exposure and health-related state or event. An environmental exposure may be a specific event that is relatively easy to measure (e.g., an infectious agent) or can be subdivided into dose or duration (e.g., the number of cigarettes smoked during pregnancy). An adverse reproductive health outcome may require a minimal level of exposure and increase in probability with longer exposure or considerable exposure at a single point in time. Although it is often desirable to isolate the association between a given exposure and disease outcome, assessing the combined effects of multiple exposures on human health is a potentially important approach from a public health perspective because public health interventions often target an overall exposure scenario. Combined effects may reflect contaminants where the total effect differs from the sum of the individual effects.[11]

Whenever possible, measurement of an exposure variable on a continuous scale is the most informative for evaluating associations. With continuous data, dose–response relationships can be measured. Yet exposure information is often only available on a nominal scale such as exposed or not exposed. This is the only option when there are perceived exposures compared with documented exposures or when the exposure occurred in the past and direct measurement is not possible. There also exists the basic question as to what to measure (e.g., peak exposure or cumulative exposure).[12]

Exposure data may be classified as direct or indirect measures. Direct measures of exposure include personal monitoring involving quantitative measurements of personal exposure to environmental physical stresses, chemical or biological agents, and psychosocial milieu, as well as biologic markers. Personal monitoring may be used that involves wearing a dosimeter to estimate total exposure to radiation in the workplace through the air, water, and food, or a personal air monitor can measure a person's exposure to air pollutants in the home. Exposure may involve an intense dose over a relatively short period of time or a low-level prolonged dose over a period from weeks to years. The effects of acute, high-dose environmental exposures may appear within hours or days (e.g., miscarriage) or low-dose exposure may appear after several years (e.g., cancers).

Biological monitoring may involve measuring concentrations in human tissues (blood lead), metabolic products (dimethylarsinic acid in urine after arsenic exposure), or markers of physiologic effects (e.g., protein adducts induced by beta-naphthylamine in cigarette smoke).[11] Sources of biologic information can involve measurement through physical examinations, laboratory assays, and medical imaging. For example, heavy metals and some pesticides can accumulate in the body, with the risk of human harm increasing with time. These pollutants leave residues in the body that can usually be measured in the blood or urine. Biomonitoring is the approach of measuring pollutant levels in tissue or fluid samples.[13]

Some indirect sources of exposure information include questionnaires, surrogates, existing records, and diaries. **Questionnaires** translate the research objectives into specific questions. Data used in data analysis are provided through answers to these questions. Questionnaires may be administered through face-to-face interviews, over the telephone, or through the mail or internet. Questionnaire data are subject to interviewer and recall bias. Response bias is also increasingly problematic with telephone interviews because of caller identification, cell phones, and a decreasing tolerance of telemarketing in the population. Although mailed questionnaires avoid interviewer influences, they are subject to low response rates, and they exclude individuals who cannot read. They also do not allow the responder to obtain item clarification. Electronic mail questionnaires are increasingly popular because of their relative speed, low cost, ability to attach pictures and sound files, and the higher response levels they often stimulate when compared to "snail" mail surveys. Yet, challenges exist with email surveys, which include obtaining (or purchasing) a list of email addresses, nonresponse to unsolicited email (which may be higher than unsolicited regular mail), and obtaining a representative sample of the population of interest.

Some exposures may be represented by **surrogate measures** such as years of employment, census track, carbon monoxide in indoor air at home, trihalomethanes in water coming out of the tap, self-reported water consumption, and hot shower use. These measures are crude and prone to errors. Although direct measures of exposure are more accurate, resource constraints may limit investigators to surrogate measures of exposure.

An ideal source of exposure information is from **existing records** such as hospital admission or discharge records, laboratory records, pathology records, and crisis intervention services because this source of information avoids the problems of interviewer bias, recall bias, and response bias.

Diaries are also a common source of exposure information. For example, a prospective cohort study involving newlywed couples in China examined associations between selected environmental and occupational exposures with reproductive outcomes. The study consisted of 165 newlywed couples. Women in the study were nonsmokers with no past history of dysmenorrhea (cramps or painful menstruation). Enrollment began when the couples began to try to become pregnant. Daily diaries were used to record exposure to environmental tobacco smoke up until clinical pregnancy occurred or for 1 year. Environmental tobacco smoke was measured as the mean number of cigarettes smoked per day at home by household members over an entire menstrual cycle before the menstrual period. Data results indicate an increased risk of dysmenorrhea among women exposed to environmental tobacco smoke, moreso with higher levels of exposure.[14]

Because pollutants are released from multiple sources (e.g., treatment storage and disposal facilities, industry, government facilities, households, and others), the fate and transport of contaminants are important issues in managing hazardous pollutants. Fate and transport consider ground water, soil, gas, and atmospheric transport of chemicals. A number of models have been developed to estimate the magnitude of pollutants in the air, water, and soil.

- The Atmospheric Sciences Modeling Division contains information about atmospheric models.

- The Center for Exposure Assessment Modeling provides predictive exposure models for aquatic, terrestrial, and multimedia pathways for organic chemicals and metals.

- The Division of Computational Toxicology applies mathematical and computer models to predict adverse effects and describe the mechanisms through which chemicals may induce harm.

- The Support Center for Regulatory Environmental Model provides model guidance, development, and application.

- The Support Center for Regulatory Air Models is a source of information on atmospheric dispersion (air quality) models.

- The ADL Migration Exposure Model was developed to estimate the migration of chemicals from polymeric materials used in the home.

- The Landfill Air Emissions Estimation Model was developed to estimate emissions of methane, carbon dioxide, nonmethane organic compounds, and hazardous air pollutants from mucipal solid waste landfills.

- The Multi-Chamber Concentration and Exposure Model was designed to estimate average peak indoor air concentrations of chemicals from products or materials in homes.

- AQUATOX is a freshwater ecosystem simulation model that predicts the fate of selected pollutants such as organic toxicants and their effects on the ecosystem.

- CHEMFLO is a model for simulating water and chemical movement in unsaturated soils.

- PRESTO-EPA-POP is a computer model for evaluating radiation exposure from contaminated soil layers and many other things.[15]

Another common model is the Physiologically-Based Pharmacokinetic Model. This is a physiologically based compartmental model (e.g., lung, liver, rapidly perfused tissues, slowly perfused tissues, fat, and kidney) that characterizes pharmacokinetic behavior (absorption, distribution, metabolism, and excretion) of a chemical. It is a commonly used tool for predicting the fate of environmental contaminants in humans. The Physiologically-Based Pharmacokinetic Model incorporates data on blood flow rates, metabolic and other processes that the chemical undergoes within each compartment to construct a mass-balance frame-work.[16–20]

Statistical Tests of Association

The study design dictates the appropriate statistical test for assessing the significance of the hypothesized association between the exposure and outcome variables. Tests of hypotheses, also called tests of significance, allow us to assess the pattern of association between exposure and outcome variables in a sample, compute the appropriate measure of association between variables, and estimate the probability that the measured association is due to chance (statistical significance). To do this, contingency tables, correlation measures, or regression techniques are used, depending on the nature of the data. Selected common statistical methods and tests for evaluating associations between variables according to variable type are presented in Appendix I.

Consider the traditional 2×2 table used in epidemiology to represent dichotomous exposure and outcome variables in case-control or cohort studies (see **Table 3-7**).

The letters in this table represent data collected in the epidemiologic study, as classified by exposure and outcome status. In cohort studies, the attack rate can be calculated as $(a + c)/n$. The attack rate for the exposed group is calculated

TABLE 3-7   2 × 2 Table Involving Either Cohort or Case-Control Data

	Outcome		
Exposed	Yes	No	
Yes	a	b	$a + b$
No	c	d	$c + d$
	$a + c$	$b + d$	$n = a + b + c + d$

In a cohort study, the row totals are fixed whereas in a case-control study the column totals are fixed.

TABLE 3-8 **2 × 2 Table Involving Cohort Person-Time Data**

	Disease		
Exposed	Yes	No	
Yes	a	—	Person-Time T_e (t_{ei})
No	c	—	Person-Time T_{ue} (t_{uei})
	$a + c$	—	$T = \Sigma(t_{ei} + t_{uei})$

t_{ei} is the follow-up time for the ith person in the exposed group, and t_{uei} is the follow-up time for the ith person in the unexposed group. Time can be measured in different units (e.g., hours, days, weeks, months, or years).

as $a/(a + b)$ and the unexposed group is calculated as $c/(c + d)$. The attack rate, also called the **cumulative incidence** rate, is a measure of risk. The ratio of risk for the exposed group compared with the unexposed group is called the **risk ratio**.

In cohort studies, it is sometimes desirable to consider the amount of time people are followed, especially when people are at risk for different lengths of time. Then, rather than counting each person equally, the time each person is at risk is used (see **Table 3-8**). The person-time rate is calculated as $(a + c)/T$. The person-time rate for the exposed group is calculated as a/T_e and the unexposed group is calculated as c/T_{ue}. When the denominators in the calculations involve person-time, we use the word "rate," rather than the word "risk." We also call the person-time rate the **incidence density rate**. The ratio of person-time rates is called a **rate ratio**.

Selected common study designs, measures of association, and test statistics are presented in **Table 3-9**. The summary risk ratio and odds ratio are used to control for confounding, where the confounding variable being controlled for has i levels. The test statistics follow a chi-square distribution. Many statistical packages readily compute these measures of association and test statistics.

When the association between categorical variables is being examined and the sample size is small, the Fisher's exact test is preferred to the conventional χ^2 test. The test is named after R. A. Fisher, who devised it. It is one of a class of exact tests. In some reproductive studies where there are small numbers of exposures or outcomes are rare, the exact test allows one to obtain a more accurate

TABLE 3-9   Common Study Designs With Selected Measures of Association and Test Statistics

Study Design	Measure of Association	Tests of Significance
Cohort Cumulative incidence	Risk ratio $= \dfrac{a/(a+b)}{c/(c+d)}$	$\chi^2 = \dfrac{(\lvert ad - bc \rvert - n/2)^2 n}{(a+b)(c+d)(a+c)(b+d)}$
Summary risk ratio	Risk ratio$_{MH} =$ $\dfrac{\sum[a_i(c_i+d_i)/n_i)]}{\sum[c_i(a_i+b_i)/n_i)]}$	$\chi^2_{MH} = \dfrac{\{\sum a_i - \sum[(a_i+c_i)(a_i+b_i)/n_i]\}^2}{\sum(a_i+b_i)(c_i+d_i)(a_i+c_i)(b_i+d_i)/n_i^2(n_i-1)}$
Incidence density	Rate ratio $= \dfrac{a/T_e}{c/T_{ue}}$	$\chi^2 = \dfrac{\{a - [T_e(a+c)]/T\}^2}{T_e[T_{ue}(a+c)]/T^2}$
Case-control Unmatched	Odds ratio $= \dfrac{a \times d}{c \times b}$	$\chi^2 = \dfrac{(\lvert ad - bc \rvert - n/2)^2 n}{(a+b)(c+d)(a+c)(b+d)}$
Summary odds ratio	Odds ratio$_{MH} =$ $\dfrac{\sum(a_i d_i/n_i)}{\sum(b_i c_i/n_i)}$	$\chi^2_{MH} = \dfrac{\{\sum a_i - \sum[(a_i+c_i)(a_i+b_i)/n_i]\}^2}{\sum(a_i+b_i)(c_i+d_i)(a_i+c_i)(b_i+d_i)/n_i^2(n_i-1)}$
Matched	Odds ratio $= \dfrac{b}{c}$	$\chi^2 = \dfrac{(\lvert b - c \rvert - 1)^2}{(b+c)}$
Cross-sectional	Prevalence ratio $= \dfrac{a/(a+b)}{c/(c+d)}$	$\chi^2 = \dfrac{(\lvert ad - bc \rvert - n/2)^2 n}{(a+b)(c+d)(a+c)(b+d)}$

MH = Mantel-Haenszel
a = number of exposed individuals with the outcome
b = number of exposed individuals without the outcome
c = number of unexposed individuals with the outcome
d = number of unexposed individuals without the outcome
n = total number of individuals in the sample
i = level of stratification

analysis. How small does that sample need to be before the chi-square test is inappropriate and the Fisher's exact test should be used? Most statisticians agree that an expected frequency of 5 or less means that the χ^2 test should not be used. Others suggest that if any expected frequency is less than 2 or if more than 20%

of the expected frequencies are less than 5, then the Fisher's exact test should be used. If the contingency table is greater than 2×2 and there are small cell sizes, it may be appropriate to combine categories of one or both variables.

If we can assume that the odds ratio or risk ratio across i strata are homogeneous (i.e., not influenced by effect modification), then the Mantel-Haenszel method of combining information is appropriate. This test combines a series of 2×2 tables into an overall test of significance. The Mantel-Haenszel method tests whether the summary odds ratio or risk ratio is equal to 1, which means that there is no association between the exposure and outcome.

The odds ratio approximates the risk ratio when the outcome of interest is rare. If the outcome is common in the study population ($>10\%$), the odds ratio is no longer a good approximation of the risk ratio. The more common the outcome, the more the odds ratio overestimates the risk ratio when it is greater than 1 or underestimates it when it is less than 1.

The use of regression is common in describing the association between variables. Morgenstern showed how the risk ratio (RR) could be approximated from the simple regression model $Y = a + bX$ involving ecologic data.[21] If $X = 1$ is exposed, 0 is unexposed and $Y =$ a continuous outcome variable, then:

$$RR \cong 1 + \left(\frac{b}{a}\right)$$

For example, suppose that a research team identified 20 communities located near waste sites and 20 communities not located near waste sites. Let $X = 1$ for each of the communities located near a waste site and $X = 0$ for each of the communities not located near a waste site. Also, suppose that the incidence rate of low birth weight children is available in each of the 40 areas. If the resulting model was $Y = 1.6 + 0.8X$, then an estimate of the RR is as follows:

$$RR \cong 1 + \left(\frac{1.6}{0.8}\right) = 1 + 0.5 = 1.5$$

Thus, we would expect that those women who reside in a community near a waste site have approximately 1.5 times the risk of having a child with low birth weight than those women residing in a community with a nearby waste site. This model also applies to cross-sectional data.

Associated with the statistical test is a P value. The **P value** is defined as the probability of obtaining a result at least as extreme as the one that was actually observed, given that the null hypothesis is true. For example, in a cohort study involving 1,041 Hispanic (primarily Puerto Rican) women who smoked during pregnancy, a significantly increased risk of preterm birth with increasing levels of smoking was observed.[22] The P value for the Mantel-Haenszel χ^2 test for trend was 0.03, meaning the role of chance was small enough that the investigators referred to this finding as statistically significant. As the sample size increases, the P value or the role of chance decreases.

Confidence intervals are also important to report with point estimates based on sample data because they indicate statistical precision in the estimate and the likely range in which the true parameter lies. The confidence interval is influenced by the selected level of significance (generally 0.05), the variability in the data, and the sample size. As the sample size increases the confidence interval or the role of chance decreases. In addition, for a measure of association, the confidence interval indicates statistical significance. For example, in the same study of Hispanic women, those who smoked 10 or more cigarettes per day during pregnancy had 3.2 times the risk of preterm birth (95% confidence interval, 1.1–9.5) as women who did not smoke during pregnancy. Because the confidence interval does not overlap 1, we can conclude that this risk ratio is statistically significant at the 0.05 level.[22]

Conclusion

The research process in reproductive epidemiology begins with a problem. The problem is identified through descriptive epidemiology. Surveillance is a way to identify a public health problem. Once the problem is established and a statement of the problem is made, exploration as to why the problem exists occurs. Descriptive epidemiology is also a means of identifying possible environments that may explain the problem. On the basis of descriptive epidemiology, hypotheses are formulated and an appropriate analytic study design is selected to evaluate the hypotheses. The analytic study design directs the researcher on data collection, analysis, and interpretation. Appropriate test statistics for assessing hypotheses of association depend on the data and statistical measure employed. The study design should provide guidance on collecting and analyzing data in such a way as to minimize chance, bias, and confounding. Some study designs better control for these effects. Some study designs also do better in allowing us to address criteria for drawing conclusions about causality.

Key Issues

1. Before an analytic study investigation, the researcher develops a statement of the research problem and identifies appropriate variables, data, and hypotheses. These basic elements of research help transform ideas into concrete research operations.

2. Descriptive epidemiology is useful for identifying public health problems and providing clues as to why they exist. Descriptive methods for measuring and describing data include frequency distributions, measures of central location and dispersion, ratios, proportions, and rates. Several statistical tests commonly used to evaluate selected variable characteristics were presented.

3. Descriptive epidemiology includes surveillance, which is a means for identifying sudden changes in occurrence and distribution of health-related states or events, following long-term trends and identifying patterns in health-related states or events, identifying changes in risk factors, and detecting changes in health behaviors.

4. Adverse reproductive health outcome measures include morbidity, mortality, and natality.

5. The study design is a road map that guides the researcher in his or her evaluation of the hypotheses that follow from a recognized public health problem. The study design provides direction on data collection, analysis, and interpretation. The type of data collected influences the type of statistics used to measure and test associations.

Exercises

Key Terms

Define the following terms.

χ^2 goodness-of-fit test

Analytic epidemiologic study

Arithmetic mean

Bias

Binomial test

Causal inference

Case definition

Chebychev's inequality

Coefficient of variation

Confidence intervals

Contingency table

Continuous data

Cumulative incidence

Data

Descriptive epidemiologic study

Diaries

Discrete data

Empirical rule

Existing records

External validity

Frequency distribution

Geographic information systems

Geometric mean

Health outcome variable

Incidence density rate

Internal validity

Kolmogorov-Smirnov test

Lilliefors test

Mean

Measure of central location

Measure of dispersion

Median

Mode

Multinomial test

Nominal data

Null hypothesis

Odds ratio

Ordinal data

P value

Parameter

Person-time rate

Point prevalence proportion

Poisson regression

Population

Power

Proportion

Public health surveillance

Questionnaires

Random error

Rate

Rate base

Rate ratio

Ratio

Relative frequency

Reproductive health problem

Research

Research hypothesis

Research problem

Research question

Risk ratio

Runs test

Shapiro-Wilk test

Statistic

Statistical inference

Study design

Surrogate measures

Systematic error

Variable

Study Questions

3.1 Define research and discuss the basic elements of research that help transform ideas into concrete research operations.

3.2 Describe what a reproductive health problem is and the importance of a standard case definition in analyzing the problem.

3.3 Identify a reproductive health issue and draft a research problem, research question, and research hypothesis for the issue.

3.4 Describe each of the four types of data: nominal, ordinal, discrete, and continuous.

3.5 Define public health surveillance and its functions in reproductive health epidemiology.

3.6 What are three common ways that morbidity (incidence) is presented in the epidemiologic literature?

3.7 Which measures provided in Question 3.6 involve a comparison group and thus allow us to test hypotheses about associations between exposure and outcome variables?

References

1. Parzen E. *Modern Probability Theory and Its Applications.* New York, NY: Wiley; 1992.

2. Templeton D. Study seeks to explain drop in male births. *Pittsburgh Post-Gazette* [serial online]. April 10, 2007. Available at: http://www.post-gazette.com/pg/07100/776561-114.stm. Accessed December 4, 2008.

3. St. Luke's Episcopal Health System. Information on infertility (men). Available at: http://www.sleh.com/sleh/Section004/index.cfm?pagename=Infertility%20Men. Accessed December 4, 2008.

4. About.com. Infertility in men. Available at: http://adam.about.com/reports/000067_6.htm. Accessed December 4, 2008.

5. Rushton G, Krishnamurthy R, Krishnamurti D, Lolonis P, Song H. The spatial relationship between infant mortality and birth defect rates in a U.S. city. *Stat Med.* 1996; 15:1907–1919.

6. Forand SP, Talbot TO, Druschel C, et al. Data quality and the spatial analysis of disease rates: congenital malformations in New York State. *Health Place.* 2002;8:191–199.

7. Centers for Disease Control and Prevention. Interactive atlas of reproductive health: geodataset selection. Available at: http://apps.nccd.cdc.gov/gisdrh/(ylc0yhujqrwlub45psxl10aa)/Default.aspx. Accessed December 4, 2008.

8. Orr M, Bove F, Kaye W, et al. Elevated birth defects in racial or ethnic minority children of women living near hazardous waste sites. *Int J Hyg Environ Health.* 2002;205:19–27.

9. Gilboa SM, Mendola P, Olshan AF, et al. Relation between ambient air quality and selected birth defects, seven county study, Texas, 1997–2000. *Am J Epidemiol.* 2005;162:238–252.

10. Wasserman CR, Shaw GM, Selvin S, et al. Socioeconomic status, neighborhood social conditions, and neural tube defects. *Am J Public Health.* 1998;88:1674–1680.

11. Hertz-Picciotto I. Environmental epidemiology. In: Rothman K, Greenland S, eds. *Modern Epidemiology.* Philadelphia, PA: Lippincott-Raven; 1998.

12. Bailar JC. Inhalation hazards: the interpretation of epidemiologic evidence. In: Bates DV, Mohr U, Dungworth DL, McClellan RO, Lee PN, eds. *Assessment of Inhalation Hazards.* New York, NY: Springer-Verlag; 1989:39–48.

13. Environmental Protection Agency. Measuring exposures to environmental pollution. Available at: http://www.epa.gov/indicate/roe/html/roeHealthMe.htm. Accessed April 6, 2007.

14. Chen C, Cho S, Damokosh AI. Prospective study of exposure to environmental tobacco smoke and dysmenorrheal. *Environ Health Perspect*, 2000;108:1019–1022.

15. Environmental Protection Agency. Modeling at EPA. Available at: http://www.epa.gov/epahome/models.htm. Accessed April 7, 2007.

16. Environmental Protection Agency. Glossary archive. Available at: http://www.epa.gov/iris/gloss8_arch.htm. Accessed April 7, 2007.

17. Shipp AM, Gentry PR, Lawrence G. Determination of a site-specific reference dose for methylmercury for fish-eating populations. *Toxicol Ind Health.* 2000;16(9–10):335–438.

18. Nordbert GF, Kjellstrom T. Metabolic model for cadmium in man. *Environ Health Perspect.* 1979;28:211–217.

19. O'Flaherty EJ. Physiologically based models for bone-seeking elements. IV. Kinetics of lead disposition in humans. *Toxicol Appl Pharmacol.* 1993;118(1):16–29.

20. Licata AC, Dekant W, Smith CE, Borghoff SJ. A physiologically based pharmacokinetic model for methyl tert-butyl ether in humans: implementing sensitivity and variability analyses. *Toxicol Sci.* 2001;62(2):191–204.

21. Morgenstern H. Uses of ecologic analysis in epidemiologic research. *Am J Public Health.* 1982;71(12):1336–1344.

22. Haskins A, Mukhopadhyay S, Pekow P, et al. Smoking and risk of preterm birth among predominantly Puerto Rican women. *Ann Epidemiol.* 2008;18(6):440–446.

FOUR

Surveillance in Reproductive Epidemiology

Learning Objectives

After completing this chapter, you should be able to:

1. Describe important objectives and operational aspects of surveillance.
2. Identify criteria for considering the usefulness of a surveillance system.
3. Describe active, passive, sentinel, and special systems surveillance.
4. Distinguish between a survey and a surveillance system.
5. Describe a cluster and the steps to a cluster investigation in reproductive epidemiology.
6. Understand some of the data and statistical challenges involved in cluster investigations.

In the previous chapter, surveillance was presented for identifying and monitoring public health problems. In the United States, surveillance programs of birth defects on the state level provide coverage for most infants. A dramatic increase in state programs since the late 1990s is attributed to the Birth Defects Prevention Act of 1998 and the funding of 26 cooperative agreements between the Centers for Disease Control and Prevention and states. At the end of 2000, 87% of states, Puerto Rico, and the District of Columbia had existing monitoring programs.[1] Surveillance programs allow statements to be made, such as 1 in 33 babies born in the United States this year will have a structural birth defect or mental retardation; the most common birth defects are of the heart, Down syndrome, cleft lip or cleft palate, spina bifida, and other neural tube defects; 1 in 10 children with birth defects will die by one year of age; and about 1% of all newborns will be diagnosed with mental retardation by school age. In addition, surveillance data provided the information that birth defects tend to increase with maternal age, are greatest in African Americans, and tend to be lower in women with more education.[2]

Although surveillance of birth defects and other reproductive health problems is relatively new, surveillance has been around a long time. Historically, surveillance involved close observation of individuals who had been exposed to a communicable disease so that early symptoms could be detected and prompt isolation and control measures imposed. This form of surveillance is referred to as **medical surveillance**. More recently, **surveillance** has also been used as a type of observational study that involves continuous monitoring of health-related states or events within a population. As defined in the previous chapter, it is the systematic collection, collation, analysis, interpretation, and dissemination of data. This form of surveillance is called **public health surveillance**. It provides a means for identifying outbreaks of health-related states or events and yields a basis for implementing control measures. Public health surveillance originally focused on communicable diseases, but now includes monitoring injuries, birth defects, chronic diseases, and health behaviors. Public health surveillance is also used to monitor changes in environmental risk factors (physical, biological, chemical, or psychosocial), evaluate prevention and control programs, monitor long-term trends, plan future resource needs for prevention, and suggest topics for future research.

The purpose of this chapter is to explore the public health surveillance of birth defects and other reproductive disorders.

Objectives and Operations

Surveillance data provide information for more effective planning, policy, and prevention and control measures; it provides information on which action may be taken. Hence, a primary objective of a surveillance program is to contribute to the understanding about the natural course and epidemiology of the health-related state or event. Surveillance systems can provide insight into who is at greatest risk, the average time of presymptomatic disease, the clinical manifestations of disease, and the average survival times. Public health surveillance is also a means of monitoring health-related states or events in order to identify sudden changes in distribution, to identify changes in exposure and host factors, and to detect changes in health behaviors. Surveillance provides baseline data that can be used to determine the presence of disease outbreaks. Public health surveillance is also used to assess whether prevention and control measures have effectively influenced incidence and mortality rates.

Clear objectives should accompany any surveillance program. For example, the state of Alaska has the following objectives for their birth defects surveillance system:

- Establish baseline and prevalence estimates within populations and identify temporal and geographic trends.
- Investigate unusual patterns of occurrence.
- Provide information to health-related programs for planning and evaluation.
- Identify areas of unmet need.
- Help prevent secondary disabilities by making recommendations regarding the need for special services in the community.
- Observe and evaluate effects of interventions and policy changes.[3]

A surveillance system of birth defects and other adverse reproductive health outcomes can:

- Detect sudden changes in the distribution of reproductive health problems.
- Identify long-term trends in the distribution of reproductive health problems.
- Detect the effects of newly introduced reproductive hazards.
- Detect increases in exposure rates of already existing hazards.
- Detect changes in health behaviors related to reproductive health.

When surveillance data are presented according to person and place, we gain further insights into who is at greatest risk and where the problem is most pronounced.

Assessing the correlation between exposure and health outcome data by person and place also provides clues about what caused the problem; however, because of the difficulty in controlling for confounding factors when survival data are correlated, analytic epidemiologic studies are generally required for more definitive consideration of cause–effect relationships. Yet surveillance data may be effective at ruling out a potential cause. For example, birth defects detected in infants born to two separate women who had used spray adhesives extensively while doing "foil art" during pregnancy led the Consumer Product Safety Commission to ban the sale of these spray adhesive compounds; however, further investigation of birth surveillance data for 1970 to 1973 showed a decrease in birth defects among infants, despite sales of the spray adhesive compounds increasing fivefold.[4]

The operational aspects of a surveillance system involve the following:

1. A case definition of the health-related state or event
2. Specification of the population under surveillance
3. Specification of the time period of data collection
4. Specification of the information that will be collected
5. Details on the reporting sources or data sources
6. Description of how the data will be handled
7. Description of how the data will be analyzed
8. Identification of those who will interpret the results
9. Description of who should be provided the results (e.g., medical and public health communities and policymakers)
10. Description of how the information will be disseminated

Case Definition

Once the objectives of an investigation are clearly identified, the cases to be included are determined. If all cases are not being used, it is important to avoid bias in the selection of cases. In surveillance systems, it is critical that a case definition be consistently applied in order to avoid changes in frequency and patterns of cases simply because of inconsistent application of the case definition. Some explanations for observed changes in the frequency and pattern of cases in a surveillance system, which are not due to changes in risk exposures, include the following:

- Inconsistent interpretation and application of the case definition
- Change in the case definition

- Change in surveillance system/policy of reporting
- Improved diagnosis (e.g., new laboratory test, increased physician awareness, a new physician in town)
- Change in diagnostic criteria
- Change in reporting requirements
- Change in the population
- Change in the level and emphasis on active case detection
- Random events
- Increased public awareness

If change in an outcome variable is not attributed to these alternative explanations, the epidemiologist can then be more confident that it is due to the introduction or increased level of exposure to a risk factor.

Population Under Surveillance

In order to set policy and plan programs effectively and efficiently, public health surveillance must represent the health of the population or community it serves. **Population** refers to a collection of individuals that share one or more observable characteristics from which data may be collected and evaluated. Population can refer to all people inhabiting a given area, or the total number of people of a particular social class, race/ethnicity, or group in a specified area. Surveillance that aims to obtain representative information from a population or community is referred to as population based.

As mentioned in the outset of this book, epidemiology includes the study of the frequency and pattern of health-related states or events in a population. In assessing frequency, it is often more informative to consider the counts in relation to the population from which the health-related states or events occurred. By dividing counts by population values, proportions and rates can be obtained. Proportions and rates are more informative than counts alone because they take into account the population size and allow for more meaningful comparisons over time and among different groups. When differences over time or among groups exist in terms of an extrinsic factor such as age or gender, these factors may be adjusted for in order to minimize their potential confounding effect.

Several measures for assessing and monitoring birth defects and other adverse reproductive health problems include population values in their calculation. For rare health-related states or events, a surveillance program should collect data from a large enough population to make it possible to monitor changes/differences in proportions or rates; however, the population needs to be defined so that detailed information that changes in unusual occurrences can be detected (accuracy). If the area or country is very large, this may be a problem. Some population-based registries trying to identify and register all birth defects in large populations may jeopardize accuracy. Although a population-based registry covering a smaller, well-defined geographic area may have high accuracy, it may not be appropriate to generalize the results of the surveillance data to the overall country.

Time Period of Data Collection

Proportions or rates of health-related states or events change over time. Surveillance is a means to evaluate whether changes occur regularly and can be predicted or are unusual events that are unexpected. Monitoring rates according to month allows the detection of seasonality. To control for seasonal affects, one method is to compare the rate during a given month with the rate reported during the same period in previous years. Monitoring rates according to year allows the identification of long-term (secular) trends.

Annual rates are typically used to monitor trends over time. For example, one study examined annual rates of Down syndrome and changes in the mother's age at the time of birth over several years. The study showed that an increase in Down syndrome paralleled an increase in maternal age at the time of birth.[5]

What Information to Collect

All forms of birth defects and adverse reproductive health outcomes that can be interpreted in a convincing way should be surveyed. On the other hand, some reproductive health outcomes may be impractical to monitor, such as spontaneous abortions (miscarriages). Registering miscarriages and interpreting their rates of occurrence are generally impractical for large-scale surveillance because of widespread underreporting. Similarly, when the time from exposure to outcome is lengthy (e.g., mild developmental delays manifesting themselves later in childhood or adolescence), intervening psychosocial factors may confound the relationship, making interpretation of the rates problematic. Hence, surveillance programs tend to concentrate on health-related states or events that can be obtained with relative ease. In addition, surveillance programs tend to be more effective at providing clues as to the causes of an adverse health outcome when the time between the exposure and outcome variables is short.

State regulations typically specify the health-related states or events that must be reported, who should submit reports, how and to whom the case reports are to be sent, and what information should be provided. Some statutes and regulations set specific control measures and penalties to be imposed on those not reporting. Although some state and local surveillance data indicate that about 3% of births in the United States are affected by any of a number of birth defects, population-based birth defects surveillance on the national level have not been available, with the exception of certain neural tube defects (spina bifida anencephaly).[6]

All births in a small population may be monitored whereas in large populations, registry data may only cover a subset of the population. In this latter situation, generalization of results to the overall population may be inappropriate. Ideally, large populations would be monitored by a combination of cooperating regional registries that employ high-quality standards of operation. These registries should be selected to provide representation of the overall population.

Reproductive health surveillance programs tend to focus on congenital malformations. Their aim is to identify epidemics quickly in order to identify causes and to remove them before a large number of damaged infants are born. The level of detailed information in the registration of malformations depends largely on the sources of available information. Specific information to be collected should include outcome information according to person, place, and time. Assessing surveillance data by person characteristics may provide clues as to the causes of the birth defects. Age, gender, and race/ethnicity information are often available and useful for identifying those at greatest risk. In the example given previously, collecting information on maternal age allowed the researchers to identify a positive association between Down syndrome and maternal age at birth.

As a practical matter, epidemiologists often analyze reproductive health problems by time and place simultaneously. This allows answers to the where and when questions in epidemiology. It is also often informative to organize data into tables, maps, or both, as well as by potential sites of exposure. By so doing, information can be more effectively communicated and clues as to the causes of the health problems more easily recognized.

Data Sources

Case information is generally ascertained by abstracting information from hospital logs, which includes labor and delivery reports, neonatal intensive care units, pathology reports, and surgery logs. States vary in the extent to which prenatally diagnosed birth defects are collected by the surveillance system. Prenatal birth defects data are obtained from prenatal diagnostic centers and sources such as genetics laboratories.

In the United States, national estimates of birth defects have historically been based on data from the Birth Defects Monitoring Program, which is based on hospital discharge data and is not population based.[7] The National Birth Defects Prevention Network (NBDPN) collects population-based surveillance data. Annual surveillance data are provided by 34 states for up to 45 major birth defects.[8] This surveillance system allows for state comparisons for selected birth defects. Thus far, these data have only provided national prevalence estimates for neural tube defects. In a study conducted by the Centers for Disease Control and Prevention (CDC), NBDPN data from 11 states were used to calculate state-specific and national prevalence estimates per 10,000 live births. These states had active case-findings for 18 selected defects during 1999 to 2001 birth years and reported this data to NBDPN for the 3 successive years.[6] Results from this study are presented in **Table 4-1**.

The CDC uses different systems to track birth defects. In turn, this information is used to inform the public about trends in birth defects. In addition to revealing patterns and trends in the surveillance data, they also present purported causes. Surveillance data provide information for planning, prevention, and control purposes. Various major systems used by the CDC to track birth defects are as follows:

- The Metropolitan Atlanta Congenital Defects Program for tracking birth defects[9]
- State Birth Defects Tracking Systems[10]
- National Birth Defects Prevention Network[8]
- International Clearinghouse for Birth Defects Monitoring Systems[11]
- The Health and Environment Linked for Information Exchange (HELIX-Atlanta)[12]

TABLE 4-1	Average Prevalence* of 18 Selected Major Birth Defects in 11 States Combined and Estimated Number of Births Affected by These Defects Each Year, by Birth Defect—United States, 1999–2001

	11 States Combined		National Estimates[‡]			
Birth Defects[†]	Average Prevalence[§]	95% Confidence Interval	Prevalence	95% Confidence Interval	Annual No. of Cases	95% Confidence Interval
Eye defects						
Anophthalmia/ microphthalmia	2.1	1.9–2.3	2.1	1.9–2.3	834	763–905
Cardiovascular defects						
Truncus arteriosus (also known as common truncus)	0.8	0.7–0.9	0.8	0.7–0.9	329	285–373
Transposition of great arteries	4.7	4.5–5.0	4.7	4.5–5.0	1,901	1,795–2,007
Tetralogy of Fallot	3.9	3.6–4.1	3.9	3.7–4.2	1,574	1,478–1,670
Atrioventricular septal defect (also known as endocardial cushion defect)	4.3	4.1–4.6	4.35	4.1–4.6	1,748	1,644–1,852
Hypoplastic left heart syndrome	2.4	2.2–2.6	2.43	2.2–2.6	975	900–1,051
Orofacial defects						
Cleft palate only	6.3	6.0–6.6	6.4	6.1–6.7	2,567	2,445–2,689
Cleft lip with or without cleft palate	10.5	10.2–10.9	10.5	10.1–10.9	4,209	4,050–4,368
Gastrointestinal defects						
Esophageal atresia/ Tracheoesoph- ageal fistula	2.3	2.2–2.5	2.4	2.2–2.6	952	878–1,027

(continued)

TABLE 4.1   *(Continued)*

Birth Defects[†]	11 States Combined		National Estimates[‡]			
	Average Prevalence[§]	95% Confidence Interval	Prevalence	95% Confidence Interval	Annual No. of Cases	95% Confidence Interval
Rectal and large intestinal atresia/ stenosis	4.8	4.6–5.1	4.8	4.5–5.1	1,931	1,824–2,039
Musculoskeletal defects Reduction defect, upper limbs	3.8	3.6–4.1	3.8	3.6–4.0	1,521	1,425–1,617
Reduction defect, lower limbs	1.9	1.8–2.1	1.9	1.7–2.1	763	695–831
Gastroschisis	3.8	3.6–4.1	3.7	3.5–4.0	1,497	1,402–1,592
Omphalocele	2.1	1.9–2.3	2.1	1.9–2.3	839	769–909
Diaphragmatic hernia	2.9	2.7–3.1	2.9	2.7–3.2	1,179	1,095–1,262
Chromosomal defects Down syndrome (trisomy 21)	12.9	12.5–13.4	13.6	13.2–14.1	5,429	5,245–5,613
Trisomy 13	1.3	1.2–1.5	1.3	1.2–1.5	528	471–585
Trisomy 18	2.3	2.1–2.5	2.4	2.2–2.6	959	881–1,037

* Per 10,000 live births.
[†] Infants with more than one major structural birth defect were included in more than one defect group.
[‡] National estimates for all defects were based on the average prevalence from the 11 states and adjusted for race-specific distribution of U.S. live births during 1999–2001 (all defects except Down syndrome, trisomy 13, and trisomy 18) or adjusted for maternal age (Down syndrome, trisomy 13, and trisomy 18).
[§]Average prevalence is a pooled estimate from Alabama, Arkansas, California, Georgia, Hawaii, Iowa, Massachusetts, North Carolina, Oklahoma, Texas, and Utah.[6]

Many other sources of data are available that can be used to monitor birth defects and other reproductive health problems, which include the following:

- National Congenital Rubella Syndrome Registry to study congenital rubella[13,14]
- Birth Defects Monitoring Program to study congenital malformations[13,15]

- Hospital records to study congenital malformations[16,17]
- Birth certificates to study spina bifida and Down syndrome[18-21]
- Death certificates to study spina bifida[18,22]
- Department of health records to study Down syndrome and birth defects[19,23-25]
- Department of mental hygiene records to study Down syndrome[19,23,24]
- Special schools to study Down syndrome and other birth defects[19,24,26]
- Hospital obstetric records to study Down syndrome and other birth defects[23,27]
- Hospital inpatient records to study birth defects[24,28]
- Private physician records to study fetal alcohol syndrome[29]
- Indian Health Service patient case files to study fetal alcohol syndrome[29]
- Counts from office of Population Census and Surveys to study neural tube defects[30,31]
- Spatial surveillance monitoring of birth defects[32]

Sometimes surveillance outcome and exposure data are linked to provide clues as to the causes of the health problem. For example, in one study, researchers linked population-based medical birth data in Norway and Sweden with cancer registry data.[33] The linkage allowed the researchers to identify subsequent cancer risk in children with birth defects. The results found that there was an increased risk of cancer among individuals with birth defects. The highest risks were observed in those with malformations of the nervous system, Down syndrome, and multiple defects. Parents and siblings of individuals with birth defects showed no increased risk of cancer. In another study, linked data allowed researchers to identify that Down syndrome was associated with increased risk of leukemia, but was not associated with increased risk of brain tumors.[34] Mental retardation excluding Down syndrome was associated with increased risk of acute nonlymphoblastic leukemia and cleft palate–lip cases developed acute lymphoblastic leukemia more often.

The sources of many surveillance systems employ **secondary data**, which are data collected for other purposes (e.g., vital records, healthcare utilization records, national and local surveys, and environmental data). **Vital records** refer to data on birth, death, marriage, and divorce. This information is available at the local and state levels. Coroners and medical examiners can be a source of information on sudden or unexpected deaths. This information is available at the local and state levels. Notifiable disease reports, laboratory data, hospital data, and outpatient healthcare data are other sources of morbidity data.

The quality of surveillance data in terms of completeness and accuracy is influenced by the type of health outcome considered. For example, malformation information on birth certificates tends to be incomplete and inaccurate, while hospital records tend to be more complete and accurate. For this reason, many population-based surveillance registries tend to rely on laboratory, hospital, and healthcare data.

Environmental data are routinely collected by many public health agencies to monitor contamination of public water, milk, and food supplies. There is also regular environmental surveillance of radiation, workplace hazards (chemicals, biological and physical agents, and psychosocial milieu), and conditions in nature that may be reservoirs or vectors of disease. The challenge, then, is associating environmental data with reproductive health problems that may have a long latency period.

Exposure information may be characterized by exploring:

- The mechanism (physical, chemical, biological, psychosocial)
- The potency or intensity of the exposure
- The duration of exposure
- The relationship between duration of exposure and an adverse health-related state or event
- The exposure pathway (air, water, soil, food)
- The pollutant portal of entry into the body
- The clinical signs, if any, associated with the exposure

In Chapter 3, "Research Process in Reproductive Epidemiology," reference was made to direct and indirect measures of environmental exposures. Briefly, direct measures such as personal monitoring and use of biologic markers are most appropriate for assessing risk factors. Personal measurement allows for assessment of the contaminant. Total dose to the body from multiple routes of exposure can be measured using biological markers. Exposure measures on a continuous scale are useful for identifying adverse health outcomes according to dose and whether a threshold exists. Quantifying concentrations of toxic contaminants in a specified environment (air, water, soil, and food) is also useful exposure data for reflecting a direct measure of dose. Indirect measures of dose are often easier to obtain but obviously less precise. Limited time and money may make it necessary to rely on indirect measures of exposure. Although causal inference is strongest when exposure information is directly measured, surrogate measures of exposure can also provide important insights into causality.

Examples of indirect measures of exposure include drinking water use, food use, distance from a site and duration of residence, residence or employment within reasonable proximity to a site where exposure can be assumed, and residence or employment in a defined geographical area of the site (e.g., a county).[35]

Handling the Data

Effective surveillance requires fast action. Timeliness is the availability of data in a time frame that is appropriate for action; however, because multiple sources of information are often desired in order to obtain sufficient detail, time of data collection is often delayed. Delays may prevent public health authorities from initiating prompt intervention or feedback. Delays may occur at any phase of the **surveillance process** (i.e., data collection, management, analysis, interpretation, or dissemination). To avoid delays, specific guidelines are needed for routing, transferring, and storing data, for appropriate methods of analysis that can be readily interpreted and communicated, and for details about the target audience. A well-planned surveillance system will minimize error and disseminate information in a timely manner.

Those who have a responsibility to report data (e.g., physicians, nurses, and laboratory staff) need to be aware of when and how this is to be done. A list of reportable diseases and the mechanisms by which to report a case need to be communicated by the health department to those who need to know. A simple reporting process where only relevant information is requested will improve reporting. Timely, informative, interesting, and relevant feedback will reinforce the importance of participating in the surveillance process.

Preliminary tabulations should be constructed and reviewed to identify obvious errors or highly unusual cases. Computer algorithms and statistical analyses are often useful for identifying inaccurate data and assisting to quickly manage, summarize, and describe the data. Accuracy in malformation registration is critical. Finally, confidentiality is necessary to protect individual privacy.

Data Analysis

Shortly after the data are collected, when the reports are evaluated and coded, strong deviations in the data from what is expected may be noticed. If so, these deviations should be checked for accuracy and, if necessary, corrected. Data analyses then follow. Surveillance data may identify sudden outbreaks that show up when the observed and expected numbers significantly differ during a given surveillance period. Unexpected health outcomes may also manifest themselves by evaluating fluctuations over the long run. Descriptive epidemiology is used to assess sudden unexpected outbreaks and fluctuations in long-term trends. Survival analyses are also used to assess the lethality of the health problem. Person, place, and time aspects are often assessed in surveillance data. Study designs and statistical techniques commonly used in descriptive epidemiology will be presented in Chapter 6, "Study Designs in Reproductive Epidemiology."

Assessment of the data typically begins by generating tables. A **table** is an orderly arrangement of values that groups data into classes. Tables should include a title, which tells as simply as possible what is in the table and answers what the data are (counts, percentage distributions, rates), who are represented in the table, where the data are from, and when the time period reflected by the data is. Summary tables are designed to present specific data for a specific use. Generally, a summary table should only use important categories, grouped data, whole numbers, and place data being compared in adjacent positions.

The best medium for presenting data that can be quickly visualized is a graph, which is a diagram that shows a relationship, often between two variables. Graphs can emphasize main points and clarify relationships that may otherwise be elusive. There are many types of graphs (e.g., bar graphs, histograms, frequency polygons, line graphs, pie charts, scatter diagrams, and pictograms). The type of graph chosen depends on the type of data being displayed. Presenting too many graphs or including graphs that fail to demonstrate anything of interest should be avoided. Graphs that depict specific relationships or trends inherent in the data, however, may be particularly useful. As with tables, a simple title should be used, with answers to: What? Who? Where? When?

Geographic maps are often an effective way to communicate surveillance data. This is a map of an area that is the reference, with certain statistical information superimposed. Dot maps and shaded maps are commonly used types of geographic maps. Dot maps are typically used to represent the location of cases, and shaded maps are most often used for incidence and mortality rates. The interested reader may wish to refer to a recent paper that specifically considered the role of geographic information systems (GIS) in surveillance and research of birth defects.[36]

Measures of central tendency and variation are standard methods for describing surveillance data.

The primary tool for measuring risk is the rate. Rates have already been described. Age-adjusted rates are commonly used to monitor risk over time, because they remove the confounding effect of a changing age distribution.

Time-series analyses are useful for organizing counts or rates of health-related states or events by time in order to identify the nature of the phenomenon represented by the sequence of observations. Once a time-series pattern is established, it can be combined with other data (e.g., exposure) as a useful means for identifying incubation or latency periods and for better understanding possible causal relationships. The **time-series design** involves a sequence of measurements of some numerical quantity made at or during two or more successive periods of time. A simple time-series design involves the collection of quantitative observations made at regular intervals through repeated observations.

Survival analysis is used for estimating survival (prognosis) in a population under study. It is the probability that an individual will survive until time t. Its primary purpose is to identify the effects of patient care, treatments, prognostic factors, exposures, or other covariates on survival over time. There are several types of survival measures. Survival time and survival rate will be discussed briefly. Survival time is the average (mean) or median survival time for a group of patients. The median survival time has the advantage of being less sensitive to extreme values. Survival rate is observed survival that measures the proportion of persons surviving regardless of cause of death. This can be calculated using the Kaplan Meier method, the direct method, or the actuarial method.

Survival results are then presented using graphs and reports. Mean and median survival time can be presented in a bar graph. Survival rates in a single period can also be presented by bars; however, if the emphasis is on pattern of change over time, it is better to use a line graph. Furthermore, the survival report should include the survival rate (or time) and also a complete description of the patients, their health problems, and their treatment.

There has been an ongoing debate about whether to publish estimated rates of birth defects for comparing rates over time or among regions. The challenge comes in random error and ascertainment bias that often accompanies birth defects surveillance data. It has been proposed that efforts should be made to develop standards for birth defects surveillance in order to minimize the variability in prevalence of birth defects caused by differences in case ascertainment methods. In turn, evaluation of real temporal and spatial variations in environmental effects can be made. In the meantime, where comparisons of rates are necessary to address public health concerns, such comparisons should only be made between regions or across time when the degree of case ascertainment can be assumed to be similar across regions and time;[37] however, it is often very difficult to estimate the ascertainment rates in a surveillance program.

Surveillance data may provide clues as to potential confounders that should be controlled for in analysis assessing possible relationships between exposures and health outcomes. For example, a strong association between maternal age and chromosomal defects has been shown using surveillance data. Hence, prevalence and rate estimates of Down syndrome, trisomy 13, and trisomy 18 should adjust for maternal age, generally less than age 35 years versus 35 years and older. Infants with more than one birth defect are typically counted once for each of the defects that they have.

Dissemination

A critical component of surveillance is disseminating information to those who need it. Surveillance information should be disseminated to healthcare providers and laboratory directors and those who can use this information for administrative, program planning, and decision making purposes. Surveillance reports targeted at medical and public health communities are intended to inform and to motivate. Summary information on health-related states or events by person, place, and time informs the public as to overall risk and helps the physician anticipate the probability of encountering specific health problems among their patients. Tabular and graphical presentations of the data often make the information more interpretable.

Surveillance reports may demonstrate that the health department is aware of and acting on the public health problem. Some reports may thank those who submitted case report information, thereby maintaining a spirit of collaboration that improves the surveillance system. Surveillance reports may also include information on selected prevention and control efforts and summarize completed epidemiologic investigations.

Usefulness of the Surveillance System

The usefulness of a surveillance system is impacted by its responsiveness to the operational aspects presented in the previous section. Additional issues that should be considered when evaluating the usefulness of a surveillance system are as follows:

1. Whether appropriate actions have been taken to date as a result of information from the surveillance system.
2. Whether the information has been used to make decisions and take action.
3. Whether monitored prevalence of the outcome variable relates to the level and distribution of services available.
4. Whether the information may be used in the future.

The surveillance system should be as simple as possible while still meeting its objectives, and it should be flexible (i.e., able to add new health outcomes and accommodate changes in operating conditions). It should also be representative in that it accurately portrays the incidence of a health-related state or event in a given population by person, place, and time; provide data in a timely manner; detect the health-related states or events it is intended to detect; measure the predictive value of a reported case or epidemic; and have a high level of willingness of individuals or organizations who participate in the surveillance system.[4] In short, the surveillance system should address an important public health need, meet its objectives, and operate efficiently.

Active, Passive, Sentinel, and Special Systems Surveillance

There are four categories of surveillance methods: active, passive, sentinel, and special systems surveillance.

Active surveillance occurs when the health department takes the initiative to contact public authorities through regular telephone calls or visits to laboratories, hospitals, and providers. Thus, the burden is taken from the healthcare provider and placed on the health department. In other words, the health department actively contacts healthcare providers on a regular basis. This form of surveillance is relatively expensive and is usually limited to short-term intensive investigation and control activities or seasonal problems; however, active surveillance has a tendency to increase the number and proportion of reported cases. It also tends to promote closer personal ties between health department staff and medical providers. Active surveillance is a reasonable method to document a suspected outbreak, to validate the representativeness of passive reports, to improve completeness, and to target and eliminate a given health problem.

Passive surveillance is the most common form of surveillance. It relies on data collected from disease observations on an ad-hoc basis. Standardized reporting forms are provided by the local or state health departments, which are returned to the health departments when a given health-related state or event is identified. Health authorities do not take action while waiting for the forms to be submitted. Factors that contribute to completeness are proper case definition and partner management. This form of reporting is relatively less expensive and less burdensome to health officials and may provide useful information for identifying trends or outbreaks. An important limitation of passive surveillance, however, is that it is prone to nonreporting or underreporting.

Sentinel surveillance is when case data are collected from only part of the population in order to obtain information about the overall population, such as disease pattern. This form of data is less expensive than collecting data from the total population and may be higher quality than data obtained through passive surveillance because it is often more logistically feasible to obtain higher quality data from a smaller population; however, obtaining a representative subset of the total population may be difficult.

Special systems may be designed to generate surveillance information if it is not possible to acquire the information through active, passive, or sentinel surveillance. For example, chlamydia is only diagnosed by testing. Hence, the population at risk for a diagnosis of the disease is those tested for chlamydia. Information would then be collected on all tests performed such as positive or negative tests.[38]

Survey Versus Surveillance

In the beginning of the chapter, we defined surveillance as a type of descriptive epidemiologic study that involves ongoing monitoring of health-related states or events within a population. In contrast, a **cross-sectional survey** is a detailed inspection or investigation at a snapshot in time. A cross-sectional survey is often referred to as a prevalence survey that is useful for estimating the prevalence of the health-related state or event under consideration. Both the surveillance system and the cross-sectional survey are commonly population based. The primary distinction between them is that the surveillance system is ongoing. Some advantages and disadvantages of survey versus surveillance data are as follows.

Survey

Advantages

- More control over the quality of data.
- More in-depth data can generally be obtained.
- A greater spectrum of health-related states or events may be considered.
- More accurate estimates of prevalence can be obtained.

Disadvantages

- It may be more costly to validate an instrument and train and supervise those carrying out the survey.
- It is limited to a single point in time and is not feasible for rare or rapidly fatal conditions.
- Unless serial surveys are used, time trends in the incidence or prevalence of a health outcome or exposure cannot be assessed over time.
- Recall and interviewer bias may result.

Surveillance

Advantages

- It is less costly for the health department.
- Existing systems and health personnel are often available for data collection.
- Time trends may be monitored.
- With ongoing data collection, an adequate number of rare cases may accumulate over time to study those at risk.

Disadvantages

- It may not be representative of the total population unless complete and representative reporting occurs.

- Data are limited according to the willingness of the data collectors, who may have other more important priorities.
- Quality control standards may be poorly defined or not enforced.
- Data quality may vary according to data collection site.

A **serial survey** is a cross-sectional survey that is routinely conducted. Serial surveys provide the means of monitoring health-related states or events over time. Several national surveys in the United States and elsewhere are conducted on an annual basis, providing repeated cross-sectional looks at the population over time. The National Health Examination Survey is a random sample of the U.S. population that collects demographic and medical history information, clinical examination information, and laboratory information. Another example is the National Hospital Discharge Survey, which provides national information on characteristics of inpatients discharged from non-federal short-term stay hospitals in the United States. It has been conducted annually since 1965. Neither survey samples all the same individuals from year to year.

Clusters of Adverse Reproductive Health Outcomes

A surveillance system can be a means of identifying a cluster of cases. A **cluster** of adverse reproductive health outcomes is an unusual aggregation, real or perceived, of reproductive health-related states or events that are grouped together in time and space and that are reported to a health agency. A cluster of an adverse reproductive health outcome tends to occur when a physical, chemical, biological, or psychosocial environment is introduced into the human environment or when some event brings people into contact with an environmental contaminant at levels not typically encountered. For example, a local increase in birth defects or miscarriage rate may be observed, along with a new chemical being manufactured in the same area.

Cluster investigations are characterized by clusters with definable health outcomes, either new or rare, a suspected environmental cause, an unusual situation confirmed by statistical testing, and a short-term public health impact that is immediate and self-evident.[39] Reproductive cluster investigations begin by confirming reported cases, determining whether there is a higher than expected level of the reproductive health problem, and if possible, identifying causal relationships.

In contrast to a disease cluster of the occurrences of seemingly unexpected health-related states or events where no clearly recognized cause exists, **sentinel events** are occurrences of serious unexpected health-related states or events that occur from specific, recognized causes that are known to be associated with the health outcome of interest. Such events are called "sentinel" because they signal the need for immediate investigation and response.[40]

For example, since 1996, there have been 40 cases of perinatal death and 7 cases of permanent disability reported to the Joint Commission for review under the Sentinel Event Policy. Cases considered reviewable under the Sentinel Event Policy are any perinatal death or major permanent loss of function unrelated to a congenital condition in an infant having a birth weight greater than 2,500 grams. The Joint Commission then conducted an investigation that led to a report of the root causes, risk reduction strategies, and recommendations.[41] The role of an epidemiologist in the investigation of sentinel health events includes the following:

1. Establishing the existence of the health-related state or event.
2. Evaluation.
3. Interpreting the results.
4. Summarizing and disseminating relevant information from the investigation to prevent similar cases elsewhere and in the future.

Process of Cluster Investigation

A four-stage process has been prescribed by the CDC for investigating clusters: (1) initial contact and response, (2) assessment, (3) major feasibility study, and (4) etiologic investigation.[39] These stages may be adapted to the specific setting where the cluster is being investigated under the discretion and judgment of local health officials. In some cases, an advisory committee may be consulted at critical decision points of the investigation.

Stage I: Initial Contact and Response

The first question to consider is whether there really is a cluster. There are many possible explanations for a purported cluster, which should be considered prior to drawing conclusions about causality. These include the following:

Variations in diagnosis—A poorly defined case definition or failure to accept a given case definition may lead to local variation; new diagnostic procedures may explain a cluster; changes in reporting practices may explain a cluster, and misdiagnosis by physicians may explain a suspected cluster.

Variation in interest—Local interest or awareness in a specific malformation or condition has the potential of increasing ascertainment and accurate diagnoses.

Variation in malformations—Assortment of unrelated malformations and disease processes means a common origin is unlikely.

Local gene pools—The genetic makeup of groups of people is not evenly distributed throughout the world. This may explain varying rates of specific malformations in different areas.

Migration—Migration patterns such as existence of a new military base or a new housing area may explain a cluster. This emphasizes the importance of considering rates rather than just cases. Short-term migration of high-risk people to specific areas may cause higher rates than expected. If information is available on the country or place of origin, a migration effect on the rates may be assessed.

Local demographic or socioeconomic conditions—Because maternal age or socioeconomic conditions have been associated with selected reproductive health problems such as Down syndrome, spontaneous abortion, and low birth weight, local clusters may arise merely because of differences in the distribution of these factors. If only women of a certain age are affected, for example, this might indicate that an environmental pollutant is an unlikely cause.

Clusters as random phenomena—Clusters of malformations or other adverse reproductive outcomes are most frequently the result of random variation; a rare disease cluster may be a result of chance and not related to a given exposure. Because of small numbers, it is often impossible to statistically test whether a putative cluster is random.

If there is not a simple explanation for the cluster and we accept that a cluster may actually exist, then we proceed to the assessment stage.

Stage II: Assessment

Assessment should include: (1) preliminary evaluation to determine whether an excess of an adverse reproductive problem has occurred, (2) case evaluation to ensure that a biological basis is present, and (3) further evaluation of some or all of the suspected cases to describe the epidemiologic characteristics.

Preliminary evaluation—Preliminary evaluation is used to identify whether a cluster exists and to provide a description of the cluster. This process involves: (1) determining the geographic area and time period for study, (2) ascertaining those cases within the established time and space boundaries, (3) identifying an appropriate reference population, (4) determining whether there is a sufficient number of cases for assessment and whether a denominator is available for calculating rates and other statistics, and (5) determining whether small numbers prevent obtaining meaningful rates or if the denominator is not available, assessing space, time, or space–time clustering. Computer software (e.g., SaTScan 2005) may be used to identify spatial or space–time clustering and to evaluate statistical significance.

Earlier in this chapter we discussed surveillance systems for adverse reproductive outcomes. Surveillance systems may make it possible to actively look for clusters of malformations or other adverse reproductive outcomes. A strong increase in a malformation rate above what is expected over a relatively short time span should be noticed by treating doctors and by the local health authorities.

Statistical methods allow us to assess the probability that there is an excess of the health event being considered; this probability is the P value. The research hypothesis of association between an environmental exposure and adverse health outcome is tested with an appropriate statistical test and a corresponding P value. If the P value is sufficiently small (generally less than or equal to 0.05), then the probability that the observed result is due to chance is small enough to conclude that the measured association is real; however, the interpretation of the conventional P value is dependent on whether the hypothesis is a priori or not. Statistical challenges of detecting reported clusters when the hypothesis is post hoc, and some methods for statistical assessment are presented later.

If there appears to be an excess of cases, the next step is to do a case evaluation.

Case evaluation—Verification of the diagnosis is the purpose of this step. Confirmation of a diagnosis often requires a laboratory test; however, some adverse reproductive health outcomes have no laboratory tests for verification. Cases may also be difficult to diagnose. If an excess of the health problem is supported by case confirmation, or if biologic plausibility persists, then proceed to the next step of occurrence evaluation.

Occurrence evaluation—Here the cluster is characterized, which typically involves: (1) identifying the appropriate geographic and temporal boundaries, (2) ascertaining all potential cases according to the specified time and space boundaries, (3) identifying numerator and denominator data and their availability, (4) identifying appropriate epidemiologic and statistical methods for describing and analyzing the data, (5) reviewing the literature and considering biologic plausibility, (6) assessing whether an exposure–event relationship can be established, (7) identifying the public perceptions, reactions, and needs, and (8) completing the descriptive investigation.

Geographic and temporal boundaries should correspond to the entire area that could have been exposed to the suspected environmental hazard. This requires the epidemiologists to become acquainted with the person-related issues and characteristics related to the reproductive health problem under investigation. Potential confounders should be considered and adjusted for in the analysis, such as inherent characteristics (age, gender, race/ethnicity), acquired characteristics (immunity or marital status), activities (occupation, leisure, use of medications), and conditions (socioeconomic status, access to health care).

It is important to establish these geographic and temporal boundaries at the beginning of the study to avoid the problem of "boundary shrinkage," which may "accentuate estimates of disease risk." Arbitrary circular distance bands around the source can be problematic. If the study region is too small, it may not include all of the potential at-risk population. On the other hand, if the study region is too large, it may include individuals exposed to other risk factors. Both situations may produce misleading results.[42] The narrower the underlying population defined is, the smaller the expected number of cases is, the greater the estimate of the excess rate is, and the more pronounced the statistical significance is.[43]

The epidemiologist also needs to ask whether the disease cluster is associated with a common source or a propagated source. The concentration of cases should be further determined according to person, place, and time. This provides insights into the causes of the health problem. The epidemiologist might choose to plot on a map the locations of each case at the time of exposure or when those exposed were identified as cases.

If an excess of events is confirmed, along with compelling epidemiologic and biologic evidence, then investigators proceed to the final stage.

Stage III: Major Feasibility Study

At this stage, we consider whether it is feasible to link the putative exposure to the adverse health problem by:

1. Reviewing the literature for putative exposures of the health event under consideration.
2. Selecting the appropriate study design and consider the attendant cost, sample size, use of previously identified cases, area and time dimensions, and selection of a control group.
3. Determining the required case and control data needed, which should include laboratory and physical measurements.
4. Considering the appropriate methods for assessment.
5. Outlining the logistics for collecting and processing the data.
6. Determining the analysis plan (e.g., hypotheses to be tested, power to detect differences).
7. Considering the current social and political climate and the potential impact of decisions and outcomes.
8. Considering the resource requirements of the study.

After an excess of cases is expected, a review of the literature can provide insight into the etiology of the problem. The environmental contaminants that might have been present need to be considered, along with the known biological effects of these contaminants, and whether there are known or potential pathways of transmission (e.g., air, water, soil, food). An environmentally caused outcome requires conditions of the environment in which the individuals spent time. If sufficient biological evidence is available, then the research hypothesis is formulated, which addresses the most probable source of the cluster. The validity of the study is based on the accuracy of the measurements of the exposure and outcome data.

The study design, data, methods, logistics, and context are a means for assessing the research hypothesis. When an investigation of a purported cluster is deemed feasible, then proceed to the etiologic investigation.

Stage IV: Etiologic Investigation

Refer to Chapter 3 for the research process in reproductive epidemiology and the causal criteria to consider. In addition, the etiologic investigation should include a final report. Tabular and graphical displays of the data or any useful and helpful displays of pertinent epidemiologic data, tests, laboratory reports, information, and characteristics should be included in the report. Finally, the report should compare the research hypotheses with the observed facts.

Public Health Response

Careful consideration among public health officials of each of the stages of a cluster investigation is necessary to allay public concerns and link the putative exposure to the reproductive health problem. By understanding the source of an adverse reproductive health outcome, public health prevention and control measures can be taken. Eliminating risk exposures is the first line of defense in environmentally founded diseases. Failed prevention and control measures in the past often contribute to disease clusters in the future.

Information about adverse reproductive problems that pose a risk or danger to the public should be communicated to public health officials, related government agencies, physicians, hospitals, health maintenance organizations, medical clinics, schools, universities, and any group of people who are at risk. Public health officials have a responsibility to warn the public and the population at risk. The cardinal rules for managing disease clusters are: (1) accepting and involving the public as a partner; (2) carefully planning and evaluating the findings; (3) listening to the public's specific concerns; (4) being honest, frank, and open; (5) working with other credible sources; (6) meeting the needs of the media; and (7) speaking clearly and with compassion.[44] Along these lines, the public should be informed of the potential health problem, possible risks, and progress made along the course of the investigation.

Data Challenges in Cluster Investigations

A sufficient number of cases are needed in order to rule out or support a cluster. Data that are used in cluster investigations include diagnostic information; case information according to person, place, and time; length of time cases lived in the selected area; potential changes in diagnostic or reporting procedures; migration patterns; and increased public awareness of the disease in question.

A lack of access to quality surveillance data is a primary hindrance to cluster investigation, thereby causing:

- Delays in the investigation
- An inability to identify trends in the reproductive health state or event
- Inhibition of identifying a true cluster
- Reduction of the number of cluster investigations that can be carried out by states, such that some purported clusters are not investigated
- Prevention of the communication of adverse reproductive cluster information to those who need it

Statistical Challenges in Cluster Investigations

Some basic epidemiologic and statistical challenges arise with cluster investigations. This is primarily due to the investigative nature of a cluster investigation such that hypotheses are post hoc rather than a priori. Post hoc hypotheses are formulated after an excess of the health outcome has been observed. It is not appropriate to use the conventional P value with post hoc hypotheses because careful selection of a suspected cluster for statistical testing is equivalent to multiple testing. This is because the probability of finding a significant result increases as we become highly selective in testing only a given area out of many. If a cluster was reported in a region with 20 subareas, we may conclude that the disease rate in the area of the cluster is statistically significant at the 5% level; however, by selectively choosing this area out of 20, we have in essence simultaneously conducted 20 tests. Thus, assuming the null hypothesis is true, we would expect 1 in 20 independent tests to be significant by chance alone at the 5% level of significance. Consequently, the unusual event may simply be a chance occurrence in the random variation of the disease; therefore, significant test results in a cluster investigation involving a post hoc hypothesis are not effective at proving that the cluster is real. On the other hand, statistical tests are useful for screening out potential clusters, which would not have been statistically significant even if the area had been selected a priori.[45]

Overestimated rates are also a potential problem in cluster investigations. This is because of a phenomenon called "boundary shrinkage," which was introduced earlier in this chapter. In order to avoid boundary shrinkage, it is important to choose appropriate geographic areas of research. For example, in a study conducted in the West Midlands region of England after reports of an excess of leukemia, a radio and television transmitter used distance bands up to 10 km to investigate the suspected cluster.[42] The distance bands reflected the geographic locality, established ahead of time to ensure that all those at risk were included in the study.

Boundary shrinkage is a problem associated with almost all cluster investigations. The problem arises because when a group of cases is observed, the underlying population corresponding to the suspected cluster is then defined. The narrower the definition of the underlying population is, the greater the estimated rate of the health outcome is and the more pronounced the statistical significance.

Some statistical approaches useful for assessing clusters are presented here.

Standardized Mortality (or Registration) Ratio

The standardized mortality ratio (SMR) is used to compare the observed number of deaths to the expected number of deaths in a defined population. If incident events are being evaluated, the standardized registration ratio (SRR) should be used. The formula for calculating these statistics is the same.

$$\text{SMR, SRR} = \theta = \frac{\text{Observed}}{\text{Expected}}$$

The z statistic is used to test whether the observed count is significantly different than the expected count, using the following equation.

$$z = 2\left(\sqrt{Observed} - \sqrt{Expected}\right)$$

The observed number of cases is assumed to be Poisson distributed with mean $(\mu) = \theta \times \text{Expected}$. The symbol θ (= SMR or SRR) represents the amount of excess risk (e.g., $q = 1$ means there is no excess risk). A one-sided P value for $\theta = 1$ is obtained from the probability of observing in a Poisson distribution, with μ = Expected, at least the number of cases observed in the suspected cluster area. This is approximated by z, where z is the standard normal distribution.[45]

The 95% confidence interval for θ is calculated as:

$$\left(\sqrt{Observed} \pm 1.96/2\right)^2 / Expected$$

A Cluster in Search of a Cause

Olsen and colleagues (1996) provide a recommendation for dealing with cluster data where clustering is tested as a feature of the disease pattern over an entire region.[43] In the context of data being categorized into subareas, the null hypothesis is that the disease or injury rate is the same in each of the subareas, the cases occur at random across the regions, the frequencies are proportional to the numbers at risk in each subarea, and variability is characterized by the Poisson distribution. Here a summary measure for total variability of the rate can be obtained across all subareas. The χ^2 can be calculated for the i subareas as follows:

$$\chi^2 = \sum_{i=1}^{n} \frac{(O_i - E_i)^2}{O_i}$$

where O_i is the observed number of cases and E_i is the expected number of cases in each subarea. The χ^2 value measures how much the observed cases differ from the expected in the subareas. Using this approach the conventional use of the P value is appropriate such that a P value less than 5% means that variability in the rates across the subareas is greater than the Poisson model allows. Thus, there appears to be a clustering within one or more of the subareas; that is, the rates vary across subareas.

Alternative Measures

In the context of post hoc hypotheses, although significance tests are not appropriate, some alternative methods of assessment may be used. The study may be performed in a different location but with a similar exposure; cases in the original cluster may be excluded and new cases may be used in the test of significance, assuming additional case ascertainment resulted. Other factors may be considered that distinguish the cases from others in the cluster, other than their residence, and assessing whether a dose–response relationship exists between an exposure and health outcome and evaluating a dose–response relationship between the exposure and health event.[45]

Finally, the relationship between an exposure and health outcome is assessed, which assumes measurable exposure and health outcome data is available. Determining whether a dose–response relationship exists in a putative cluster is independent of whether the study used a post hoc or a prior hypothesis. Dose–response relationships provide support for a causal association.

Conclusion

Public health surveillance is a type of descriptive epidemiology that involves monitoring health-related states and events in the population, thereby identifying unusual occurrences and patterns. Monitoring environmental information can further facilitate formulating hypotheses and assessing correlations between exposure and adverse health outcome variables. This chapter described the surveillance process and concluded with cluster investigations, which find their impetus from public health surveillance.

Key Issues

1. Medical surveillance refers to monitoring of individuals, whereas public health surveillance refers to monitoring of populations.
2. Surveillance is a means to evaluate whether changes occur regularly and can be predicted or are unusual events that are unexpected. Surveillance data provide information for more effective planning, policy, and prevention and control measures; it provides information upon which action may be taken.
3. After the objectives of an investigation are clearly identified, we determine the cases to be included. All forms of birth defects and adverse reproductive health outcomes that can be interpreted in a convincing way should be surveyed. On the other hand, some reproductive health outcomes may be impractical to monitor, such as spontaneous abortions (miscarriages).
4. Case information is generally ascertained by abstracting information from hospital logs, which includes labor and delivery reports, neonatal intensive care units, pathology reports, and surgery logs. The sources of many surveillance systems employ secondary data, which are data collected for other purposes (e.g., vital records, healthcare utilization records, national and local surveys, and environmental data).
5. Effective surveillance requires timely data collection, management, analysis, interpretation, and dissemination.
6. There are four categories of surveillance methods: active, passive, sentinel, and special systems surveillance.
7. A surveillance system can be a means of identifying a cluster of cases. A cluster of adverse reproductive health outcomes is an unusual aggregation, real or perceived, of reproductive health–related states or events that are grouped together in time and space and that are reported to a health

agency. Data and statistical challenges associated with cluster investigations were considered.

Exercises

Key Terms

Define the following terms.

Active surveillance	Sentinel surveillance
Cluster	Serial survey
Cluster investigation	Special systems
Cross-sectional survey	Surveillance
Medical surveillance	Surveillance process
Passive surveillance	Survival analysis
Population	Table
Public health surveillance	Time-series designs
Secondary data	Vital records
Sentinel events	

Study Questions

4.1 Describe the difference between medical surveillance and public health surveillance, and identify some of the health-related states or events public health surveillance monitors.

4.2 Explain why it is important for a surveillance program to define clear objectives.

4.3 Identify the 10 operational aspects of a surveillance system. Choose two aspects, and explain why each is important to include.

4.4 Describe each of the four categories of surveillance methods: active, passive, sentinel, and special systems surveillance (include benefits and limitations in the use of each).

4.5 Discuss cluster investigations. Present the four-stage process, and discuss management issues, data, and statistical challenges associated with cluster investigations.

References

1. Meaney JF. Introduction: birth defects surveillance in the United States. *Teratology.* 2001;74:S1–S2.

2. California Birth Defects Monitoring Program. Overview: the problem of birth defects. Available at: http://www.cbdmp.org/pbd_overview.htm. Accessed December 5, 2008.

3. *Alaska Birth Defects Monitor.* Anchorage, AK: Alaska Birth Defects Registry. 2008; 1(1):1–4.

4. Centers for Disease Control and Prevention. *Principles of Epidemiology*, 2nd ed. Atlanta, GA: U.S. Department of Health and Human Services; 1992. Available at: http://www2a .cdc.gov/phtn/catalog/pdf-file/Epi_Course.pdf.

5. Melve KK, Lie RT, Skjaerven R, et al. Registration of Down syndrome in the Medical Birth Registry of Norway: validity and time trends. *Acta Obstet Gynecol Scand.* 2008; 87(8):824–830.

6. Centers for Disease Control. Improved national prevalence estimates for 18 selected major birth defects—United States, 1999–2001. *MMWR.* 2006;54(51&52);1301–1305. Available at: http://www.cdc.gov/mmwr/preview/mmwrhtml/mm5451a2.htm. Accessed February 28, 2009.

7. Edmonds LD, James LM. Temporal trends in the prevalence of congenital malformations at birth based on the birth defects monitoring program, United States, 1979–1987. *MMWR Surv Summ.* 1990;39(SS-4):19–23.

8. National Birth Defects Prevention Network. Birth defects surveillance data from selected states, 1997–2001. *Birth Defects Res A Clin Mol Teratol.* 2004;70:677–771.

9. Centers for Disease Control. Birth defects. Available at: http://www.cdc.gov/ncbddd/BD/ macdp.htm. Accessed December 5, 2008.

10. Centers for Disease Control. State Birth Defects Tracking Systems. Available at: http://www.cdc.gov/ncbddd/BD/state.htm. Accessed December 5, 2008.

11. International Clearinghouse for Birth Defects: Surveillance and research. Latest news. Available at: http://www.icbdsr.org/page.asp?p=9895&l=1. Accessed December 5, 2008.

12. Centers for Disease Control. National Environmental Public Health Tracking Program. Available at: http://www.cdc.gov/nceh/tracking/helix.htm. Accessed December 5, 2008.

13. Cochi SL, Edmonds LE, Dyer K, et al. Congenital rubella syndrome in the United States, 1970–1985. *Am J Epidemiol.* 1989;129:349–361.

14. Reef SE, Redd SB, Abernathy E, Zimmerman L, Icenogle JP. The epidemiological profile of rubella and congenital rubella syndrome in the United States, 1998–2004: the evidence for absence of endemic transmission. *Clin Infect Dis.* 2006;43(Suppl 3):S126–S132.

15. Yang J, Carmichael SL, Kaidarova Z, Shaw GM. Risks of selected congenital malformations among offspring of mixed race-ethnicity. *Birth Defects Res A Clin Mol Teratol.* 2004;70(10):820–824.

16. Chapman CJ. Ethnic differences in the incidence of cleft lip and/or cleft palate in Auckland, 1960–1976. *New Z Med J.* 1983;96:327–329.

17. Rawashdeh MA, Jawdat Abu-Hawas B. Congenital associated malformations in a sample of Jordanian patients with cleft lip and palate. *J Oral Maxillofac Surg.* 2008;66(10): 2035–2041.

18. Hook EB, Albright SG, Cross PK. Use of Bernoulli census and log-linear methods for estimating the prevalence of spina bifida in live births and the completeness of vital record reports in New York State. *Am J Epidemiol.* 1980;112:750–758.

19. Huether CA, Gummere GR. Influence of demographic factors on annual Down's syndrome in Ohio, 1970–1979, and the United States, 1920–1979. *Am J Epidemiol.* 1982; 115:846–860.

20. Roecker GO, Huether CA. An analysis for paternal-age effect in Ohio's Down syndrome births, 1970–1980. *Am J Hum Genet.* 1983;35:1297–1306.

21. Mathews TJ, Honein MA, Erickson JD. Spina bifida and anencephaly prevalence— United States, 1991–2001. *MMWR Recomm Rep* 2002;51(RR-13):9–11.

22. Martínez de Villarreal LE, Arredondo P, Hernández R, Villarreal JZ. Weekly administration of folic acid and epidemiology of neural tube defects. *Matern Child Health J.* 2006;10(5):397–401.

23. Hook EB, Regal RR. Validity of Bernoulli census, log-linear, and truncated binomial models for correcting for underestimates in prevalence studies. *Am J Epidemiol.* 1982; 116:168–176.

24. Wittes JT, Colton T, Sidel VW. Capture-recapture methods for assessing the completeness of case ascertainment when using multiple information sources. *J Chronic Dis.* 1974; 27(1):25–36.

25. Henry GP, Britt DW, Evans MI. Screening advances and diagnostic choice: the problem of residual risk. *Fetal Diagn Ther.* 2008;23(4):308–315.

26. Buckley S, Bird G, Sacks B, Archer T. A comparison of mainstream and special education for teenagers with Down syndrome: implications for parents and teachers. *Downs Syndr Res Pract.* 2006;9(3):54–67.

27. Wong SF, Chan FY, Cincotta RB, Lee-Tannock A, Ward C. Factors influencing the prenatal detection of structural congenital heart diseases. *Ultrasound Obstet Gynecol.* 2003; 21(1):19–25.

28. So SA, Urbano RC, Hodapp RM. Hospitalizations of infants and young children with Down syndrome: evidence from inpatient person-records from a statewide administrative database. *J Intellect Disabil Res.* 2007;51(Pt 12):1030–1038.

29. Egeland GM, Perham-Hester KA, Hook EB. Use of capture–recapture analyses in fetal alcohol syndrome surveillance in Alaska. *Am J Epidemiol.* 1995;141(4):335–341.

30. Murphy M, Seagroatt V, Hey K, et al. Neural tube defects 1974–94—down but not out. *Arch Dis Childhood Fetal Neonatal Ed.* 1996;75(2):F133–F134.

31. Shaw GM, Nelson V, Olshan AF. Paternal occupational group and risk of offspring with neural tube defects. *Paediatr Perinat Epidemiol.* 2002;16(4):328–333.

32. Gardner BR, Strickland MJ, Correa A. Application of the automated spatial surveillance program to birth defects surveillance data. *Birth Defects Res A Clin Mol Teratol.* 2007;79(7):559–564.

33. Bjørge T, Cnattingius S, Lie RT, Tretli S, Engeland A. Cancer risk in children with birth defects and in their families: a population based cohort study of 5.2 million children from Norway and Sweden. *Cancer Epidemiol Biomarkers Prev.* 2008;17(3):500–506.

34. Nishi M, Miyake H, Takeda T, Hatae Y. Congenital malformations and childhood cancer. *Med Pediatr Oncol.* 2000;34(4):250–254.

35. National Research Council. *Environmental Epidemiology: Use of the Gray Literature and Other Data in Environmental Epidemiology* (Vol. 2). Washington, DC: National Academy Press; 1997.

36. Siffel C, Strickland MJ, Gardner BR, Kirby RS, Correa A. Role of geographic information systems in birth defects surveillance and research. *Birth Defects Res*. 2006;76(Pt A):825–833. Available at: http://www3.interscience.wiley.com/cgi-bin/fulltext/113455766/PDFSTART. Accessed February 28, 2009.

37. Correa-Villaseñor A, Satten GA, Rolka H, Langlois P, Devine O. Random error and undercounting in birth defects surveillance data: implications for inference. *Birth Defects Res A Clin Mol Teratol*. 2003;67(9):610–616.

38. Centers for Disease Control. Program Operations Guidelines for STD Prevention: Surveillance and Data Management. Available at: http://www.cdc.gov/STD/Program/surveillance/4-PGsurveillance.htm. Accessed December 5, 2008.

39. Centers for Disease Control. Guidelines for investigating clusters of health events. *MMWR*. 1990;39(RR-11):1–23.

40. Joint Commission on Accreditation of Healthcare Organizations. Setting the Standards for Quality in Health Care: Sentinel Event. Available at: http://www.jointcommission.org/SentinelEvents/. Accessed February 28, 2009.

41. JCAHO. Preventing infant death and injury during delivery. *Sentinel Event Alert*. 2004:30. Available at: http://www.jointcommission.org/SentinelEvents/SentinelEventAlert/sea_30.htm. Accessed February 28, 2009.

42. Elliott P, Wakefield J. Disease clusters: should they be investigated, and, if so, when and how? *J R Stat Soc Series A (Stat Soc)*. 2001:164(1);3–12.

43. Olsen SF, Martuzzi M, Elliott P. Cluster analysis and disease mapping—why, when, and how? A step by step guide. *Br Med J*. 1996;313:863–866.

44. Covello V, Allen F. *Seven Cardinal Rules of Risk Communication*. Washington, DC: U.S. Environmental Protection Agency, Office of Policy Analysis; 1988.

45. Wilkinson P, ed. *Environmental Epidemiology*. New York, NY: Open University Press; 2006.

FIVE

Descriptive Reproductive Health Indicators

Learning Objectives

After completing this chapter, you should be able to:

1. Define the term "health indicator" and be familiar with various indicators that reflect reproductive health.
2. Define monitoring.
3. Recognize the Millennium Development Goals and understand the influence they have in providing direction in the field of reproductive health.
4. Differentiate between ratios, proportions, and rates, and understand their importance in understanding and monitoring reproductive health.
5. Calculate and interpret rates useful in reproductive health.

In the 16th century, the "**Bills of Mortality**" were introduced in London as a way to warn people about plague epidemics. Parish clerks collected and published the information every week. In 1570, the bills consisted of baptisms, and in 1629, the cause of death was added. From the "Bills of Mortality," John Graunt (1620–1674), one of the first known demographers, assessed deaths according to age, gender, residence, and season in order to better understand who was dying and why they were dying. He was the first to develop and calculate life tables and life expectancy and classify deaths into two categories: those that occurred suddenly (acute) and those that followed a long period of illness (chronic).[1,2]

After John Graunt's death, little was done to continue his work until William Farr (1807–1883) was appointed registrar general in England, some 200 years later. Farr extended the use of vital statistics and organized and developed a modern vital statistics system.[3] Today, data derived from certificates and reports reflecting important events in human life (e.g., births, deaths, fetal deaths, and induced termination of pregnancy) are regularly collected and made available to the public.

Reproductive health is related to various dimensions of health. Hence, a number of health indicators have been developed to describe reproductive health. **Reproductive health indicators** are useful in that they describe reproductive health status and provide a comparison with health-related policy, program, and service goals. In addition, when reproductive health indicators are reported according to person, place, and time variables, it is possible to better understand who is at greatest risk and how they have become more susceptible to the reproductive health problem.

Health Indicator

A **health indicator** is a marker of health status, service provision, or resource availability. It is designed to enable the monitoring of service performance or program goals.[4] The term "health status" may refer to death, disease (mental, physical), impairments or disability, and social well-being. **Monitoring** is a process where changes in health status over time or among populations are identified in order to assess progress toward health goals or objectives.

Selecting a health indicator that best reflects health status is complicated because of the many aspects of health. Although it would be much simpler if one indicator was available to reflect health, this is not the case. In addition, selecting a "best" reproductive health indicator is further complicated by the fact that to understand reproductive health fully, it should be studied in the context of economic circumstances, education and employment status, living conditions, social support, sexual relationships, and cultural norms and legal structures. For instance, the status women have in society and the control that they have over their own health and fertility is largely influenced by their socioeconomic opportunities.

Because of the various dimensions of public health (and of reproductive health), several categories of indicators are in use:

- Health and well-being (e.g., fertility, miscarriage, physical fulfillment, and psychosocial comfort and closeness)
- Health resources (e.g., family planning, opportunities for choice, satisfaction with and perceived quality of services)
- Collective justice (e.g., level of disparity in individual health indicators)
- Social capital (e.g., community involvement, trust in others, perceived enabling factors)
- Collective capacity (e.g., community participation)
- Resiliency (e.g., a community's ability to cope with natural disasters that may adversely affect reproduction)
- Functionality (e.g., peace, safety, and factors associated with poor reproductive health such as abuse, exploitation, unwanted pregnancy, disease, and death)

Thus, reproductive epidemiology involves consideration of reproductive health indicators that are complimentary and in combination reflect the broad scope of reproductive health and the various dimensions of health.

The health issues facing society are constantly changing, and the indicators under consideration typically reflect the prevailing health issues or challenges of greatest concern where an intervention is sought. Reporting a health indicator such as infant mortality helps us understand the problem and create ways to intervene and improve the situation. As a given health problem is improved, new indicators reflecting other major health concerns may surface as priorities. For example, as infant mortality rates fall, congenital malformations, growth retardation, child mental development, and gender ratio become increasingly important issues, and new indicators are needed.

For practical reasons, health indicators tend to involve data that are required by law (like death certificates, hospital discharge information, and notifiable disease) and that have data quality standards and collection methods in place. Summary statistics of these data tend to be complete and reliable. Concerns about data quality arise with:

- Small sample size
- Nonrepresentative sample
- Poor response rate
- Changes in reporting over time
- Differential nonresponse
- Changes in procedures for data collection
- Revisions in definitions and values related to health
- Changes in the socioeconomic characteristics of the population
- Long-term stability of aggregate levels of health statistics
- Lack of data to control for confounding factors
- Changes in the organization and delivery of health care[4]

Indicators for Global Health Monitoring

Health indicators are usually presented in the form of a ratio, proportion, percentage, or rate.

At the Millennium Summit in September 2000, members of the United Nations reaffirmed their commitment to achieving significant and measurable improvements in people's lives, including greater survival for mothers and their infants. Millennium Development Goal (MDG) reproductive health indicators that were agreed on for reporting by the 147 heads of state and government and 189 nations in total for measuring progress toward the MDGs are presented in **Table 5-1**. This short list is intended to provide a set of indicators that are complementary and representative of all areas of reproductive health. A more extensive list of reproductive health indicators is presented in Appendix II.

In the remainder of this chapter, each of these MDG reproductive health indicators will be defined and discussed.

Total Fertility Rate

The **total fertility rate** (TFR) is the total number of children a woman would have by the end of her reproductive period if she experienced the currently prevailing age-specific fertility rates (ASFRs) throughout her childbearing life (ages 15–49

TABLE 5-1   A Shortlist of Indicators for Global Monitoring of Reproductive Health

1. Total fertility rate
2. Contraceptive prevalence
3. Maternal mortality ratio
4. Antenatal care coverage
5. Births attended by skilled health personnel
6. Availability of basic essential obstetric care
7. Availability of comprehensive essential obstetric care
8. Perinatal mortality rate
9. Prevalence of low birth weight
10. Prevalence of positive syphilis serology in pregnant women
11. Prevalence of anemia in women
12. Percentage of obstetric and gynecological admissions owing to abortion
13. Reported prevalence of women with genital mutilation
14. Prevalence of infertility in women
15. Reported incidence of urethritis in men
16. Prevalence of HIV infection in pregnant women
17. Knowledge of HIV-related preventive practices

Source: World Health Organization. Reproductive Health Indicators: Guidelines for their generation, interpretation and analysis for global monitoring. Geneva, Switzerland: World Health Organization Press; 2006. Available at: http://www.who.int/reproductive-health/publications/rh_indicators/guidelines.pdf. Accessed February 28, 2009.

years); in other words, it is the average number of births per woman. The ASFR is the fertility rate within selected age groups and is calculated as:

$$\text{ASFR} = \frac{\text{Births in year to women aged } X}{\text{No. of women aged } X \text{ at mid-year}} \times 1000 \text{ women}$$

$$X = 15\text{--}19, 20\text{--}24, 25\text{--}29, 30\text{--}34, 45\text{--}39, 40\text{--}44, 45\text{--}49 \text{ years}$$

The TFR per woman is then calculated as:

$$\text{TFR} = \frac{\sum \text{ASFRs} \times 5}{1000}$$

The TFR is a commonly used indicator of reproductive health and population momentum, and is also a proxy for the effectiveness of family planning services. The primary strength of this summary measure is its independence of age structure, unlike the crude birth rate. Hence, it is useful for monitoring trends over time and for making international comparisons.

Data sources come from vital registrations (on births only), population census, and population-based surveys.

The TFR has slightly decreased in recent years from 2.8 in 2000 to 2.6 in 2007. TFRs throughout the world are presented in **Figure 5-1**. The highest TFRs in the world are in Mali (7.38), Niger (7.37), Uganda (6.84), Somalia (6.68), and Afghanistan (6.64). The lowest TFRs in the world are in Lithuania (1.21), Taiwan (1.12), Singapore (1.07), Macau (1.03), and Hong Kong (0.98). The TFR in the United States is 2.09.[5]

In developed countries, the TFR has fallen from above 6 per woman in the 1960s to under 3 today. In developing countries, the TFR averages 5 per woman with nearly 7 per woman in Uganda, Afghanistan, and Niger.[6]

The TFR in the United States is presented by calendar year in **Figure 5-2**. It fell from 2.5 in 1970 to 1.7 in 1976 and then increased to slightly above 2 between

FIGURE 5-1   **Total Fertility Rates in the World**

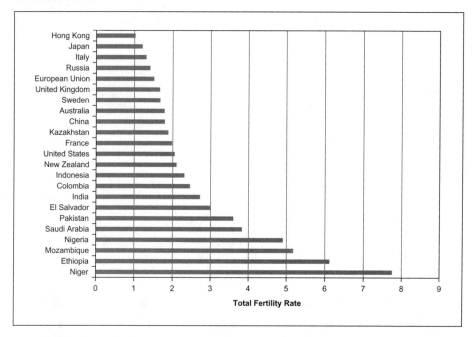

Source: Central Intelligence Agency. The World Factbook. https://www.cia.gov/library/publications/the-world-factbook/rankorder/2127rank.html. Accessed June 9, 2009.

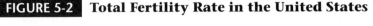

FIGURE 5-2   **Total Fertility Rate in the United States**

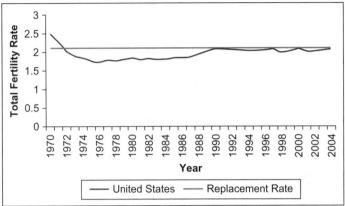

Source: Total fertility rates: Number of children born to women aged 15 to 29: United States. Available at: http://www.swivel.com/data_columns/show/2417583. Accessed January 2, 2009.

1989 and 2004. In theory, if the TFR = 2, then each couple exactly replaces itself and change in the population is constant; however, because some die before they reach an age where they can have their own two children, it actually takes a TFR = 2.1 (or higher in countries with low life expectancy) to replace each generation. This number is referred to as the **replacement rate**.[7]

In order for a TFR of 2.1 to ensure zero population growth, the distribution of the population needs be fairly constant across the childbearing ages; however, if there are at any given time an unusually large number of children born who pass through the childbearing years, the population will increase even if the TFR remains at 2.1. For example, in the United States the percentage of the population in their childbearing years ages 15 to 49 increased from 46% in 1960 to 53% in 1990.[8] In 2001, the percentage decreased slightly to 51%, and by 2050, it is expected to fall to 44%.[9] This large cohort of people moving through reproductive ages has kept the United States population growing. In many developing regions of the world where a larger proportion of their population is in their childbearing years, even if the TFR remains constant the population will continue to grow. The tendency for population growth to continue after the replacement rate has occurred because of a comparatively high concentration of the population in the childbearing years is called **population momentum**.

The average annual percentage change in the population in the United States was 1% in 2008. In 2025, it is expected to be 0.9%. The TFR is expected to remain near 2.1 between 2008 and 2025.[10]

Contraceptive Prevalence

Contraceptive prevalence (CP) is the proportion of women of reproductive age (i.e., 15 to 49 years) who are using (or whose partner is using) a contraceptive method at a given point in time. Contraceptive methods include sterilization, intrauterine devices, hormonal methods, condoms and vaginal barrier methods, rhythm, withdrawal, abstinence, and lactational amenorrhea (a lack of menstruation during breastfeeding). It is calculated as:

$$CP = \frac{\text{No. of women of reproductive age at risk of pregnancy who are using (or whose partner is using) a contraceptive method at a point in time}}{\text{No. of women of reproductive age at the same point in time}}$$

This indicator measures utilization of contraceptive methods. It is useful for measuring progress toward child and maternity health goals. Population-based sample surveys are typically used to estimate contraceptive practice. Smaller scale or more focused group surveys and records kept by organized family planning programs are other sources of information about contraceptive practices.

Family planning can have a positive impact on contraceptive use. In developing countries, CP has increased from 10% in the early 1960s to 59% in 2000.[11] From the mid-1990s there has been a 1% annual increase in CP.[12] Based on survey data collected on contraceptive use in the 1990s from 94 countries in Africa, Asia and the Pacific, and Latin America and the Caribbean, a 1% increase in contraception is associated with a 0.06 birth decrease in TFR.[13]

In 1997–2005, CP in developing countries was 59% and in the least developed countries was 29%. In Sub-Saharan Africa the prevalence was 24%, in the Middle East and North Africa 53%, in South Asia 46%, in East Asia and Pacific 79%, in Latin America and the Caribbean 71%, and in Central and Eastern Europe/Commonwealth of Independent States (CEE/CIS) 65%. In contrast, CP was 75% in Canada, Germany, France, and New Zealand; 79% in the Netherlands;

81% in Spain; 82% in Switzerland; 84% in the United Kingdom; and 76% in the United States.[14]

Maternal Mortality Rate

Maternal mortality rate is the number of maternal deaths (i.e., death of a woman while pregnant or within 42 days of termination of pregnancy) per 100,000 live births. Maternal mortality consists of death from any cause related to or aggravated by the pregnancy state (pregnancy, labor, puerperium) or its management (interventions, omissions, or incorrect treatment).[15]

$$\text{MMR} = \frac{\text{No. of maternal deaths occuring in a period (usually a year)}}{\text{No. of live births occurring in the same period}} \times 100,000$$

The tendency for underreporting and selection bias makes vital registration and health service data problematic. Hence, population-based surveys are the primary source of data used for calculation of maternal mortality rate in several developing countries.

This indicator is the most widely used measure of maternal death. It is a general indicator of the overall health of a population. It further represents the status of women in society and the functioning of the health system.

In 2000, the maternal mortality rate was 13 in industrial countries, 440 in developing countries, and 890 in the least developed countries. In Sub-Saharan Africa, the rate was 940, in the Middle East and North Africa 220, in South Asia 560, in East Asia and Pacific 110, in CEE/CIS 64, and in Latin America and the Caribbean 190. In contrast, the rates were 6 in Canada, 17 in France, 16 in the Netherlands, 7 in New Zealand, 4 in Spain, 7 in Switzerland, 13 in the United Kingdom, and 17 in the United States.[14]

Antenatal Care Coverage

Antenatal care coverage is the proportion of women attended to, at least once during their pregnancy, by **skilled health personnel** for reasons relating to pregnancy. A skilled health attendant is an accredited health professional (midwife, doctor, nurse) who had the necessary training to proficiently manage normal pregnancies, childbirth, and the immediate postnatal period and to identify, manage, and refer complications in women and newborns.[16]

$$ACC = \frac{\text{No. of pregnant women attended, at least once during their pregnancy, by skilled personnel for reasons related to pregnancy during a fixed period}}{\text{Total number of live births during the same period}}$$

National population-based (household) surveys are typically used to provide data on maternity care. This indicator provides useful information on the proportion of women who use antenatal care services.

In 2000, antenatal care coverage (%) was 71 in developing countries and 59 in the least developed countries. During 1997–2005, antenatal care coverage was 68 in Sub-Saharan Africa, 70 in the Middle East and North Africa, 53 in South Asia, 88 in East Asia and Pacific, 87 in CEE/CIS, and 93 in Latin America and the Caribbean. This information was not available for many industrial countries like the United States.[14]

Births Attended by Skilled Health Personnel

Births attended by skilled health personnel refer to the proportion of births attended to by skilled health personnel. These are midwives, doctors, or nurses who have been educated and received training in the skills needed to manage normal pregnancies, childbirth, and the immediate postnatal period. They are also trained to identify, manage, and refer complicated cases.[16] Trained or untrained birth attendants are excluded from this definition.

$$BASHP = \frac{\text{Births attended by skilled health personnel during a specified period}}{\text{Total number of live births during the specified period}}$$

The main data sources come from vital registration and household surveys.

This indicator informs program management whether safe motherhood programs are available and used and whether the health system is properly functioning in providing adequate coverage for deliveries.

In 2000, the percentage of births attended by skilled health personnel was 99 in industrial countries, 60 in developing countries, and 35 in the least developed countries. The rate was 43 in Sub-Saharan Africa, 76 in the Middle East and

North Africa, 37 in South Asia, 87 in East Asia and Pacific, 93 in CEE/CIS, and 87 in Latin America and the Caribbean.

Availability of Basic Essential Obstetric Care

Availability of **basic essential obstetric care** (BEOC) is the number of facilities with functioning BEOC per 500,000 people. BEOC facilities are facilities that have performed the following six services (also called signal functions) at least once in the previous 6 months: administration of parenteral antibiotics, parenteral oxytocic drugs, parenteral sedatives for eclampsia, manual removal of the placenta, manual removal of retained products (e.g., manual vacuum aspiration), and assisted vaginal delivery (vacuum extraction or forceps).[17]

$$\text{BEOC} = \frac{\text{No. of facilities with functioning basic care}}{\text{Total population}} \times 500{,}000$$

Data are obtained from service records and/or registers.

This indicator is primarily used in needs assessment to determine the adequacy of facilities for meeting minimum recommendations for essential obstetric care.

Availability of Comprehensive Essential Obstetric Care

Availability of **comprehensive essential obstetric care** (CEOC) is the number of facilities with functioning CEOC per 500,000. CEOC facilities are facilities that have performed surgery (caesarean section) and blood transfusion, in addition to all six BEOC services, at least once in the past 3 months.[17]

$$\text{CEOC} = \frac{\text{No. of facilities with functioning comprehensive essential obstetric care}}{\text{Total population}} \times 500{,}000$$

Data are obtained from service records and/or registers.

This indicator is primarily used in needs assessment to determine the adequacy of facilities for meeting minimum recommendations for essential obstetric care.

Perinatal Mortality Rate

Perinatal mortality rate is the number of perinatal deaths per 1,000 births. The perinatal period commences at 22 completed weeks (154 days) of gestation and ends at 7 completed days after birth.

$$PMR = \frac{\text{No. of perinatal deaths (fetal deaths and early neonatal deaths)}}{\text{Total number of births}} \times 1,000$$

Data are obtained from vital registration systems. Where these are not complete, population-based surveys are used to obtain information about pregnancy and birth outcomes.

This indicator measures the outcome of pregnancy with respect to the infant. It is also a widely used statistic for evaluating the effectiveness of perinatal care.

The perinatal mortality rate per 1,000 is 10 in industrial regions, 50 in developing regions, and 61 in the least developed countries. The rate is 62 in Africa, 50 in Asia, 13 in Europe, 21 in Latin America and the Caribbean, 7 in North America, and 42 in Oceania.[18]

Prevalence of Low Birth Weight

Prevalence of low birth weight is the percentage of live born babies who weigh less than 2,500 g. It is the first weight of the infant immediately after birth.[15]

$$LBW = \frac{\text{No. of live born babies who weigh less than 2500 g}}{\text{Total number of live births}} \times 100$$

Very low birth weight is less than 1,500 g, and extremely low birth weight is less than 1,000 g. Data for this statistic are obtained from population-based surveys, where mothers are asked to report their babies' weight at birth.

This is a rough indicator of many factors, including maternal nutrition, lifestyle, and other exposures during pregnancy. Assessment of maternal nutrition should consider nutrition during childhood, adolescence, prepregnancy, and pregnancy. Alcohol, tobacco, and drug use are primary lifestyle variables that are often considered. Finally, environmental exposures may include infectious diseases, toxic chemicals, ionizing radiation, and altitude.

In 2000, the percentage of low birth weight infants was 7 in industrial regions, 16.5 in developing regions, and 18.6 in the least developed countries. The percentage was 14.3 in Africa, 18.3 in Asia, 6.4 in Europe, 10 in Latin America and Caribbean, 7.7 in North America, and 10.5 in Oceania.[19]

Prevalence of Positive Syphilis Serology in Pregnant Women

This is the percentage of pregnant women aged 15–24 years attending antenatal clinics with a positive serology for syphilis.

$$PS = \frac{\text{No. of pregnant women aged } 15-24 \text{ years attending antenatal clinics, whose blood has been screened for syphilis, with a positive serology for syphilis during a specified period}}{\text{Total number of pregnant women aged } 15-24 \text{ years attending antenatal clinics, whose blood has been screened for syphilis, during the same time period}} \times 100$$

Data are obtained from sentinel surveillance approaches where pregnant women attending antenatal clinics are routinely tested for syphilis.

This indicator may serve as a proxy at national and international levels for the burden of sexually transmitted infections.

Prevalence of Anemia in Women

This is the percentage of women of reproductive age (i.e., 15–49) screened for hemoglobin levels who have levels below 110 g/L (pregnant women) and 120 g/L (nonpregnant women).

$$\text{Anemia} = \frac{\text{No. of women of reproductive age screened for hemoglobin levels who have levels below } 110 \text{ g/L (pregnant women) and } 120 \text{ g/L (nonpregnant women) during a specified time}}{\text{Total number of women of reproductive age screened for hemoglobin levels during the specified time}} \times 100$$

Data are obtained from health facilities, where there is routine screening of hemoglobin levels for all women and population-based surveys, and specific groups are targeted.

This indicator provides an initial identification of women with iron deficiencies who should take iron supplementation or receive other care.

Percentage of Obstetric and Gynecological Admissions Caused by Abortion

This is the percentage of admissions for (spontaneous or induced) abortion-related complications to service delivery points providing inpatient obstetric and gynecological services, among all obstetric and gynecological admissions (except for planned termination of pregnancy).

$$\text{ARC} = \frac{\text{Admissions for abortion-related complications}}{\text{All admissions, except those for planned termination of pregnancy}} \times 100$$

Routinely kept and maintained hospital records may provide this information; however, there are no existing sources of routinely collected data that will allow us to create this indicator accurately worldwide.

This indicator may represent trends in obstetric complications in general, but would not necessarily be informative about changes that are specific to abortion complications.

Reported Prevalence of Women With Genital Mutilation

This is the percentage of women interviewed in a community survey, preferably ages 15–49, who report having undergone genital mutilation. **Genital mutilation** results from any procedure that involves partial or total removal of external female genitalia or other injury to the female genital organs.

$$\text{GM} = \frac{\text{No. of women interviewed in a community survey who reported having undergone genital mutilation}}{\text{Total number of women interviewed in the survey}} \times 100$$

The WHO/UNICEF/UNFPA Joint Statement classifies female genital mutilation into four types:

- Type I—Partial or total removal of the clitoris and/or the prepuce (clitoridectomy).

- Type II—Partial or total removal of the clitoris and the labia minora, with or without excision of the labia majora (excision).

- Type III—Narrowing of the vaginal orifice with creation of a covering seal by cutting and appositioning the labia minora and/or the labia majora, with or without excision of the clitoris (infibulation).

- Type IV—All other harmful procedures to the female genitalia for non-medical purposes, for example: pricking, piercing, incising, scraping, and cauterization.[20]

Types I, II, and III have been documented in 28 countries in Africa, as well in selected countries in Asia and the Middle East. Data are obtained from large-scale national surveys. The World Health Organization estimates that between 100 million and 140 million girls and women have been subjected to one of the first three types of female genital mutilation. Approximately 3 million girls in Africa are at risk of undergoing female genital mutilation each year. The reported prevalence rates range from as low as 5% in Niger to as high as 99% in Guinea. The practice in generally concentrated in Africa with cases also being reported in Asia, the Middle East, and among people who have immigrated from practicing countries (see **Figure 5-3**).[21,22]

Prevalence of Infertility in Women

This is the percentage of women of reproductive age (15–49 years) at risk of becoming pregnant (not pregnant, sexually active, not using contraception, and not lactating) who report trying for a pregnancy for two years or more.

$$ARP = \frac{\text{No. of women of reproductive age at risk of becoming pregnant who report trying unsuccessfully for a pregnancy for two years or more}}{\text{Total number of women of reproductive age at risk of becoming pregnant}} \times 100$$

Data are obtained from a community survey, and the indicator is used to measure the level of infertility in the community. Both women and their partners are asked about sexual practices, contraceptive use, previous births, lactation, and so on.

FIGURE 5-3 **Female Genital Mutilation in African Women Ages 15–49 Years**

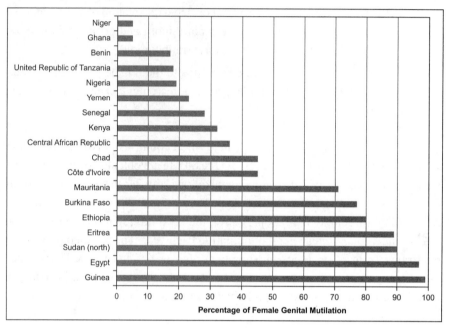

Source: UNICEF. *Female Genital Mutilation/Cutting: A Statistical Exploration.* New York, NY: UNICEF; 2005.

Some disorders that have been associated with infertility in women include ovulation disorder, pelvic inflammatory disease, endometriosis, polycystic ovarian syndrome, hormone imbalance responsible for repeated spontaneous miscarriages, congenital anomalies affecting the reproductive structures, certain environmental and occupational exposures, older age, underweight or overweight, excessive physical exercise, stress and psychological factors, and tobacco, alcohol, and substance use and abuse.[23] In men, infertility results from sexual dysfunction, inadequate semen or sperm quality, smoking, exercise, or other activities leading to prolonged increased scrotal temperature, stress, and other psychological factors resulting from sexual dysfunction, and alcohol and substance use and abuse.[23]

Reported Incidence of Urethritis in Men

This is the percentage of men aged 15–49 years, interviewed in a community survey, who reported having one or more episodes of urethritis (discharge from the penis while passing urine) in the previous 12 months.

$$\text{Urethritis} = \frac{\text{No. of men aged } 15-49 \text{ years who reported having one or more episodes of urethritis in the previous 12 months}}{\text{No. of men aged } 15-49 \text{ years interviewed in the survey}} \times 100$$

Data are generally obtained from community surveys at the national or specific population level.

This indicator is useful for measuring the impact of preventive services for sexually transmitted diseases.

Prevalence of HIV Infection in Pregnant Women

This is the percentage of blood samples taken from women aged 15–24 years that test positive for HIV during routine sentinel surveillance at selected antenatal clinics.

$$\text{PHIV} = \frac{\text{No. of HIV-positive blood samples taken from pregnant women aged } 15-24 \text{ years from selected antenatal clinics that were tested for HIV}}{\text{Total number of blood samples taken from pregnant women aged } 15-24 \text{ years from selected antenatal clinics that were tested for HIV}} \times 100$$

This indicator can be used as a proxy for HIV incidence.

Knowledge of HIV-Related Preventive Practices

This is the percentage of survey respondents who correctly identify all three major ways of preventing sexual transmission of HIV and who also reject all three major misconceptions about HIV transmission or prevention. The three major ways of preventing sexual transmission of HIV are as follows:

1. Having no penetrative sex.
2. Using a condom.
3. Limiting sexual activity to one faithful, uninfected partner.

The three major misconceptions about HIV transmission or prevention are as follows:

1. Not understanding that a healthy-looking person can carry the AIDS virus.
2. A major misconception to be determined in the local cultural context.
3. A second major misconception to be determined in the local cultural context.

Knowledge about HIV is obtained from population-based surveys. This indicator provides information about knowledge of preventive practices in HIV/AIDS that is prerequisite in behavior change. The knowledge about HIV indicator is derived as follows:

$$\text{Knowledge HIV} = \frac{\begin{array}{c}\text{No. of survey respondents (women and men) who}\\ \text{correctly identify all three major ways of preventing}\\ \text{sexual transmission of HIV and who also reject all}\\ \text{three major misconceptions about HIV transmission}\\ \text{or prevention}\end{array}}{\text{Total number of respondents included in the survey}} \times 100$$

Conclusion

Reproductive health indicators are useful in that they describe reproductive health status and provide a comparison with health-related policy, program, and service goals. When reproductive health indicators are reported according to person, place, and time variables, it is possible to better understand who is at greatest risk and why and how they have become more susceptible to the reproductive health problem. Identifying health status through reproductive health indicators is a starting point in the research process, which leads to the research question and formulation of hypotheses. The next step is to select an appropriate study design for assessing the research hypothesis, which is the focus of the next chapter.

Key Issues

1. Reproductive health indicators are markers that are used to determine the status and needs of reproductive health.
2. There are many dimensions of reproductive health, and thus, in order to create a comprehensive understanding, we use indictors in several

categories, including health and well-being, health resources, collective justice, social capital, collective capacity, resiliency, and functionality.
3. Ratios, proportions, and rates are important commonly used measures for describing the indicators of reproductive health.
4. The United Nations' MDG reproductive health indicators can be summarized into a short list of 17 indicators that are complementary and representative of all areas of reproductive health.

Exercises

Key Terms

Define the following terms.

Antenatal care coverage

Basic essential obstetric care

Bills of mortality

Comprehensive essential obstetric care

Contraceptive prevalence

Genital mutilation

Health indicator

Maternal mortality rate

Monitoring

Perinatal mortality rate

Population momentum

Replacement rate

Reproductive health indicators

Skilled health personnel

Total fertility rate

Study Questions

5.1 Calculate the ASFR (see **Table 5-2**).
5.2 Calculate the TFR.

TABLE 5-2   **Questions 1–2**

Age of Women	Estimated Females	Births	ASFR	ASFR × 5
15–19	10,611	442		
20–24	10,680	1,081		
25–29	10,545	1,182		
30–34	10,092	950		
35–39	10,076	499		
40–44	10,500	105		
45–49	11,430	7		

5.3 Calculate the maternal mortality rate given the following fictional information: The small nation of Iritaniba, population 4,500,000, reported 1,300,000 women of childbearing age, 136,000 live births, and 200 maternal deaths in 2001.

5.4 Refer to the Human Development Report for the United States (http://hdrstats.undp.org/countries/data_sheets/cty_ds_USA.html). Identify the statistics involving CP and births attended by skilled health personnel, and then refer to these statistics for other countries. What is the general relationship?

5.5 Refer to the article by Stanley K. Henshaw, Susheela Singh, and Taylor Haas. (Recent trends in abortion rates worldwide. *International Family Planning Perspectives* 1999;25(1). Available at: http://www.guttmacher .org/pubs/journals/2504499.html.) What do the authors predict will cause a rapid fall in abortion rates in developed countries? Do the authors believe that legalization of abortion and access to abortion services will lead to an increased reliance on abortion for fertility control over the long run?

5.6 Why might a country with a fertility rate less than 2.1 continue to have an increase in its population?

5.7 If the TFR is below the replacement rate and assuming in-migration remains constant, will the population eventually fall, even if there is currently a high percentage of the population in the childbearing ages?

5.8 According to the paper by Sonya Norris (http://dsp-psd.pwgsc.gc.ca/ Collection-R/LoPBdP/EB-e/prb0032-e.pdf), can reproductive infertility be reversed? What are some treatments for reproductive infertility?

References

1. Glass DV. Graunt's life table. *J Inst Actu.* 1950;76:60–64.
2. Greenwood M. *Medical Statistics from Graunt to Farr.* New York, NY: Cambridge University Press; 1948.
3. Fox JP, Hall CE, Elveback LR. *Epidemiology: Man and Disease.* New York, NY: Macmillan Company; 1970.
4. World Health Organization. Reproductive health indicators: Guidelines for their generation, interpretation and analysis for global monitoring. Geneva, Switzerland: World Health Organization Press; 2006. Available at: http://www.who.int/reproductive-health/publications/ rh_indicators/guidelines.pdf. Accessed February 28, 2009.
5. Index Mundi. Country comparison: Total fertility rate. Available at: http://www.indexmundi .com/g/r.aspx?c=xx&v=31. Accessed December 5, 2008.

6. United Nations. *The World Population Prospects: The 2004 Revision*, 4th ed. New York: United Nations; 2005.

7. Wikipedia. Total fertility rate. Available at: http://en.wikipedia.org/wiki/Total_fertility_ rate. Accessed December 31, 2008.

8. OECD. Total fertility rates: Number of children born to women aged 15 to 49: United States. Available at: http://www.swivel.com/data_columns/show/2417583. Accessed January 2, 2009.

9. U.S. Census Bureau, International Data Base. U.S. data are based on official estimates and projections. Population estimates for 1950–1999 are based on the resident population plus the armed forces overseas. Population data in the IDB for 2000–2050 are projections based on the resident population. Official population estimates for the United States for 2000 through 2007 can be found at http://www.census.gov/popest/estimates.php.

10. U.S. Census Bureau, International Data Base. *Country Summary: United States.* Available at: http://www.census.gov/ipc/www/idb/country/usportal.html. Accessed January 3, 2009.

11. United Nations. *World Contraceptive Use 2001*. New York, NY: United Nations Department of Economic and Social Affairs; 2002.

12. United Nations. *World Contraceptive Use 2003*. New York, NY: United Nations Department of Economic and Social Affairs; 2003.

13. U.S. Census Bureau. Contraceptive prevalence in the developing world. Available at: http://www.census.gov/ipc/prod/wp02/wp-02005.pdf. Accessed December 5, 2008.

14. United Nations Children's Fund. *The State of the World's Children 2007: Women and Children, The Double Dividend of Gender Equality.* New York, NY: United Nations Children's Fund; 2006.

15. World Health Organization. *ICD-10. International Statistical Classification of Diseases and Related Health Problems*, 10th revision. Geneva, Switzerland: World Health Organization; 1992.

16. World Health Organization. *Making Pregnancy Safer: The Critical Role of the Skilled Attendant. A Joint Statement by WHO, ICM and FIGO.* Geneva, Switzerland: World Health Organization; 2004.

17. UNICEF/WHO/UNFPA. *Guidelines for Monitoring the Availability and Use of Obstetric Services.* New York, NY: UNICEF; 1997.

18. World Health Organization. *Neonatal and Perinatal Mortality: Country, Regional and Global Estimates.* Geneva, Switzerland: World Health Organization; 2006.

19. UNICEF/World Health Organization. Low Birthweight: Country, Regional and Global Estimates. New York, NY: UNICEF; 2004. Available at: http://www.unicef.org/publications/files/low_birthweight_from_EY.pdf.

20. World Health Organization. Classification of female genital mutilation. Available at: http://www.who.int/reproductive-health/fgm/terminology.htm. Accessed December 31, 2008.

21. World Health Organization. Female genital mutilation. Available at: http://www.who.int/reproductive-health/fgm/prevalence.htm. Accessed December 12, 2008.

22. UNICEF. *Female Genital Mutilation/Cutting: A Statistical Exploration.* New York, NY: UNICEF; 2005.

23. Norris S. Reproductive infertility: prevalence, causes, trends and treatments. Parliamentary Research Branch, Library of Parliament, 2001. Available at: http://dsp-psd.pwgsc.gc.ca/Collection-R/LoPBdP/EB-e/prb0032-e.pdf. Accessed January 2, 2009.

SIX

Study Designs in Reproductive Epidemiology

Learning Objectives

After completing this chapter, you should be able to:

1. Distinguish between descriptive and analytic study designs.
2. Distinguish between observational and experimental study designs.
3. Understand how and when to apply selected study designs and describe their potential strengths and weaknesses.

A fundamental part of the research process is the study design. In the previous chapters, reference was made to descriptive and analytic study designs in reproductive epidemiology. The study design is used to provide structure to the research and depends on the question being studied; it is a plan of action. The study design dictates the type of data that will be employed and the appropriate statistical approach to be taken. **Descriptive study designs** include case reports and case series, cross-sectional surveys, and exploratory ecologic designs. These designs provide a means for obtaining descriptive statistics, which are used to assess the distribution of data without typically attempting to test particular hypotheses.

Analytic study designs include observational case-control and cohort studies, case-crossover studies, and experimental studies. A statistically significant result is an important piece of evidence used in causal inference.

Understanding how and why disruptions in reproductive health occur is achieved through analytic epidemiology; that is, analytic study designs and statistical methods are used to assess associations between selected health outcomes and different environments (see Chapter 2, "Environments in Reproductive Epidemiology"). Once an environmental risk factor has been established, it may be classified according to whether its exposure can be avoided through personal behavior. Identifying the routes of transmission of physical, chemical, and biological agents is also achieved through analytic epidemiologic methods. Finally, understanding biologic mechanisms and processes of observed relationships between exposures and health outcomes can be further explored through laboratory studies.

The purpose of this chapter is to explore study designs used in reproductive epidemiology. We will also consider some of the challenges encountered in applying these study designs in human reproduction.

The Study Design

Descriptive

Several descriptive study designs that direct the researcher along the path of systematically describing data are presented in **Table 6-1**. Each of these designs can

TABLE 6-1 **Epidemiologic Descriptive Study Designs**

	Description	Strengths	Weaknesses
Case study	A snapshot description of a problem or situation for an individual or group; qualitative descriptive research of the facts in chronological order	• In-depth description • Provides clues to identifying a new disease or adverse health effect resulting from an exposure or experience • Identifies potential areas of research	• Conclusions limited to the individual, group, and/or context under study • Cannot be used to establish a cause–effect relationship

TABLE 6-1 *(Continued)*

Cross-sectional	All the variables are measured at a point in time; there is no distinction between potential risk factors and outcomes	• Control over study population • Control over measurements • Several associations between variables can be studied at same time • Short time period required • Complete data collection • Exposure and injury/disease data collected from same individuals • Produces prevalence	• No data on the time relationship between exposure and injury/disease development • Potential bias from low response rate • Potential measurement bias • Higher proportion of long-term survivors • Not feasible with rare exposures or outcomes • Does not yield incidence or relative risk
Ecologic	Aggregate data involved (i.e., no information is available for specific individuals); prevalence of a potential risk factor compared with the rate of an outcome condition	• Takes advantage of preexisting data • Relatively quick and inexpensive • Can be used to evaluate programs, policies, or regulations implemented at the ecologic level • Allows estimation of effects not easily measurable for individuals	• Susceptible to confounding • Exposures and disease or injury outcomes not measured on the same individuals

provide information about the health problem. An important aim of the **case study** is to identify an emerging health problem resulting from an exposure or experience. The case study can also provide insights by describing the characteristics of a person or group of people, the setting or community, the circumstances, and the problem. The case study may also be useful for investigating an unusual event such as a cluster—that is, "an unusual aggregation, real or perceived, of health events that are grouped together in time and space and that are reported to a health agency."[1]

A **cross-sectional study** provides data that can be correlated and reflect the prevalence of an exposure or outcome in a selected population. For example, a recent cross-sectional survey identified that the prevalence of miscarriages among women in Jordanian refugee camps was 2.3%.[2] Because exposure and outcome data are collected at the same point in time, establishing a time sequence of events between variables is problematic, which limits drawing conclusions about causality.

An **ecologic study** is where the units of analysis are populations or groups of people rather than individuals. Comparisons are then made among groups rather than individuals. For example, one study estimated the association between the incidence of caesarean sections in 19 Latin American countries and the countries' gross national product per capita. The correlation between aggregated population-level socioeconomic conditions and caesarean section rates among these countries was significantly positive.[3]

Analytic

Once the research problem has been established and research hypotheses formulated, analytic study designs are employed for assessing associations. In these study designs, a comparison group is employed that has been explicitly collected. A brief overview of common analytic study designs is presented in **Table 6-2**.

In the analytic study design, the unit of analysis is the individual. There are two types of analytic studies: observational and experimental. In observational studies, the observed variables are beyond the control or influence of the investigator, such as in a case-control or cohort study. On the other hand, in experimental studies some of the participants are deliberately manipulated in order to evaluate the intervention effect. Because many environmental exposures are suspected to produce adverse health outcomes, it would be unethical to assign the exposure to the participants. For this reason, reproductive epidemiology predominately involves observational studies.

Experimental Study

The randomized blinded controlled **experimental study** is considered to be the "gold standard" in epidemiology because randomization can balance out

TABLE 6-2	Epidemiologic Analytic Study Designs		
	Description	**Strengths**	**Weaknesses**
Experimental	Examines the relationship between the intervention and outcome variables in a cohort of people followed over time	• Produces the strongest evidence for causal associations • May produce a faster and less costly answer to the research question than a cohort study • The only appropriate research design for answering certain research questions	• Ethical barriers • Infeasible because the outcome is too rare • Relatively costly and time-consuming • Limited generalization to common practice • Potential bias due to loss to follow-up
Cohort	People are followed over time to describe the incidence or the natural history of a condition; assessment can also be made of risk factors for various conditions	• Establishes time sequence of events • Avoids bias in measuring predictors from knowing the outcome • Several outcomes can be assessed • Allows assessment of incidence and the natural history of disease • Yields relative risk	• Large samples often required • May not be feasible in terms of time and money • Not feasible with rare outcomes • Limited to one risk factor • Potential bias due to loss to follow-up
Case-control	Presence of risk factor(s) for people with a condition is compared with that for people who do not	• Effective for rare outcomes • Compared with the cohort study, requires less time, money, and size	• Limited to one outcome condition • Does not provide incidence, relative risk, or natural history

(continues)

TABLE 6-2   *(Continued)*

	Description	*Strengths*	*Weaknesses*
Case-control		• Yields the odds ratio (when the outcome condition is rare, a good estimate of the relative risk)	• Less effective than a cohort study at establishing time sequence of events • Potential recall and interviewer bias • Potential survival bias • Does not yield incidence or prevalence
Case-crossover	Exposure frequency during a window immediately prior to an outcome event is compared with exposure frequencies during a control time or times at an earlier period	• Controls for fixed individual characteristics that may otherwise confound the association • Effective at studying the effects of short-term exposures on the risk of acute events	• Does not automatically control for confounding from time-related factors

confounding factors and blinding can minimize bias. Blinding the intervention status will minimize special attention to the treatment group or seeking other treatment for those in the placebo group. Blinding the health outcome eliminates incorrect conclusions of a study because of the way the data were collected.

It may be readily apparent that applying the experimental study design for assessing physical, chemical, biological, and psychosocial environments can pose ethical challenges. Because carrying out controlled experiments on pregnant women is ethically impossible, conclusions have to be made from observational studies. It may also be that the outcome of interest is too rare to adequately capture in an experimental study. Hence, observational studies and analytic studies may be necessary.

Cohort Study

Cohort studies are forward looking in that people are followed from exposure status to health outcome. As time passes, the number of potential health outcomes connected with the exposure increases. This study design is useful for assessing rare exposures and health outcomes that have a short latency period. On the other hand, for health-related states or events involving a long latency period, the case-control study design is more efficient. Several strengths and weaknesses of the cohort study design are presented in the table.

In reproductive epidemiology, it may be convenient to compare cohorts from two separate populations, where the first population reflects people exposed to a potential risk factor and the second population reflects people not exposed or exposed at lower levels of the potential risk factor. For example, from 1989 to 1997, a cohort study was conducted to determine whether an association existed between the incidence of stillbirths and maternal alcohol consumption during pregnancy. The level of stillbirths was compared between mothers from two distinct populations: One population involved mothers who consumed alcohol during pregnancy, and the other population included mothers who did not. This study found a higher risk of stillbirths among mothers in the population who consumed alcohol during pregnancy.[4]

In another cohort study involving Danish women, exposure to polychlorinated biphenyls with fatty fish consumption was associated with reduced fetal growth. This result is consistent with previous studies linking fatty fish intake with decreased fetal growth. This may cause dietary recommendations that encourage weekly consumption of fatty fish among pregnant women to be altered.[5]

When the potential exposure associated with a given adverse health outcome is very rare, a **double cohort study** may be appropriate. This involves selecting the exposed and unexposed groups from two distinct populations. For example, in the study by Bernier, Crawford, and Dewey (2005) on the developmental outcome of children who had choroid plexus cysts that were detected prenatally via ultrasound, the researchers used a retrospective double cohort design. Because the exposure (prenatally discovered choroid plexus cysts) is so rare, researchers selected the control group from children who had a normal second-trimester ultrasound scan.[6] The presence of the cysts was suspected of causing developmental problems in childhood. The children with choroid plexus cysts detected prenatally were monitored (retrospectively) for developmental outcomes. The children with a normal ultrasound served as the comparison of unexposed persons; they too were monitored and the developmental outcomes were compared with those children with the choroid plexus cysts.[6]

Ten to 15% of lung cancer deaths occurs in nonsmokers.[7] In a cohort study of 71,314 Chinese women aged 40 to 70 years who were lifetime nonsmokers, selected menstrual and reproductive factors (i.e., later age at menopause, longer reproductive period, and higher parity) were associated with decreased risk of lung cancer.[8] The study implicates hormonal factors in the etiology of lung cancer among women who do not smoke.

Case-Control Study

Case-control studies are backward looking. With this study design, the presence of a potential risk factor or factors is compared between those with and those without the health problem of interest. The study begins by identifying cases and controls and then identifies whether the cases were more likely to have been exposed than were the controls. This study design is better than the cohort study design for chronic conditions where the latency period from exposure to disease is years or decades. An example of a case-control study involved a study where cases of women with Hodgkin's disease were compared with controls in a hospital setting. A significant protective effect was observed between Hodgkin's disease and three or more pregnancies compared with nulligravidae and for women with at least one spontaneous or induced abortion compared with women having had no abortions. The study also showed that earlier age at first birth (i.e., less than 20 years old) was protective against Hodgkin's disease.[9]

A nested case-control study (also called a case-cohort study) is a case-control study "nested" within a cohort study. Levels of the risk factor or factors are compared between cases and a sample of noncases. For example, the University of Minnesota's Department of Pediatrics did a study to determine the association between neuroblastoma and selected birth record variables. They performed a nested case-control study by linking Minnesota's birth and cancer registries. The study used children born 1976–2004 who were diagnosed with neuroblastoma before they were 14 years old and then used a randomly sampled comparison group and controlled for gender, birth year, and other potential confounding variables. They found that the risk of neuroblastoma was significantly greater for women who had used drugs during pregnancy as was a child's small size for gestational age.[10]

Nested case-control studies have the scientific benefits of a cohort design but are less expensive to conduct than cohort studies.

Case-Crossover Design

A **case-crossover study** involves comparing the exposure status of a case immediately before its occurrence with that of the same case at a prior time. The idea here is that if precipitating events exist, they should occur more frequently immediately prior to the onset of a health-related state or event rather than during a period more distant from the outcome. This design is especially appropriate where individual exposures are intermittent, the health outcome occurs abruptly, and the incubation period for detection is short.

Individuals serve as their own controls in this study design, with the analytic unit being time. The time just before the acute event is the "case" time compared with some other time, referred to as the "control" time. The case-crossover design assumes there are no confounding time-related factors. The simplest case-crossover design is similar to a matched-pair case-control design.

In Missouri, a case-crossover design was done to determine the association between prenatal smoking and stillbirth. A case-control design and case-crossover design were combined to determine the association. They used the Missouri maternally linked cohort data set. First, for the case-control study, each woman only counted one birth to study. Then, in the case-crossover design, they used only women who had a stillbirth. It was determined that the use of smoking while pregnant increases risk of stillbirth.[11]

Conclusion

This chapter presented various study designs. A description, along with strengths and weaknesses of both descriptive and analytic study designs, was presented. A study design provides a plan of action that gives structure to the research. The study design is influenced by the questions being studied. Descriptive designs are used to answer "who," "what," "when," and "where" questions. Analytic designs are used to answer "how" and "why" questions.

Key Issues

1. The study design is used to provide structure to the research and depends on the question being studied; it is a plan of action.
2. These designs provide a means for obtaining descriptive statistics, which are used to assess the distribution of data without typically attempting to test particular hypotheses.

3. Understanding how and why disruptions in reproductive health occur is achieved through analytic epidemiology.
4. After the research problem is established and research hypotheses formulated, analytic study designs are employed for assessing associations.
5. In the analytic study design, the unit of analysis is the individual. There are two types of analytic studies: observational and experimental.

Exercises

Key Terms

Define the following terms.

Analytic study designs	Cross-sectional surveys
Case-control study	Descriptive study designs
Case-crossover study	Double cohort study
Case study	Ecologic study
Cohort study	Experimental study

Study Questions

6.1 Describe the difference between observational and experimental studies.

6.2 Compare and contrast cross-sectional surveys and ecologic studies.

6.3 Compare and contrast case-control and cohort studies. Discuss the strengths and weaknesses of each.

6.4 Discuss the general steps for constructing a cross-sectional study, case-control study, and cohort study.

6.5 Match the following:

  ____ Yields prevalence   a. Cross-sectional study

  ____ Unit of analysis the population   b. Ecologic study

  ____ Potential bias from low response rate   c. Case study

  ____ Not feasible for rare outcomes

  ____ In-depth description

  ____ Takes advantage of preexisting data

6.6 Match the following:

  ____ Useful for identifying a time   a. Case-control study
     sequence of events   b. Cohort study

_____ Relatively less expensive

_____ Several outcomes can be studied

_____ Not feasible for rare outcomes

_____ Not feasible for long latency periods

_____ Useful for studying rare outcomes

_____ Bias may result from loss to follow-up

_____ Yields odds ratio

_____ Yields incidence (risk), relative risk, attributable risk

_____ Potential bias in measuring exposure variables

_____ Prone to recall and interviewer bias

6.7 In a case-control study conducted in South Africa, 89 women with a child having a birth defect were identified (cases), and 178 women with a child without a birth defect were identified (controls). Among the cases, 53 women used agricultural chemicals (pesticides) during pregnancy. Among controls, 22 had used pesticides during pregnancy.[12] Calculate an appropriate measure of association between pesticide use and birth defect. How might bias influence your result?

References

1. Centers for Disease Control and Prevention. Guidelines for investigating clusters of health events. *MMWR.* 1990;39(RR-11):1–23. Available at: http://cdc.gov/mmwr/preview/mmwrhtml/00001797.htm. Retrieved October 16, 2008.
2. Khawaja M, Barazi R. Prevalence of wife beating in Jordanian refugee camps: reports by men and women. *J Epidemiol Community Health.* 2005;59:840–841.
3. Belizan JM, Althabe F, Barros FC, Alexander S. Rates and implications of caesarean sections in Latin America: ecologic study. *Br Med J.* 1999;319:1397–1402.
4. Aliyu MH, Wilson RE, Zoorob R, Chakrabarty S, Alio AP. Alcohol consumption during pregnancy and the risk of early stillbirth among singletons. *Alcohol.* 2004;42. Available at: http://www.ncbi.nlm.nih.gov/sites/entrez. Accessed October 29, 2008.
5. Halldorsson TI, Thorsdottir I, Meltzer HM, Nielsen F, Olsen SF. Linking exposure to polychlorinated biphenyls with fatty fish consumption and reduced fetal growth among Danish pregnant women: a cause for concern? *Am J Epidemiol.* 2008;168(8):958–965.
6. Bernier FP, Crawford SG, Dewey D. Developmental outcome of children who had choroid plexus cysts detected prenatally. *Prenatal Diagn.* 2005;25:322–326.
7. Annual smoking-attributable mortality, years of potential life lost, and productivity losses—United States, 1997–2001. *MMWR.* 2005;54(25):625–628.
8. Weiss JM, Lacey JV, Shu XO, et al. Menstrual and reproductive factors in association with lung cancer in female lifetime nonsmokers. *Am J Epidemiol.* 2008;168:1319–1325.
9. Tavani A, Pregnolato A, La Vecchia C, Franceschi S. A case-control study of reproductive factors and risk of lymphomas and myelomas. *Leuk Res.* 1997;21(9):885–888.

10. Johnson KJ, Puumala SE, Soler JT, Spector LG. Perinatal characteristics and risk of neuroblastoma. *Int J Cancer.* 2008;123. Available at: http://www.ncbi.nlm.nih.gov/pubmed/18546287?ordinalpos=1&itool=EntrezSystem2.PEntrez.Pubmed.Pubmed_ResultsPanel.Pubmed_DefaultReportPanel.Pubmed_RVDocSum. Accessed November 1, 2008.

11. Salihu HM, Sharma PP, Getahun D, Hedayatzadeh M, Peters S. Prenatal tobacco use and risk of stillbirth: a case-control and bidirectional case-crossover study. *Nicotine and Tobacco Res.* 2008;10. Available at: http://www.ncbi.nlm.nih.gov/sites/entrez. Accessed November 3, 2008.

12. Heeren GA, Tyler J, Mandeya A. Agricultural chemical exposures and birth defects in the Eastern Cape Province, South Africa: a case-control study. *Environ Health Global Access Sci Source.* 2003;2:11.

SEVEN

Causal Inference in Reproductive Epidemiology

Learning Objectives

After completing this chapter, you should be able to:

1. Identify and describe selected criteria that may be used to draw conclusions about causal associations.
2. Identify some of the limitations associated with the selected criteria for drawing conclusions about causality.
3. Describe common types of bias and confounding and the best methods of controlling for them.
4. Describe predisposing, reinforcing, and enabling factors in the context of causal inference.
5. Know the meaning of "risk factor" and how it relates to a component cause.

In the previous two chapters, selected study designs were presented for addressing the research problem. The study design provides a framework for collecting, analyzing, and interpreting data. The first step in detecting a causal association is to identify a valid statistical association. When a statistical association is demonstrated between exposure and outcome variables, consideration should be given as to whether it is a causal association.

A primary aim in reproductive epidemiology is to identify causes of health-related states or events, based on the totality of evidence from scientific inquiry. The connection between human health and physical, chemical, biological, social, and psychosocial factors in the environment is based on causal inference. **Causal inference** is a conclusion about the presence of an outcome and reasons for its existence. To better understand this term, consider that in our daily lives each of us infers that something is true or highly probable based on our expectations and experiences. We may exercise on a regular basis expecting that it will help us maintain good physical and mental health. Inference in reproductive epidemiology is similar to inference in daily life in that it also is based on expectations and experience; however, expectations are referred to as hypotheses and experiences are called data. Causal inferences provide a scientific basis for medical and public health action. By identifying the existence and cause of a health problem, priorities can be established for implementing and evaluating interventions designed to address the health needs of the affected population and provide care for that population in a manner that is sensitive to cultural and political values, as well as resource constraints.

In contrast to causal inference, **statistical inference** draws a conclusion about a population based on sampled data and uses probability to indicate the level of reliability in the conclusion. Sampled data are evaluated using statistical methods such as regression and correlations, decision theory, and time-series analysis. Causal inferences are made with methods comprising lists of criteria or conditions applied to the results of scientific studies. Causal inference then takes into account the totality of evidence in order to make a "judgment" about causality.

The purpose of this chapter is to present selected concepts and criteria for discussing causal theories and establishing cause–effect associations.

Causation

Although a valid statistical association between an exposure and disease outcome is necessary for there to be a causal association, it does not necessarily mean a causal association exists. That is, not all statistically significant associations between exposure and outcome variables amount to causal relations. More than just a statistical association needs to be considered before we can draw conclusions about causality.

A **cause** is a specific event, condition, or characteristic that precedes the health outcome and is necessary for its occurrence. Reduction in the exposure leads to a reduction in the adverse health outcome. If an environmental exposure is required for the outcome to occur, the causative factor is "necessary." If the health-related state or event always occurs because of the exposure, the causative factor is "sufficient." For example, a mother's exposure to rubella virus (rubivirus) is necessary for rubella to develop; however, exposure to rubella virus is not sufficient to cause rubella because not everyone infected develops the disease. The host must be susceptible and other host factors may also influence risk.

Several disease causation models have been presented. These models are purposely simplified representations, with the express purpose to facilitate our understanding of complex causal associations. The **epidemiology triangle** is a traditional model that characterizes infectious disease causation (see **Figure 7-1**). This model is useful for showing the interaction and interdependence of agent, host, environment, and time. The **agent** is a causative factor such as a pathogen or chemical. The **host** is an organism and usually a human. This may be expanded to groups or populations and their characteristics. **Host factors** are intrinsic factors that influence a person's exposure, susceptibility, or response to a causative agent, such as age, race/ethnicity, gender, sexual practice, eating habits, smoking, and many others. **Environmental factors** are extrinsic factors that affect the agent

FIGURE 7-1 **The Triangle of Epidemiology**

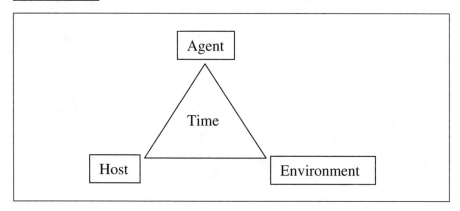

and the opportunity for exposure. These factors often involve physical factors such as physical surroundings, climate, and geology; biological factors, such as vectors; and psychosocial factors such as crowding, sanitation, and socioeconomic status. The agent, host, and environment interact in complex ways to produce adverse health-related states or events in humans. When we look for causes of disease we must consider all three components. In addition, each component has time-related issues (e.g., duration of exposure, time the pathologic changes occur prior to clinical symptoms, and the time in which a vector is capable of spreading an infectious agent). The interrelatedness of these four epidemiological factors influences birth defects and other adverse reproductive health outcomes.

The epidemiologic triad does not work well for certain noninfectious diseases. Thus, other models have been developed to capture the multifactorial nature of causation for many health-related states or events. One such model is Rothman's causal pies (1976).[1] In **Figure 7-2**, the factors that cause the adverse health outcome are pieces of a pie, with the entire pie making up the sufficient cause for a health problem or one causal mechanism. The health-related state or event may have more than one sufficient cause, as illustrated in the figure, with each sufficient cause consisting of multiple contributing factors that are called **component causes**. The different component causes include the agent, host factors, and environmental factors. Where a given component cause is required in each of the different sufficient causes, it is referred to as a necessary cause. In the figure, the letter "A" represents a necessary cause since it is included in each of the three sufficient causes for the adverse health outcome. Exposure to the rubivirus is necessary for rubella-related birth defects to occur but not sufficient to cause birth

FIGURE 7-2   **Three Sufficient Causes of an Adverse Health Outcome**

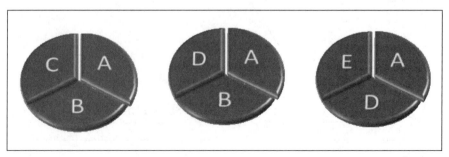

defects. Component causes that may be required to make a sufficient cause may include a susceptible host who is not immune and illness during the first few months of pregnancy.

Prevention and control measures do not require identifying every component of a sufficient cause because the health problem can be prevented by blocking any single component of a sufficient cause.

Causal Criteria

A primary aim in epidemiologic research is to uncover the cause of adverse health outcomes in human populations. Thus, how do we determine whether a given relation is causal? Various authors have established criteria for evaluating whether an association is a causal association.[2–7]

The most widely cited causal criteria were presented by Hill, which he adapted from the U.S. Surgeon General's report in 1964, linking smoking with adverse health outcomes. The causal criteria developed by Hill are presented in this section.[2–7]

Strength of Association

A valid statistical association is prerequisite to there being a causal association. Although a valid statistical association does not necessarily mean that a causal association exists, it is a requirement for causality.

Underlying a valid statistical association are accurate measures of exposure and outcome data. The outcome measure is relatively easy to measure; however, although causal inference is strongest when exposure information is directly measured, epidemiologists often must rely on indirect measures of exposure. Yet insights into causality may still be made with indirect measures of exposure.

The quality of the exposure measurements relates to the **validity** ("truthfulness") of the study. Challenges in collecting exposure data or an imperfect definition of the level of exposure experienced may result in bias. Exposure assessment is complicated for many reasons. First, exposures at different times in gestation result in a range of possible outcomes. Second, with lower levels of exposure, repair or compensation for the damage can occur, which may not be possible at higher levels of exposure. Exposure may involve an intense dose over a relatively short period of time or a low-level prolonged dose over a period from weeks to years. The effects of acute, high-dose environmental exposures may appear within seconds or minutes (e.g., an acute dose of ionizing radiation). On the other hand, the effects of chronic, low-dose exposures may not appear until years later (e.g., cancers). Third, a given exposure may result in several outcomes, each with its own chance of occurring, depending on the combination of time and dose of the exposure.

Assessing exposures is particularly complicated for those exposures that occurred in the distant past. Reconstructing past exposures may be complicated because of limited recall, incomplete measurements, inaccurate records, and variability of exposure from person to person. In this situation, a direct measure of the past exposure may not be possible and can require estimation through modeling.

Reproductive health problems may require a minimal level of exposure and an increase in probability with longer exposure. Such a relationship between exposure and disease may be missed with a dichotomous measure characterizing the presence or absence of the exposure. For this reason, it is often more appropriate to use ordinal or continuous measures of the exposure, particularly in a dose–response assessment. Measurement of an exposure variable on a continuous scale is the most informative for evaluating associations. Continuous-level data allow measurement of a dose–response relationship; however, in some cases, exposure information is only available on a nominal scale—exposed versus not exposed. This may be the only alternative when there are perceived versus documented exposures or the exposure occurred in the past and direct measurement is not feasible.

Assuming valid measures of exposure and outcome variables, a valid statistical association requires an analytic study design where a comparison group is involved. The comparison group allows better control for the presence of confounding and provides a meaningful reference. The analytic study design should be based on the research hypothesis, defined prior to data collection. This will help focus the study and has implications as to the significance level.

The randomized controlled trial is the best method in controlling for confounding because randomization balances out confounding factors between or among groups. The use of blinding is also helpful for controlling for bias. For analytic study designs that do not involve randomization or blinding, such as the case-control and cohort study designs, confounding is often controlled for by matching and restriction at the design level of the study, and stratification and multiple-regression at the analysis level of the study.

Case-control studies are subject to bias through selection and observation. With selection bias, the association between exposure and outcome variables differs from what the relationship would have been among individuals in the population of interest. Recruiting from all individuals in the population of interest avoids selection bias. Observation bias results from differential accuracy of recall between cases and controls (**recall bias**) or because of differential accuracy of exposure information because an interviewer probes cases differently than controls (interviewer bias). The use of medical records or other recorded health information rather than recalled information about exposure can avoid recall bias. When this is not possible, those from which information is being obtained should be unaware of the specific hypotheses being tested. In addition, proper training and blinding of interviewers as to case-control status can minimize bias. This is because an interviewer may subconsciously probe or scan records more intensively for a history of exposure among the cases compared with the controls.

Cohort studies are also prone to bias because of selection. For example, the healthy worker effect is a type of selection bias that occurs in cohort studies when workers represent the exposed group and a sample from the general population represents the unexposed group. This is because workers tend to be healthier on average than the general population; that is, initial employment and continued work often require a certain level of health. Alternatively, many in the general population are unable to get or keep a job because of health problems. If we were interested in whether a job requiring standing is related to miscarriages in pregnant women, rather than comparing these women with pregnant women in the general population, we could compare them with other women employed by the company but in jobs that do not require standing.

Selection of participants in a study may also lead to bias because of loss to follow-up, which is a circumstance in which researchers lose contact with participants. Loss to follow-up in cohort studies increases with longer follow-up times. Bias can result in an estimate of association between exposure and outcome variables if the extent of loss to follow-up is associated with both the exposure and the outcome.

As a general rule, the validity of a study requires that loss to follow-up not exceed 20%. Approaches for minimizing loss to follow-up include excluding those not likely to remain in the study, having periodic contact with participants, and providing incentives for participation.

The potential effect of confounding needs to be considered when assessing the validity of a statistical association. **Confounding** occurs when the relationship between a risk factor and outcome is influenced by a third variable. A third variable is a confounder if it is associated with the outcome variable and, independent of that association, is also associated with the exposure. Variables such as age, gender, race/ethnicity, education, and income are some of the more common confounding variables that are often considered when assessing the relationship between exposure and health outcome variables. For example, suppose that we were interested in evaluating whether birth order is associated with Down syndrome. A positive statistical association between birth order and Down syndrome, however, may be because maternal age is associated with Down syndrome, and independent of that relationship, maternal age is also related to birth order. Hence, it may be that maternal age and not birth order increases the risk of Down syndrome. Failure to adjust for age would result in a misleading result.

The positive association between maternal age at pregnancy and Down syndrome is well established (see **Table 7-1**).[8–10]

TABLE 7-1   **Maternal Age at Pregnancy and Down Syndrome**

Age (years)	Frequency of Fetuses With Down Syndrome to Normal Fetuses at 16 Weeks of Pregnancy	Frequency of Live Births of Babies With Down Syndrome to Normal Births
15–19	—	1/1250
20–24	—	1/1400
25–29	—	1/1100
30–31	—	1/900
32	—	1/750
33	1/420	1/625
34	1/325	1/500
35	1/250	1/350
36	1/200	1/275
37	1/150	1/225
38	1/120	1/175
39	1/100	1/140
40	1/75	1/100
41	1/60	1/85
42	1/45	1/65
43	1/35	1/50
44	1/30	1/40
45 and older	1/20	1/25

Source: Hook EB, Cross PA, Schreinemachers DM. Chromosomal abnormality rates at amniocentesis and in live-born infants. *JAMA.* 1983;249:2034–2038.

There is also evidence of a positive association between paternal age and Down syndrome.[9,11] Fisch and colleagues (2003) found no parental age affect on Down syndrome until age 35 years and older, whereupon there was a paternal age effect in association with a maternal age of 35 years and older.[11] The paternal age effect was most pronounced when maternal age was 40 years and older. The paternal contribution to Down syndrome where the mother was at least 40 years was 50%. Hence, adjusting for paternal age at the study design or analysis levels is important to avoid potentially misleading results.

When sampled data are used to assess relationships between/among variables, then chance needs to be considered. Specifically, **chance** is the probability the results are due to the "luck of the draw" and are not necessarily real. This is a greater concern when the sample size is small. As the sample size increases, the role of chance as an explanation of the results decreases. A statistical association may also be biased, which means the measured association does not reflect the truth. Bias is controlled by carefully designing and carrying out the study. Bias needs to be controlled for at the design level of the study because it cannot be corrected for thereafter.

A strong direct association between an exposure and disease outcome increases the likelihood of there being a causal association. On the other hand, a weak statistical association provides little support of causal association. Stronger associations are less likely explained by chance, bias, or confounding.

Measuring the intensity and duration of exposure is often necessary for supporting causal association. A causal association may be implied in a descriptive study without a direct measure of exposure; however, greater confidence in causal associations between environmental factors and human health requires accurate identification of the primary mechanism (physical, chemical, biological, psychosocial) of the environmental contaminant or stress, and determination of how and in what form the environmental contaminant or stress comes in contact with people.

Identifying an association between dose and an adverse health outcome provides support for causality. The quality of the exposure measurements influences the validity of the study. Validity refers to the "truthfulness" of a measure. A valid measure of a concept measures what it claims to measure. This is often a challenge when the environmental exposure, such as a hazardous chemical or radiation fallout, occurred in the distant past. Reconstructing past exposures may be complicated by limited recall, incomplete measurements, inaccurate records, and variability of exposure from person to person. In this situation, a direct measure of the past exposure may not be possible and can require estimation through modeling.

Removal of the exposure should reduce or eliminate the disease risk, unless irreversible damage has occurred.

Although a strong statistical association may not reflect a causal association, a weak statistical association may be causal. Some component causes making up sufficient causes of an adverse health outcome may be weak.[12]

Consistency

Consistency occurs when associations are replicated by different investigators in different settings and populations and using different methods. If similar associations are consistently replicated, it is unlikely that the results could be due to chance, bias, or confounding. Meta-analysis is used to combine relations found across several studies and can also be used to give an overall picture of consistency among studies; however, this assumes that similar study designs and statistical methods were used in order to avoid bias.

Specificity

Specificity of association means that an exposure is associated with only one health outcome or that the health outcome is associated with only one exposure. Although this condition may support a causal hypothesis, failure to satisfy this criterion cannot rule out causality because many exposures are related to a given health outcome or many health outcomes are related to a given exposure. To illustrate the misleading nature of this criteria, consider that the more diseases smoking is associated with, the greater the evidence is against smoking as a cause of any of the diseases.[12]

Temporality

Establishing a temporal sequence of events is fundamental to there being a causal association; that is, for an environmental factor to cause a reproductive health problem, it must precede the problem at a reasonable interval. Incubation periods from exposure to the onset of clinical symptoms can be a few hours, days, weeks, or years. (The word "latency" is used instead of "incubation" in the context of chronic disease.) The best analytic study design for establishing a time sequence of events is the cohort study or the experimental study, which is a special type of cohort study that involves an intervention. In a cohort study, exposure status is first identified and persons with the health outcome of interest are excluded from the study. Exposed and unexposed groups are then followed to see whether there is a difference in the risk of an adverse health outcome.

Establishing a temporal sequence of events is typically more difficult with diseases having longer latency periods.

Biologic Gradient

A **dose–response relationship** is where the health problem changes in direct proportion to the level of exposure. If an association is causal, we would expect an increasing gradient of risk associated with greater exposure; however, it is possible that a biologic gradient may be entirely explained by confounding, such as was the case between birth order and Down syndrome, where maternal age confounded this relationship.

Biological Plausibility

Consistent with the inner versus the outer environment presented in the previous chapter, biological plausibility is the association between an exposure and disease outcome supported in terms of basic human biology. This is a vague and subjective criterion that may be difficult or impossible to apply.

Coherence

A causal association should be consistent with known epidemiologic patterns of health-related states or events. This is a vague criterion that is difficult to distinguish from consistency or biological plausibility.

Experimental Evidence

Analytic epidemiology is used to search for causes of disease. The ideal study design for providing information about causality is the randomized, blinded experimental control trial. This is because randomization balances the effect of confounding factors between/among groups, blinding helps minimize bias, and the comparison group allows evaluation of the strength of statistical association. Furthermore, a temporal sequence of events and a dose–response relationship between exposure and health outcome can be effectively assessed. The next best study design for supporting causality is the cohort study followed by the case-control study. The cohort study is better than the case-control study for supporting causal associations because temporality and risk can be determined. All analytic epidemiologic study designs are better able to determine temporality and to control for confounding and bias than descriptive epidemiologic study designs.

Although the randomized, blinded experimental control trial may be ideal, it does not apply in many settings.

Analogy

The idea here is that an association is more likely to be causal if it is analogous to causal associations that have already been identified; however, this criterion is questionable, given that numerous analogies abound.

Predisposing, Reinforcing, and Enabling Factors

Any of several factors may be associated with the causation of health behaviors and adverse health outcomes. These factors are classified as predisposing, reinforcing, enabling, and risk factors. Green and Kreuter (1999) define predisposing factors as "antecedents to behavior that provide the rationale or motivation for the behavior."[13] These factors include peoples' knowledge, attitudes, beliefs, preferences, skills, and self-efficacy beliefs. From an epidemiologic perspective, predisposing factors may be thought of as those factors that are already present that produce a susceptibility or disposition in a host to a health-related state or event without actually causing it. For example, in a retrospective analysis of case records, a higher risk of fetal loss after amniocentesis was identified in women ages greater than 40 years compared with those aged 20 to 34 years. In addition, bleeding during the current pregnancy, a history of three or more abortions during the first trimester, a second trimester miscarriage or termination of pregnancy were significantly predisposing factors for fetal loss after an amniocentesis.[14] Reinforcing factors are "those factors following a behavior that provide continuing reward or incentive for the persistence or repetition of the behavior."[13] These factors include social support, peer influence, and vicarious reinforcement.

Health education and economic assistance are examples of positive reinforcing factors that can promote behavior change to reduce health problems. On the other hand, negative reinforcing factors such as social acceptance or poor economic conditions may increase the negative behaviors.

Enabling factors are "antecedents to behavior that allow a motivation to be realized."[13] Enabling factors can affect behavior through an environmental factor in either a positive or a negative way. These factors include services, living conditions, programs, societal supports, skills, and resources that facilitate a behavior's or health outcome's occurrence.

Risk Factors

In the first section of this chapter, Rothman's causal pie model was introduced.[1] The primary message this model represents is that every causal mechanism involves the joint effects of a multitude of component causes. The factors that result in the adverse health outcome are pieces of the pie, with the entire pie making up the sufficient cause for an adverse health outcome. The component causes likely involve a combination of physical, chemical, biological, and psychosocial environmental components.

A related term is **risk factor**, which is a variable associated with the increased probability of a human health problem. It may be thought of as a component cause because it must be combined with other factors before an adverse health outcome occurs. It is not the same as a sufficient cause because not everyone who has the risk factor will experience the health problem. Risk factors are identified through analytic epidemiologic studies. After they have been identified, prevention and control measures can then be taken.

Conclusion

In order to prevent and control reproductive health problems, epidemiologists seek to understand causal relationships. Indeed, a primary aim in reproductive epidemiology is to understand determinants of reproductive health problems. With the use of study designs, statistical methods, and theory, causal inferences are made. Some of the criteria commonly employed in epidemiology to draw conclusions about causality were presented in this chapter. On the basis of these criteria, causal inferences are made and efficient and effective individual and public health decisions can be made in human reproduction.

Key Issues

1. When looking for a cause, consideration should be given to all contributing or component factors, which include the host, agent, environmental factors, and time.

2. A causal association implies that a valid statistical association exists between an exposure and outcome variable. On the other hand, a valid statistical association does not necessarily mean there is a causal association.

3. Hill described the criteria for causation by linking smoking with adverse health outcomes. These criteria include strength of association, consistency, specificity, temporality, biologic gradient, biological plausibility, coherence, experimental evidence, and analogy.

4. To ensure validity, bias should be controlled at the design level of the study. An effective way to control for bias includes blinding. Bias that results from confounding is best controlled at the design level of a study through randomization, but if randomization is not feasible, restriction and matching are commonly employed. At the analysis level of a study confounding, common ways to adjust for confounding include stratification and multiple regression analysis.

5. Predisposing, reinforcing, and enabling factors contribute to health behaviors and outcomes by encouraging them to occur, rewarding them for occurring, and allowing them to occur.

6. A risk factor is a variable in any environmental exposure associated with the increased probability of a human health problem. It may be thought of as a component cause because it must be combined with other factors before an adverse health outcome occurs.

Exercises

Key Terms

Define the following terms.

Agent

Causal inference

Cause

Chance

Component causes

Confounding

Consistency

Dose–response relationship

Environmental factors

Epidemiology triangle

Host

Host factors

Recall bias

Risk factors

Statistical inference

Validity

Study Questions

7.1 What are some challenges in obtaining valid exposure measurements, and how can these be overcome?

7.2 What is the ideal study design for attempting to determine causality, and what makes it effective?

7.3 Describe two models that are used to describe causation.

References

1. Rothman KJ. Causes. *Am J Epidemiol.* 1976;104:587–592.
2. Lilienfeld AM. On the methodology of investigations of etiologic factors in chronic diseases—some comments. *J Chronic Dis.* 1959;10:41–46.
3. Sartwell PE. On the methodology of investigations of etiologic factors in chronic diseases—further comments. *J Chronic Dis.* 1960;11:61–63.
4. Surgeon General's Advisory Committee on Smoking and Health. Smoking and health: 1964. Rockville, MD: U.S. Public Health Service; 1964 (DHEW publication no. PHS 1103).
5. Susser M. *Causal Thinking in the Health Sciences.* New York, NY: Oxford University Press; 1973.
6. Hill AB. The environment and disease: association or causation? *Proc R Soc Med.* 1965; 58:295–300.
7. MacMahon B, Pugh TF. *Epidemiology: Principles and methods.* Boston, MA: Little, Brown, and Company; 1970.
8. Rich-Edwards JW, Buka SL, Brennan RT, Earls F. Diverging associations of maternal age with low birth weight for black and white mothers. *Int J Epidemiol.* 2003;32:83–90.
9. National Institute of Child Health and Human Development. Facts about Down syndrome. Available at: http://www.nichd.nih.gov/publications/pubs/downsyndrome.cfm# TheOccurrence. Accessed December 5, 2008.
10. Hook EB, Cross PA, Schreinemachers DM. Chromosomal abnormality rates at amniocentesis and in live-born infants. *JAMA.* 1983;249:2034–2038.
11. Fisch H, Hyun G, Golden R, Hensle TW, Olsson CA, Liberson GL. The influence of paternal age on Down syndrome. *J Urol.* 2003;169(6):2275–2278.
12. Rothman K. *Epidemiology: An Introduction.* Oxford: Oxford University Press; 2002.
13. Green LW, Kreuter, MW. *Health Planning: An Educational and Ecological Approach,* 3rd ed. Mountain View, CA: Mayfield Publishing Company; 1999:153.
14. Papantoniou NE, Daskalakis GJ, Tziotis JG, Kitmirides SJ, Mesogitis SA, Antsaklis AJ. Risk factors predisposing to fetal loss following a second trimester amniocentesis. *Br J Obst Gynaecol.* 2001;108(10):1053–1056.

TWO

Applications of Reproductive Epidemiology

EIGHT

Nutrition and Reproductive Health

Learning Objectives

After completing this chapter, you should be able to:

1. Describe what human nutrition is and how malnutrition may involve either undernutrition or overnutrition.
2. Describe obesity rates and trends in selected geographic regions of the world.
3. Describe the association between excessive weight and reproductive health.
4. Describe the influence of maternal undernutrition during pregnancy and potential health consequences to the child.

Human nutrition is the process by which people obtain food and use it for growth, metabolism, and repair.[1] A **nutrient** is a food, chemical, or substance that is required for an organism to live and grow. Nutrients required of the human body to function properly include protein, carbohydrates, fat, fibers, vitamins, minerals, and water. Protein supplies amino acids, which build and maintain body tissue; fat supplies energy and transports nutrients; carbohydrates are a person's main source of energy; insoluble fiber speeds up the transit through the digestive system; and soluble fiber can lower blood cholesterol levels. Vitamins are organic substances found in food that are used by the body to regulate metabolism and maintain normal growth and functioning; minerals are the building blocks that make up muscles, tissues, and bones and are important to life-supporting systems (e.g., hormones, oxygen transport, and enzyme systems); and water helps transport nutrients to cells, regulate body temperature, and rid the body of waste materials.[2]

Malnutrition is caused by an improper or inadequate diet such that the body does not get the right amounts of the vitamins, minerals, and other nutrients that it needs to maintain healthy organ function and tissues.[2] Malnutrition results in people who are either undernourished or overnourished. **Undernutrition** occurs when too few essential nutrients are consumed or if essential nutrients are excreted from the body faster than they are replaced. This latter situation may result because of diarrhea, excessive sweating, heavy bleeding, or kidney failure. Nutrient intake may also be restricted because of excessive dieting, food allergies, severe injury or illness, or substance abuse. A leading cause of death in developing countries is malnutrition, which is the result of an insufficient intake of calories from proteins, vitamins, and minerals. A lack of food due to poverty is a primary reason for undernutrition. On the other hand, **overnutrition** is a type of malnutrition in which nutrients supplied to the body are greater than required for normal growth, development, and metabolism. Overnutrition occurs from eating too much, not exercising, or taking too many vitamins. The risk of overnutrition may also result from a high consumption of fat and salt, niacin to lower elevated cholesterol levels, vitamin B_6 to relieve premenstrual syndrome, vitamin A to clear up skin problems, or iron or other trace minerals.

A number of symptoms are associated with malnutrition, including anemia, **amenorrhea** (cessation of menstrual periods), easy bruising, easily bleeding gums, a swollen or shriveled and cracked tongue, visual disturbances, disorientation, irritability, anxiety, attention deficits, goiter (enlarged thyroid gland), loss of reflexes and lack of muscular coordination, muscle twitches, and scaling and cracking of the lips and mouth. Malnourished children may have weakened immune systems and may be short for their age, thin, and listless.[2]

Nutrition has historically played a direct role in improving or impeding human reproductive health. There are several different reproduction problems related to nutrition. This chapter focuses on malnutrition (overnutrition and undernutrition) during pregnancy as well as reproductive health problems.

Obesity and Reproduction

Obesity Patterns and Trends

Body mass index (BMI) is a conventional way to categorize a person as overweight or obese. Adult males or females who have a BMI between 25.0 and 29.9 are considered overweight, and those that have a BMI greater than 30 are considered obese.

Overnutrition is associated with an increased risk of obesity. Miyawaki et al. (2002) show that the gastric inhibitory polypeptide directly links overnutrition to obesity.[3] The World Health Organization (WHO) estimated in 2005 that approximately 1.6 billion adults (ages 15 years and older) were overweight and that at least 400 million adults were obese.[4] A shift toward obesity is global, with the current levels of overweight people in countries such as Mexico, Egypt, and South Africa at levels as high or higher than the United States.[5] In addition, the rates of change in obesity are much greater in lower and middle-income countries than in higher income countries.[6] In the United States and European countries, the annual increase in prevalence of overweight and obese men and women is about 0.25 for each. The prevalence of obesity in Asia, North Africa, and Latin America is two to five times greater than in the United States.[5] Adults living in lower income or lower education households are more likely to be overweight or obese, based on 37 nationally representative surveys.[7,8] Overweight prevalence among children and adolescents is also increasing. For example, increases were observed in Brazil (4.2% in 1974 to 14.3% in 1997), China (6.4% in 1991 to 7.7% in 1997), and the United States (15.4% in 1971 to 25.6% in 1994).[5]

Obesity and Health

Both women and men are more likely to suffer from reproductive problems if they are overweight or obese.

In women, several studies demonstrate that women who are overweight or obese have increased risk of amenorrhea, fertility problems, pregnancy complications, miscarriages, and birth defects compared with women of normal weight.[9,10] According to data from the Nurses' Health Study, obese women have 2.7 times the risk of infertility compared with women of normal weight.[11] Obesity also has a detrimental effect in a woman's success in infertility treatments. Studies show that obese women who are treated for fertility problems are less likely to get pregnant through artificial insemination methods, and if they do get pregnant, they have a greater risk of losing the fetus early on in the pregnancy.[11]

Studies have found that one of the causes of infertility in women is polycystic ovary syndrome (PCOS), which is an endocrine disorder in premenopausal women that is characterized by symptoms such as infertility, irregular menstruation, and being overweight. Women who are obese are more susceptible to PCOS. It is estimated that 5% to 20% of all women suffer from PCOS, and 50% of women who have PCOS are overweight or obese.[12] PCOS has other side effects that negatively affect reproduction, which is another factor that makes obese women more susceptible to reproduction problems.

Overweight or obese women have a greater risk for miscarriages. In a study conducted by Hamilton-Fairley, the risk of having a miscarriage before the first living born child was 25% to 37% higher in women who are obese.[13] In addition, complications during pregnancy are greater among overweight and obese women. Obese pregnant women are at an increased risk for gestational diabetes, which has a negative effect on both the mother and the baby and can lead to type II diabetes later in the mother's life.[14] Obese pregnant women are also more susceptible during pregnancy to hypertension disorders. Hypertension disorders include higher arterial blood pressure and altered cardiac function.[15] These disorders can cause serious complications to the fetus by limiting blood flow as well as other health complications. Furthermore, hypertension disorders can lead to a risk of cardiovascular disease in the mother.

A recent study conducted a systematic review and meta-analysis of studies examining the possible link between maternal overweight and obesity and the risk of congenital anomalies.[16] The study found that, compared with mothers of recommended BMI, obese mothers were significantly more likely to have pregnancies affected by neural tube defects, spina bifida, cardiovascular anomalies, septal anomalies, cleft lip and palate, anorectal atresia, hydrocephaly, and limb reduction anomalies. The risk of gastroschisis was significantly lower among these women. Although obesity is significantly associated with an increased risk of many birth disorders, this study found the absolute increase to be small.

In men, obesity has been associated with reduced sperm count and erectile dysfunction. In the United States, sperm counts have decreased by approximately 1.5% each year in recent decades. Similar trends have occurred in other Western countries with high levels of obesity (Swan et al., 2000).[17] Comparatively, the trend of decreased sperm count has not been as prevalent in countries where there are fewer incidents of obesity among the population.[17] Several studies have shown that obesity in males is a source of altered spermatogenesis and erectile dysfunction, which plays a major role in couples' abilities to reproduce.[18] Male infertility may also be due to obesity-related conditions such as increased sedentary living and dietary changes.

Male factors make up 25% to 30% of all cases of infertility and constitute some 30% in combination with female factors.[19]

Erectile dysfunction is directly associated with infertility. In reports in which men indicated that they suffer from erectile dysfunction, 79% have been categorized as overweight or obese.[20] In another study involving health professionals, obesity was associated with a 30% increased risk of erectile dysfunction.[21]

Undernutrition During Pregnancy and Health

Hunger causes malnourished mothers to give birth to malnourished children. Maternal malnutrition can endanger both the mother and the child. Each year approximately 18.4% of maternal deaths worldwide are attributed to iron deficiency.[22] Over 13 million children are born each year with a low birth weight. This is often the result of the mothers having inadequate nutrition before and during pregnancy.[23] A low birth weight baby is four times more likely to die within a week of birth because of infections.[24] Of those low birth weight babies who survive, they are more likely to remain malnourished throughout childhood and go on to face a greater likelihood of health and learning difficulties.[24]

The most prevalent form of malnutrition worldwide is iron deficiency, which affects an estimated 2 billion people.[25] Iron deficiency is a primary concern among women during their reproductive ages and their children, adversely affecting health, productivity, and learning.[24] Iodine deficiency is the primary cause of mental retardation and brain damage.[24] Approximately 1.9 billion people worldwide are at risk of iodine deficiency, which can be easily prevented through adding iodine to salt.[26] The United Nations has sponsored efforts to reduce iron and iodine deficiencies in order to improve maternal survival and children's cognitive development. A program selling weekly iron and folic acid supplements to women of reproductive age in Vietnam has significantly reduced the prevalence of anemia and has improved iron status during pregnancy and birth weights.[27]

The requirements for folate and iron among pregnant women have increased by 50% or more.[28] The U.S. Food and Drug Administration's (FDA's) **Daily Value** (dietary reference numbers to show the amounts of given nutrients in a serving of food) for folic acid is 400 micrograms for nonpregnant women. For pregnant women, the Daily Value is 800 micrograms. Folate (or folic acid) is a B vitamin that is found in small amounts in leafy green vegetables like spinach, watercress and curly kale, some fruits (especially oranges and satsumas), yeast, liver, and breads or breakfast cereals that have been fortified with vitamins (see **Table 8-1**).[29]

The daily value (DV) for folate is 400 µg. The percent DV (%DV) listed on the table indicates the percentage of the DV provided in one serving. A food providing 5% of the DV or less is a low source, whereas a food that provides 10% to 19% of the DV is a good source. A food that provides 20% or more of the DV is high in that nutrient.[30] Refer to the U.S. Department of Agriculture's Nutrient Database website for information on other foods: http://www.nal.usda.gov/fnic/cgi-bin/nut_search.pl.

Folate is needed by the body before and during the first weeks of pregnancy to reduce neural tube defects affecting the brain and spinal cord. These defects are called anencephaly and spina bifida. Babies with the first type of defect do not develop a brain and are stillborn or die shortly after birth. Spina bifida is a defect of the spinal column, which can cause varying degrees of handicap. Approximately 2,500 infants born each year in the United States have spina bifida.[31] Neural tube defects may also be caused by:

- A family history of neural tube defects
- Prior neural tube defect–affected pregnancy
- The use of certain antiseizure medications
- Being severely overweight
- Hot tub use in early pregnancy
- Fever during early pregnancy
- Diabetes

The folate link with neural tube birth defects was first made in the 1950s, when the condition was observed to occur in low socioeconomic groups where women

TABLE 8-1 Selected Food Sources of Folate (Folic Acid)

Food	Micrograms Per Serving	Percent DV
Breakfast cereals fortified with 100% of the DV, ¾ cup*	400	100
Beef liver, cooked, braised, 3 ounces	185	45
Cowpeas (blackeyes), immature, cooked, boiled, ½ cup	105	25
Breakfast cereals, fortified with 25% of the DV, ¾ cup*	100	25
Spinach, frozen, cooked, boiled, ½ cup	100	25
Great Northern beans, boiled, ½ cup	90	20
Asparagus, boiled, four spears	85	20
Rice, white, long-grain, parboiled, enriched, cooked, ½ cup*	65	15
Vegetarian baked beans, canned, 1 cup	60	15
Spinach, raw, 1 cup	60	15
Green peas, frozen, boiled, ½ cup	50	15
Broccoli, chopped, frozen, cooked, ½ cup	50	15
Egg noodles, cooked, enriched, ½ cup*	50	15
Broccoli, raw, two spears (each 5 inches long)	45	10
Avocado, raw, all varieties, ½ cup sliced	45	10
Peanuts, all types, dry roasted, 1 ounce	40	10
Lettuce, Romaine, shredded, ½ cup	40	10
Wheat germ, crude, 2 tablespoons	40	10
Tomato juice, canned, 6 ounces	35	10
Orange juice, chilled, includes concentrate, ¾ cup	35	10
Turnip greens, frozen, cooked, boiled, ½ cup	30	8
Orange, all commercial varieties, fresh, one small	30	8
Bread, white, one slice*	25	6
Bread, whole wheat, one slice*	25	6
Egg, whole, raw, fresh, one large	25	6
Cantaloupe, raw, ¼ medium	25	6
Papaya, raw, ½ cup cubes	25	6
Banana, raw, one medium	20	6

Items marked with an asterisk (*) are fortified with folic acid as part of the Folate Fortification Program; that is, since January 1998, the FDA has required folic acid fortification of all enriched cereal grain products in the United States.

Source: U.S. Department of Agriculture, Agricultural Research Service, 2003, as cited by the Office of Dietary Supplements, National Institutes of Health. Available at: http://ods.od.nih .gov/factsheets/folate.asp. Accessed March 2, 2009.

had poorer diets. Furthermore, babies conceived in the winter and early spring had a greater risk of spina bifida. Studies conducted in England, Hungary, and the United States in the early 1990s found that mineral supplements with folic acid reduced the risk of neural tube birth defects.[31] A more recent study has shown that folic acid fortification also improves survival of neural tube–defected children.[32]

Insufficient vitamin B_{12} in a folic acid–fortified population has also been shown to increase the risk of neural tube defects.[33] Other research has shown that vitamin B_{12} fortification, in addition to folic acid, may reduce neural tube defects more than folic acid fortification alone.[34] Vitamin B_{12} is found in many naturally occurring foods from animals (e.g., fish, meat, poultry, eggs, milk, and milk products; see **Table 8-2**).[35] Fortified foods such as breakfast cereals are an important

TABLE 8-2 **Selected Food Sources of Vitamin B_{12}**

Food	Micrograms Per Serving	Percent DV
Mollusks, clam, mixed species, cooked, 3 ounces	84.1	1400
Liver, beef, braised, 1 slice	47.9	780
Fortified breakfast cereals, 100% fortified, 3/4 cup	6.0	100
Trout, rainbow, wild, cooked, 3 ounces	5.4	90
Salmon, sockeye, cooked, 3 ounces	4.9	80
Trout, rainbow, farmed, cooked, 3 ounces	4.2	50
Beef, top sirloin, lean, choice, broiled, 3 ounces	2.4	40
Fast food, cheeseburger, regular, double patty and bun, one sandwich	1.9	30
Fast food, taco, one large	1.6	25
Fortified breakfast cereals (25% fortified), 3/4 cup	1.5	25
Yogurt, plain, skim, with 13 grams protein per cup, 1 cup	1.4	25
Haddock, cooked, 3 ounces	1.2	20
Clams, breaded and fried, 3/4 cup	1.1	20
Tuna, white, canned in water, drained solids, 3 ounces	1.0	15
Milk, 1 cup	0.9	15
Pork, cured, ham, lean only, canned, roasted, 3 ounces	0.6	10
Egg, whole, hard boiled, one	0.6	10
American pasteurized cheese food, 1 ounces	0.3	6
Chicken, breast, meat only, roasted, 1/2 breast	0.3	6

Source: U.S. Department of Agriculture, Agricultural Research Service, 2003, as cited by the Office of Dietary Supplements, National Institutes of Health. Available at: http://ods.od.nih.gov/factsheets/VitaminB12.asp. Accessed March 2, 2009.

TABLE 8-3 **Recommended Dietary Allowances (RDA) for Vitamin B$_{12}$ for Children and Adults**

Age (Years)	Males and Females (μg/day)	Pregnancy (μg/day)	Lactation (μg/day)
1–3	0.9	N/A	N/A
4–8	1.2	N/A	N/A
9–13	1.8	N/A	N/A
14–18	2.4	2.6	2.8
19 and older	2.4	2.6	2.8

Source: Institute of Medicine, Food and Nutrition Board. *Dietary Reference Intakes: Thiamin, Riboflavin, Niacin, Vitamin B6, Folate, Vitamin B12, Pantothenic Acid, Biotin, and Choline.* Washington, DC: National Academy Press; 1998, as cited by the Office of Dietary Supplements, National Institutes of Health. Available at: http://ods.od.nih.gov/factsheets/VitaminB12.asp. Accessed March 2, 2009.

source of the vitamin for vegetarians. Recommended dietary allowances of B$_{12}$ according to categories of age, gender, pregnancy, and lactation are presented in **Table 8-3**.[36] The FDA's DV for iron is 18 mg. For pregnant women the recommended daily intake of iron is 27 mg.[37] The greater need for iron during pregnancy is because the developing fetus draws enough iron from the mother to last through the first 5 or 6 months after birth. Foods rich in iron include liver, meat, beans, nuts, dried fruit, whole grains (such as brown rice), fortified breakfast cereals, and most dark-green leafy vegetables (such as watercress and curly kale).

Dietary iron is classified as heme and nonheme. Heme iron is derived from hemoglobin. **Hemoglobin** is the protein in red blood cells that delivers oxygen to cells. Primary sources of heme iron are in animal foods that originally contained hemoglobin (e.g., red meats, fish, and poultry). On the other hand, nonheme iron includes iron in plants (e.g., lentils and beans). Nonheme iron is the form of iron added to iron-enriched and iron-fortified foods.[38] Various food sources of heme and nonheme iron are presented in **Tables 8-4** and **8-5**.[39]

Iron deficiency is associated with anemia, and if it occurs during pregnancy, it is also associated with morbidity and premature birth to infants with low birth weight.[40–43] The Centers for Disease Control and Prevention (CDC) recommends a low-dose iron supplementation (30 mg/day) for pregnant women (CDC, 1998).[44]

TABLE 8-4   **Selected Food Sources of Heme Iron**

Food	Milligrams Per Serving	Percent DV
Chicken liver, cooked, 3.5 ounces	12.8	70
Oysters, breaded and fried, 6 pieces	4.5	25
Beef, chuck, lean only, braised, 3 ounces	3.2	20
Clams, breaded, fried, 3/4 cup	3.0	15
Beef, tenderloin, roasted, 3 ounces	3.0	15
Turkey, dark meat, roasted, 3.5 ounces	2.3	10
Beef, eye of round, roasted, 3 ounces	2.2	10
Turkey, light meat, roasted, 3.5 ounces	1.6	8
Chicken, leg, meat only, roasted, 3.5 ounces	1.3	6
Tuna, fresh bluefin, cooked, dry heat, 3 ounces	1.1	6
Chicken, breast, roasted, 3 ounces	1.1	6
Halibut, cooked, dry heat, 3 ounces	0.9	6
Crab, blue crab, cooked, moist heat, 3 ounces	0.8	4
Pork, loin, broiled, 3 ounces	0.8	4
Tuna, white, canned in water, 3 ounces	0.8	4
Shrimp, mixed species, cooked, moist heat, four large	0.7	4

The CDC recommends larger doses of supplemental iron when low hemoglobin or hematocrit is confirmed through repeated testing.

Studies involving nutrition and birth weight of infants born during wartime famine indicate that the timing of nutritional deprivation is critical. During the winter of 1944–1945, a famine occurred in western Holland. Babies born to mothers where famine exposure occurred during the first half of their pregnancy tended to have babies of normal birth weight. On the other hand, those mothers experiencing nutritional deprivation in the second half of their pregnancy had babies with birth weight 10% below average.[45] However, Stein and Lumey (2000) studied the effect of famine on infant birth weight, concluding that the trimester of exposure does not influence offspring birth weight other than through its effects on the mother's weight.[46]

Painter, Roseboom, and Bleker (2005) found more coronary heart disease, raised lipids, altered clotting, and obesity associated with maternal undernutrition because of famine during early gestation.[47] Exposure during mid-gestation in-creased the risk of obstructive airways disease and microalbuminuria. In addition,

TABLE 8-5 **Selected Food Sources of Nonheme Iron**

Food	Milligrams Per Serving	Percent % DV
Ready-to-eat cereal, 100% iron fortified, 3/4 cup	18.0	100
Oatmeal, instant, fortified, prepared with water, 1 cup	10.0	60
Soybeans, mature, boiled, 1 cup	8.8	50
Lentils, boiled, 1 cup	6.6	35
Beans, kidney, mature, boiled, 1 cup	5.2	25
Beans, lima, large, mature, boiled, 1 cup	4.5	25
Beans, navy, mature, boiled, 1 cup	4.5	25
Ready-to-eat cereal, 25% iron fortified, 3/4 cup	4.5	25
Beans, black, mature, boiled, 1 cup	3.6	20
Beans, pinto, mature, boiled, 1 cup	3.6	20
Molasses, blackstrap, 1 tablespoon	3.5	20
Tofu, raw, firm, 1/2 cup	3.4	20
Spinach, boiled, drained, 1/2 cup	3.2	20
Spinach, canned, drained solids 1/2 cup	2.5	10
Black-eyed peas (cowpeas), boiled, 1 cup	1.8	10
Spinach, frozen, chopped, boiled 1/2 cup	1.9	10
Grits, white, enriched, quick, prepared with water, 1 cup	1.5	8
Raisins, seedless, packed, 1/2 cup	1.5	8
Whole wheat bread, 1 slice	0.9	6
White bread, enriched, 1 slice	0.9	6

Source: U.S. Department of Agriculture, Agricultural Research Service, 2003, as cited by the Office of Dietary Supplements, National Institutes of Health. Available at: http://www.nal .usda.gov/fnic/foodcomp. Accessed March 2, 2009.

decreased glucose tolerance occurred in people exposed to famine in late gestation. Hence, maternal undernutrition during gestation has important effects on health in later life, with the affected organ system depending on the timing of the nutritional insult.

Other studies have found that famine exposure during early gestation is associated with impaired glucose tolerance,[48] addictive behaviors later in life,[49] hypertension in middle age,[50] antisocial disorders,[51] and cardiovascular disease, metabolic disease, breast cancer, and higher obesity later in life.[52] Lumey and Stein (1997) found no adverse consequences to a woman's fertility exposed to famine in utero.[53]

Conclusion

Nutrients essential for the human body include protein, carbohydrates, fat, fibers, vitamins, minerals, and water. Malnutrition occurs when a person's diet does not supply the body with the right amounts of the vitamins, minerals, and other nutrients required to maintain healthy organ function and tissues. Malnutrition can occur because of either undernutrition or overnutrition. Both causes of malnutrition can result in reproductive health problems in men and women. Adverse behavior and health effects have also been associated with exposure to malnutrition in utero.

Key Issues

1. In women, being overweight or obese is associated with an increased risk of amenorrhea, infertility, pregnancy complications, miscarriage, hypertensive disorders, and birth defects than when compared with regular weight women; obese pregnant women are at increased risk of gestational diabetes, which has a negative effect on both the mother and the baby and can lead to type II diabetes later in the mother's life.

2. In men, obesity is associated with lower sperm count and erectile dysfunction.

3. The most prevalent form of malnutrition worldwide is iron deficiency. Iron deficiency is associated with anemia and, if it occurs during pregnancy, morbidity, premature birth, and infants with low birth weight.

4. Iodine deficiency is a primary cause of mental retardation and brain damage.

5. Folate is needed by the body before and during the first weeks of pregnancy to reduce neural tube defects affecting the brain and spinal cord. These defects are called anencephaly and spina bifida.

6. Insufficient vitamin B_{12} in a folic acid–fortified population has also been shown to increase the risk of neural tube defects.

7. Undernutrition exposure during early gestation is associated with impaired glucose tolerance, addictive behaviors later in life, hypertension in middle age, antisocial disorders, and cardiovascular disease, metabolic disease, raised lipids, obesity, breast cancer, and higher obesity later in life. There is no adverse consequence to a woman's fertility exposed to famine in utero.

8. Maternal undernutrition during gestation has important effects on health in later life, with the affected organ system depending on the timing of the nutritional insult.

Exercises

Key Terms

Define the following terms.

Amenorrhea	Malnutrition
Body mass index	Nutrients
Daily Value	Overnutrition
Hemoglobin	Undernutrition
Human nutrition	

Study Questions

8.1 The human body requires certain types of nutrients to function properly. List these and describe their function.

8.2 Describe the effects of overweight and obesity on the reproductive health of women.

8.3 Describe the effects of overweight and obesity on the reproductive health of men.

8.4 Why is iron deficiency a serious concern?

References

1. *The American Heritage Science Dictionary Copyright*. Wilmington, MA: Houghton Mifflin Company; 2005.
2. Farlex, Inc., 2009. Available at: http://medicaldictionary.thefreedictionary.com/Human+nutrition. Accessed February 26, 2009.
3. Miyawaki K, Yamada Y, Ban N, et al. Inhibition of gastric inhibitory polypeptide signaling prevents obesity. *Nat Med*. 2002;8(7):738–742.
4. World Health Organization. Obesity and overweight, 2005. Available at: http://www.who.int/mediacentre/factsheets/fs311/en/index.html. Accessed February 26, 2009.
5. Popkin BM, Gordon-Larsen P. The nutrition transition: worldwide obesity dynamics and their determinants. *Int J Obesity*. 2004;28:S2–S9.
6. Popkin BM. An overview on the nutrition transition and its health implications: the Bellagio meeting. *Public Health Nutr*. 2002;5:93–103.

7. Monteiro CA, Conde WL, Lu B, Popkin BM. *Is Obesity Fueling Inequities in Health in the Developing World?* Chapel Hill, NC: University of North Carolina; 2004.

8. Mendez MA, Monteiro CA, Popkin BM. *Overweight Now Exceeds Underweight Among Women in Most Developing Countries!* Chapel Hill, NC: University of North Carolina; 2004.

9. Lake JK, Power C, Cole TJ. Women's reproductive health: the role of body mass index in early and adult life. *Int J Obes Relat Metab Disord.* 1997;21:432–438.

10. Pasquali R, Pelusi C, Genghini S, Cacciari M, Gambineri A. Obesity and reproductive disorders in women. *Hum Reprod Update.* 2003;9:359–372.

11. Rich-Edwards JW, Goldman MB, Willett WC, et al. Adolescent body mass index and infertility caused by ovulatory disorder. *Am J Obstet Gynecol.* 1994;171:171–177.

12. Gambineri A, Pelusi C, Vencennati V, Pagotto U, Pasquali R. Obesity and the polycystic ovary syndrome. *Int J Obes Relat Metab Disord.* 2002;26:883–896.

13. Hamilton-Fairley D, Kiddy D, Watson, H, Paterson C, Franks S. Association of moderate obesity with a poor pregnancy outcome with women in polycystic ovary syndrome treated with low dose gonadotrophin. *Br J Obstet Gynaecol.* 1992;99:128–131.

14. Perlow JH, Morgan MA, Montgomery D, Towers CV, Porto M. Prenatal outcomes in pregnancy complicated by massive obesity. *Am J Obstet Gynecol.* 1992;167:958–962.

15. Tomoda S, Tamura T, Sudo Y, Ogita S. Effects of obesity on pregnant women: maternal hemodynamic change. *Am J Perinatol.* 1996;13:73–78.

16. Stothard KJ, Tennant PW, Bell R, Rankin J. Maternal overweight and obesity and the risk of congenital anomalies: a systematic review and meta-analysis. *JAMA.* 2009;301(6): 636–650.

17. Swan SH, Elkin EP, Fenster L. The question of declining sperm density revisited: an analysis of 101 studies published 1934–1996. *Environ Health Perspect.* 2000;108:961–966.

18. Jensen TK, Andersson AM, Jorgensen N, et al. Body mass index in relation to semen quality and reproductive hormones among 1,558 Danish men. *Fertil Steril.* 2004;82:863–870.

19. Oehninger S. Clinical and laboratory management of male infertility: an opinion on its current status. *J Androl.* 2000;21:814–821.

20. Feldman HA, Johannes CB, Derby CA, et al. Erectile dysfunction and coronary risk factors, prospective results from the Massachusetts male aging study. *Prev Med.* 2000;30:328–338.

21. Bacon CG, Mittleman MA, Kawachi I, Giovannucci E, Glasser DB, Rimm EB. Sexual function in men older than 50 years of age: results from the health professionals follow-up study. *Ann Intern Med.* 2003;139:161–168.

22. Sanghvi T, Ross J, Heyman H. Why is reducing vitamin and mineral deficiencies critical for development? The links between VMD and survival, health, education, and productivity. *Food Nutr Bull.* 2007;28(1):S170.

23. Fishman SM, Caulfield LE, de Onis M, et al. Childhood and maternal underweight. In M Ezzati, AD Lopez, A Rodgers, CJL Murray, eds. *Comparative Quantification of Health Risks.* Geneva, Switzerland: WHO; 2004.

24. World Food Programme. Division of Communications and Public Policy Strategy, 2008. Available at: http://www.wfp.org/sites/default/files/Impact_of_Malnutrition_on_Women_and_Children_English_0.pdf. Accessed February 27, 2009.

25. Stoltzfus RJ, Dreyfuss ML. *Guidelines for the Use of Iron Supplements to Prevent and Treat Iron Deficiency Anaemia.* Washington, DC: ILSI Press; 1998.

26. United Nations Standing Committee on Nutrition. World Nutrition Situation 5th report, 2005. Available at: http://www.unscn.org/Publications/AnnualMeeting/SCN31/ SCN5Report.pdf. Accessed February 27, 2009.

27. United Nations. Maternal and child nutrition in Viet Nam, 2006. Available at: http://www.un.org.vn/index.php?option=com_content&task=view&id=339&Itemid=238. Accessed February 27, 2009.

28. U.S. Department of Agriculture, Agricultural Research Service, 2003, as cited by the Office of Dietary Supplements, National Institutes of Health. Available at: http://ods.od. nih.gov/factsheets/folate.asp. Accessed March 2, 2009.

29. Dietrich M, Brown CJ, Block G. The effect of folate fortification of cereal-grain products on blood folate status, dietary folate intake, and dietary folate sources among adult non-supplement users in the United States. *J Am Coll Nutr.* 2005;24(4):266–274.

30. U.S. Food and Drug Administration. How to understand and use the nutrition facts label. Available at: http://www.cfsan.fda.gov/~dms/foodlab.html#see6. 2004. Accessed February 27, 2009.

31. Kurtzweil P. How folate can help prevent birth defects. U.S. Food and Drug Administration, 1999. Available at: http://www.fda.gov/Fdac/features/796_fol.html. Accessed February 27, 2009.

32. Bol KA, Collins JS, Kirby RS, National Birth Defects Prevention Network. Survival of infants with neural tube defects in the presence of folic acid fortification. *Pediatrics.* 2006;117(3):803–813.

33. Ray JG, Wyatt PR, Thompson MD, et al. Vitamin B12 and the risk of neural tube defects in a folic-acid-fortified population. *Epidemiology.* 2007;18(3):362–366.

34. Thompson MD, Cole DE, Ray JG. Vitamin B-12 and neural tube defects: the Canadian experience. *Am J Clin Nutr.* 2009;89(2):697S–701S.

35. U.S. Department of Agriculture, Agricultural Research Service, 2003, as cited by the Office of Dietary Supplements, National Institutes of Health. Available at: http://ods .od.nih.gov/factsheets/VitaminB12.asp. Accessed March 2, 2009.

36. Institute of Medicine, Food and Nutrition Board. *Dietary Reference Intakes: Thiamin, Riboflavin, Niacin, Vitamin B6, Folate, Vitamin B12, Pantothenic Acid, Biotin, and Choline.* Washington, DC: National Academy Press, as cited by the Office of Dietary Supplements, National Institutes of Health. Available at: http://ods.od.nih.gov/factsheets/ VitaminB12.asp. Accessed March 2, 2009.

37. Institute of Medicine, Food and Nutrition Board. *Dietary Reference Intakes for Vitamin A, Vitamin K, Arsenic, Boron, Chromium, Copper, Iodine, Iron, Manganese, Molybdenum, Nickel, Silicon, Vanadium and Zinc.* Washington, DC: National Academy Press; 2001.

38. Office of Dietary Supplements. Dietary supplement fact sheet: iron. National Institutes of Health, 2007. Available at: http://ods.od.nih.gov/factsheets/iron.asp#en10. Accessed February 27, 2009.

39. U.S. Department of Agriculture, Agricultural Research Service, 2003, as cited by the Office of Dietary Supplements, National Institutes of Health. Available at: http://www .nal.usda.gov/fnic/foodcomp. Accessed March 2, 2009.

40. Allen LH. Pregnancy and iron deficiency: unresolved issues. *Nutr Rev,* 1997;55:91–101.

41. Blot I, Diallo D, Tchernia G. Iron deficiency in pregnancy: effects on the newborn. *Curr Opin Hematol.* 1999;6:65–70.

42. Malhotra M, Sharma JB, Batra S, Sharma S, Murthy NS, Arora R. Maternal and perinatal outcome in varying degrees of anemia. *Int J Gynaecol Obstet*. 2002;79:93–100.

43. Cogswell ME, Parvanta I, Ickes L, Yip R, Brittenham GM. Iron supplementation during pregnancy, anemia, and birth weight: a randomized controlled trial. *Am J Clin Nutr*. 2003;78:773–781.

44. Centers for Disease Control and Prevention. Recommendations to prevent and control iron deficiency in the United States. *MMWR Recomm Rep*. 1998;47:1–29.

45. No author listed. Prenatal nutrition and the human fetus. *Nutr Rev*. 1971;29(9):197–199.

46. Stein AD, Lumey LH. The relationship between maternal and offspring birth weights after maternal prenatal famine exposure: the Dutch Famine Birth Cohort Study. *Hum Biol*. 2000;72(4):641–654.

47. Painter RC, Roseboom TJ, Bleker OP. Prenatal exposure to the Dutch famine and disease in later life: an overview. *Reprod Toxicol*. 2005;20(3):345–352.

48. de Rooij SR, Painter RC, Phillips DI, et al. Impaired insulin secretion after prenatal exposure to the Dutch famine. *Diabetes Care*. 2006;29(8):1897–1901.

49. Franzek EJ, Sprangers N, Janssens AC, Van Duijn CM, Van De Wetering BJ. Prenatal exposure to the 1944–45 Dutch "hunger winter" and addiction later in life. *Addiction*. 2008;103(3):433–438.

50. Stein AD, Zybert PA, van der Pal-de Bruin K, Lumey LH. Exposure to famine during gestation, size at birth, and blood pressure at age 59 y: evidence from the Dutch Famine. *Eur J Epidemiol*. 2006;21(10):759–765.

51. Neugebauer R, Hoek HW, Susser E. Prenatal exposure to wartime famine and development of antisocial personality disorder in early adulthood. *JAMA*. 1999;282(5):455–462.

52. Painter RC, Osmond C, Gluckman P, et al. Transgenerational effects of prenatal exposure to the Dutch famine on neonatal adiposity and health in later life. *BJOG*. 2008;115(10):1243–1249.

53. Lumey LH, Stein AD. In utero exposure to famine and subsequent fertility: the Dutch Famine Birth Cohort Study. *Am J Public Health*. 1997;87(12):1962–1966.

NINE

Contraception and Reproductive Health

Learning Objectives

After completing this chapter, you should be able to:

1. Identify common types of contraception.
2. Identify and describe various methods of contraception by geographic area.
3. Identify health risks and benefits associated with selected forms of contraception.
4. Describe contraceptive use by geographic regions throughout the world.

As the world population approaches 7 billion, contraception is becoming an increasingly important issue. **Contraception** (sometimes referred to as birth control) is any strategy or device that reduces the chance of fertilization of an ovum by a spermatozoon. Contraception falls into five main categories: sterilization, hormonal methods, barrier methods, intrauterine devices (IUDs), and traditional family planning methods. Each of these methods brings with it attendant issues related to health, economics, and culture. Contraception may have unintended consequences that can be harmful to a woman's health, such as some hormonal methods that can increase the risk of certain chronic conditions later in life. Other types of contraception have important economic repercussions. In some areas of the world, women who use any form of contraception are breaking traditional cultural and social norms and must cope with the consequences of that behavior. We address each of the issues associated with contraception by examining snapshots of particular countries in most of the regions throughout the world. By comparing these regions, we hope to paint an accurate portrait of contraceptive use in our world today.

Types of Contraception

Sterilization

Sterilization is the act of making an organism infertile in that it is no longer able to reproduce. Tubal ligation in women and vasectomy in men provide permanent sterilization. Tubal sterilization involves surgery to block a woman's fallopian tubes. This procedure stops the egg from traveling to the uterus from the ovary and prevents sperm from reaching the fallopian tube and fertilizing the egg. A vasectomy prevents the release of sperm when a man ejaculates.[1]

Hormonal Methods

Birth control **hormonal methods** include the patch, vaginal rings, implant injections, and birth control pills. Hormonal birth contraceptives are popular because of the ease of their use and efficacy. Hormonal birth contraceptives have three or more mechanisms of action. The active ingredients in all hormonal contraceptives are estrogen and progestin. Some hormonal contraceptions contain both estrogen and progestin, whereas others may just contain progestin. Both hormones together are more effective than progestin alone; however, the estrogen component is linked to most of the health complications associated with hormonal methods. Oral contraceptives prevent pregnancy by inhibiting ovulation (release of an egg). Oral contraceptives are available by prescription only; individuals are typically given a physical exam in addition to a prescription to ensure that they are healthy enough to benefit from the pill. Women over 35 and those who smoke are discouraged from using the pill as a form of contraception.[2]

The hormones (synthetic estrogen and progestin) stop the ovaries from releasing eggs and thicken the cervical mucus to prevent sperm from reaching the egg and prevent fertilization from occurring.[2] If a woman using oral contraception ovulates anyway, the hormones may still prevent fertilization by changing the consistency of natural secretions in the vagina, thereby making it more difficult for the sperm to reach the egg. In addition, if a woman ovulates anyway and the sperm reaches the egg, hormonal contraceptives make it difficult for the embryo to implant in the uterus by keeping the lining of the uterus thin.[3]

Barrier Methods

There are several **barrier methods** of birth control, including the female condom (a prelubricated pouch-like device that lines the walls of the vagina), the male condom (latex or polyurethane sheath that contains sperm during intercourse), the diaphragm (a round piece of thin rubber attached to a round rim held in place by the muscles of the vagina), the cervical cap (a small piece of rubber with a hard rim and soft, domed top, which is held in place by suction over the cervix), the sponge (releases spermicide for up to 12 hours while it is in place), Lea's contraceptive (a reusable soft silicone device that is inserted into the vagina to cover the cervix), and spermicides (chemicals that either kill sperm or leave it inactive).[4]

Intrauterine Devices

An **intrauterine device** (IUD) is a small device that is inserted by a doctor through the cervix and placed in the uterus to prevent pregnancy. IUDs are most often metal T-shaped devices that do not contain hormones, but new methods, namely Mirena, are made of plastic and contain slow-releasing hormones. They work by changing the lining of the uterus and fallopian tubes, affecting the movements of eggs and sperm such that fertilization does not occur; that is, the IUD prompts the release of leukocytes and prostaglandins by the endometrium, which is hostile to both sperm and eggs. A single device may be effective for 10 or more years. The IUD is the most widely used method of reversible birth control; it is used by approximately 160 million women worldwide. IUDs are 99% effective when properly inserted.[5,6]

The device is initially inserted by a trained clinician and can stay in place for 3 to 10 years, depending on the model and the individual. The IUD can be removed at any time, which restores fertility. The Mirena, or hormone-releasing variety, may require 2 to 3 months before fertility is entirely restored.[7] IUDs have been associated with several health risks, including expulsion without warning, cramping, menstrual irregularities, perforation of the uterus, pelvic infections, an increased risk of pelvic inflammatory disease, and an increased risk of ectopic pregnancy. IUDs do not prevent against sexually transmitted infections and are often used in conjunction with male condoms.[8] Very little information is available about the effect of the IUD on the baby when conception accidentally occurs.

Traditional Family Planning Methods

Sperm can live up to 7 days in a woman's reproductive system. An egg can live up to 3 days (usually 24 hours). Hence, the time period that sexual intercourse can result in a woman getting pregnant each month lasts for about 9 days. On the basis of this information, four **traditional family planning methods** have been used to prevent pregnancy. First, a woman's body temperature varies through the menstrual cycle. On the day of ovulation, body temperature rises between 0.4°F and 0.8°F and remains elevated until a few days before the next period. Abstention from intercourse should last from 7 days before until 4 days after the temperature rise. Second, cervical mucus changes across the menstrual cycle. It is usually cloudy and tacky, but before ovulation it becomes clear and slippery. Third, if a woman's period is the same length every month, it may be possible to predict the day of ovulation (calendar or rhythm method). The time when a woman may get pregnant is from 7 days before to 4 days after ovulation. Fourth, the postovulation method is based on the fact that ovulation always occurs 12 to 16 days before a woman's period (typically 14 days). On this basis, the day of ovulation may be predicted. Hence, to avoid pregnancy, women abstain from having intercourse from the beginning of their period until the morning of the fourth day after the predicted ovulation day.[9]

Contraception and Health

Spacing or limiting the number of pregnancies and births promotes a woman's health and well-being as well as her social and economic circumstances while improving pregnancy outcomes.[10] Although contraception promotes various aspects of health, well-being, and social and economic circumstances, it also may contribute to selected health problems, such as increased risk of heart disease, stroke, and blood clots.[11–13] A recent study showed that oral contraceptive use impaired the endothelial function (i.e., thin layer of cells that line the interior surface of the heart, lymph vessels, serious cavities, and blood vessels) in young women.[14] Other serious potential effects, albeit rare, include breast and cervical cancers, liver tumors, and gallbladder disease.[13] The most commonly reported adverse effects of oral contraception use are weight gain, depression or mood disturbances, nausea, spotting between menstrual periods, painful or missed menstrual periods, decreased sexual desire or response, acne, and breast tenderness.[13,15]

The relationship between the use of the birth control pill and breast cancer in young women is controversial. In a large prospective cohort study (Nurses' Health Study), no increased risk of breast cancer was found to be associated with the use of oral contraceptive pills or the duration of use.[16] On the other hand, in a population-based case-control study of breast cancer, long-term oral contraceptive use or use beginning near menarche was associated with a small excess risk of breast cancer.[17] In another large population-based, case-control study conducted in the United States, the total duration of oral contraception was not associated with an increased risk of breast cancer. Oral contraception before a woman's first pregnancy or among nulliparous women was not associated with increased risk of breast cancer; however, a slight increased risk was observed among selected subgroups of women (e.g., among women with a body mass index [kg/m^2] less than 20.4 and among recent users who were aged 35 to 45 years).[18]

Although the relationship between oral contraceptive use and cervical cancer has been controversial, recent studies support there being an increased risk for the disease among current and extended users of oral contraception. In a case-control study conducted in Jamaican women, hormonal contraceptives by use of the pill or injection were associated with an increased risk of cervical cancer.[19] In another study involving women in Thailand, oral contraceptive pill use for more than 3 years was associated with increased risk of cervical cancer.[20] In a cohort study in the United Kingdom, an increased risk of cervical cancer was associated with an increased duration of oral contraception.[21] In a systematic review of the literature, the risk of cervical cancer increased with increasing duration of oral contraceptive use.[22] In a collaborative reanalysis of individual data from 24 epidemiologic studies, among current users of oral contraceptives, the risk of invasive cervical cancer increased with longer duration of use. The risk decreased when oral contraceptive use ceased, and the risk became similar to those who never used oral contraception by 10 or more years after ending oral contraception.[23]

Oral contraceptives have been suggested previously in the etiology of liver cancer. Liver neoplasia occurring in young women was very rare before oral contraception was introduced in the early 1960s. Thereafter, several case reports of liver tumors in women who had used oral contraceptives were reported. These case reports and two U.S. case-control studies indicated that liver cancer risk increased sharply with increasing duration of oral contraceptive use; nevertheless, a number of subsequent studies have had conflicting results.[24] A recent hospital-based case-control study conducted in Italy showed that use of oral contraceptives and the duration of use were positively associated with risk of liver cancer;[25] however, in an age-matched case-control study conducted in Israel, oral contraceptive use was not significantly associated with liver hemangioma.[26] In two case-control studies conducted in Germany, there was also little evidence of an increased risk for liver cancer in women using oral contraceptives.[27]

Studies have concluded that on a public health scale, oral contraceptive use is unlikely to have an important influence on the etiology of gallbladder disease;[28,29] however, a significantly higher rate of surgical removal of the gallbladder has been recently shown in women who are postpartum at the time of initiation of oral contraceptive use.[30] In addition, the risk of developing gallbladder disease, although small, has been demonstrated in women using levonorgestrel-releasing contraceptive implants.[31] Furthermore, in a large cohort study involving Chinese women, oral contraceptive use has been positively associated with gallbladder cancer.[32]

Oral contraceptives do not offer any protection from sexually transmitted infections; women that engage in sexual contact with multiple partners should use condoms in addition to oral contraception. A majority of women with multiple sexual partners do report using an additional form of contraception to prevent sexually transmitted infections.[33]

On a positive note, oral contraceptives have been associated with decreased risks of ovarian and uterine cancer.[34,35] The association is not entirely clear, but many scientists postulate that this correlation is due to the connection between ovarian cancer and infertility: Fertility greatly decreases the risk of ovarian cancer and women that use contraceptives are usually fertile.[36] Another theory about the correlation is that decreasing the number of ovulation cycles decreases the risk of ovarian cancer.[37] Oral contraceptives prevent ovulation when used correctly and therefore reduce the number of ovulation cycles a woman has in her lifetime.[33]

The pill has been associated with economic and social consequences. Today the pill is commonly used by married women for increasing the amount of time between births.[15] This increase in spacing has reduced the number of unintended and unwanted pregnancies each year in the United States. Morbidity and mortality rates are higher among children that resulted from unwanted, unintended pregnancies, and these pregnancies are often more costly to tax payers.[38] Increasing access to oral contraception has been associated with decreases in the rates of elective abortions among young American women.[39] Oral contraceptive use has also been associated with the growing number of women receiving professional graduate degrees (business, law, medicine, engineering) and the increasing number of women entering the professional workplace.[15] The pill has been associated with increased productivity and prosperity of American women.[15] Trends show that the pill has also been associated with an increase in the rates of women who have never been married. Women are no longer encouraged to be married to explore their sexuality; they can now explore without worrying about pregnancy.[15] Oral contraceptives were originally thought to contribute to increasing divorce rates in America, but new research shows that this may not be entirely true.[7] The pill has been shown to contribute to decreased family size and increased age at time of marriage, but couples that marry later tend to be more stable and have a lower divorce rate than younger couples.[15]

The United States

According to the National Center for Health Statistics, 98% of American women have access to some form of contraception.[8] In the United States, hormonal contraception is the most popular form of birth control. Among the different choices for hormonal contraceptives, the oral contraceptive pill is the most popular—53% of American women who use contraceptives use the oral contraceptive pill.[8] The pill became widely available in the United States following U.S. Food and Drug Administration (FDA) approval in February 1961.[15] An estimated 11.6 million American women use oral contraceptives as their main or only source of contraception; an additional 44.5 million American women have used the oral contraceptive pill at some point during their lifetime.[8] The oral contraceptive pill is increasingly popular with younger women—it is the main source of contraception used by women ages 15–19 years. Rates of use decrease with age. Trends in U.S. contraception use show that older women (ages 40 to 44 years) prefer female sterilization to oral contraceptives.[8] The rates of oral contraceptive use are higher among White women, and slightly lower in non-Hispanic Black and Hispanic Americans (both of these groups tend to use **Depo-Provera**, the trimonthly hormonal contraceptive shot, at a slightly higher rate than White females).[8] Higher levels of education are associated with oral contraceptive use; approximately

43% of women with a 4-year college degree use the oral contraceptive pill as their primary source of birth control, as compared with 11% of women with less than a high school education.[8] The difference may be associated with socioeconomic status and access to reliable medical care.[38] Additionally, oral contraceptive pills are among the most reliable forms of contraception available to American women.[40] If used correctly, 1 in 100 women will become pregnant during the first year of continued use. If used incorrectly, such as missing one or more pills, 5 in 100 women can expect to become pregnant during the first year of continued use.[40] In a country such as the United States, where the majority of people have access to the most effective reversible method of birth control, live above the poverty line, and have at least a basic education, it is not surprising that the most prevalent form of family planning is the oral contraceptive pill.

The second most popular form of contraception in the United States is female sterilization.[7] Approximately 10.3 million American women use sterilization as a form of contraception. This method is most popular among women over 35 years and among women who are currently married or have been married.[8] This method is often employed after a woman is finished having children. Women in this age group view this method as a safe and effective way to assuredly prevent future pregnancies.[41] Sterilization is more popular in non-Hispanic Blacks and Hispanics than in Whites. Approximately 22% of non-Hispanic Black women, 20% of Hispanic women, and 16% of White women depend on sterilization as an effective form of birth control.[8] This is explained by the fact that male sterilization is a common form of contraception among White women's partners.

Like the oral contraceptive pill, the rates of sterilization are influenced by education level; women with higher levels of education are less likely to employ this method as a form of effective birth control. An estimated 55% of women using sterilization have less than a high school degree; only 13% of those using this method have a 4-year college degree.[8]

There are currently two forms of FDA-approved female sterilization in the United States: transabdominal surgical sterilization (tubal ligation) and sterilization implant (Essure System manufactured by Conceptus, Inc., San Carlos, CA). Transabdominal surgical sterilization involves abdominal surgery to cut or crimp the fallopian tubes. This causes released eggs to get stuck, and fertilization in the fallopian tubes cannot occur.[42] In some cases, the procedure can be reversed; if the fallopian tubes were merely crimped, the clamps can be removed, and in most cases, the process is reversible. An estimated 84% of procedures can be successfully reversed and result in unaided conception.[41] Cut fallopian tubes cannot be repaired, and permanent infertility will result.[42] The Essure System involves minor abdominal surgery to implant two small spring-like coils to block the fallopian tubes. These implants cause the growth of scar tissue and blockage of fallopian tubes. This method cannot be reversed. Both methods of sterilization have been associated with increased risk of ectopic pregnancy and a decreased risk of ovarian cancer.[41] This procedure does not prevent against sexually transmitted infection.

Male condoms are the third most commonly used form of contraception in the United States. An estimated 9 million American couples use this as their primary method of birth control.[8] The earliest known condom is over 3,000 years old, and the concept has not changed since then.[43] Condoms are a barrier method of birth control, meaning that they block the sperm from entering the female. They are available in a wide variety of materials, but only the latex condom is preventative against sexually transmitted infections, including HIV. If used correctly, condoms are almost 100% effective in preventing sexually transmitted infections.[8] Condoms are often paired with other forms of contraception, including oral contraceptives. Female condoms are also available but they are not as widely accepted or available as male condoms and are not examined here.

Condoms are a common choice for birth control for several reasons. They are relatively inexpensive—between 50 and 75 cents each for a single lubricated condom and between 20 and 35 cents for a nonlubricated condom. Because condoms are so readily available and accessible, they are the number one choice of contraception for first sexual encounters;[8] however, condoms become decreasingly popular with age; approximately 27% of sexually active teens regularly use condoms, as opposed to 11% of women aged 40 to 44. Much of the difference is accounted for by the decrease in the number of sexual partners with age. As individuals enter into monogamous relationships, they are less likely to be concerned with sexually transmitted infection, thus limiting the need for condoms.[8]

Condoms are a reversible form of birth control, and thus, use does not impact either partner's fertility. Because of this, pregnancy can result from improper use or handling of the condom. One out of every 100 couples that correctly use condoms can expect to become pregnant during 1 year of continued use; some couples use early withdrawal to increase the efficacy. In comparison, 15 out of 100 couples that incorrectly or inconsistently use condoms can expect to become pregnant during 1 year of continued use. American women's ease of access and accessibility to the most effective forms of contraception give them control over their reproductive lives.

Western Europe

Contraception practices are very similar between Western Europe and the United States; the main noticeable difference occurs with regard to rates of sterilization. Sterilization is not as popular in Europe as it is in the United States; instead, the IUD has taken its place. Because of their ease of use and efficacy, IUDs are becoming increasingly popular among Western European women who wish to limit their family size or increase spacing between children. The use of this device has greatly decreased the numbers of unplanned or unwanted children born to Western European mothers, which in turn has decreased the economic burden placed on the region and its available resources.[44] Moving eastward on the globe we see differences in birth control trends and consequences.

Asia

India's burgeoning population of 1.15 billion is growing at a remarkable rate.[45] Soon India will surpass China as the country with the largest population. Much of that growth will come because of the relative infrequent use of contraception among Indians. In contrast to common misconceptions, the lack of contraception use is not due to a lack of knowledge, but limited access. A recent study among married women in Maharashtra showed that 99% had knowledge about modern contraception.[46] The underlying reasons for not using contraception are embedded within the cultural and social norms of Indian society.

Among those who practice contraception, the most commonly used form of birth control in India is tubal ligation. This form is used much more frequently when the family does not want to have any more children. In rural Bihar, 11.6% of married women between the ages of 21 and 30 years had been sterilized, but between the ages of 31 and 40, the incidence of sterilization was 51%. Only 6.8% of women in the study used the pill, IUDs, or condoms.[47] In Maharashtra, 80% of the contraception used was sterilization, 4% used condoms, 1.9% used IUDs, and 1.7% used the pill.[46] In Maharashtra, 40.1% of the families do not practice any form of birth control at all.[46]

There is enormous social and cultural pressure on women in India to bear many children. It is particularly important that women conceive in the first year of marriage, produce a son, and continue to have children throughout their fertile years.[46] Most women do not get to choose when or how frequently to conceive. India is a male-dominated society in which the husband is allowed to beat his wife if she covertly uses a form of contraception or refuses to have sex.[46] He is often afraid of how he will be perceived if his wife is not conceiving, and this fear leads him to overcompensate, which leads to frequent pregnancies.[46] There is also a significant amount of verbal abuse from extended family as a result of a woman's choice to use contraception.[46] There is no significant attention paid to the health of the mother or her ability to endure more pregnancies or pregnancies in close proximitiy. As a result of the lack of contraceptive use, women are at risk in two ways—physical abuse and potential complications or problems with the pregnancy.

Although we have already examined India for our snapshot of Asia, China's contraceptive practices are unique because of the policy of one child per family. When Mao Zedong came to power in 1949, one of his policies encouraged people to have as many children as possible; however, after a devastating 3-year famine (1958–1960) that killed 30 million people, the rationale of the regime shifted. The Chinese Communist Party began to mandate a one-child policy for those living in urban areas. The regulations were less strict for those in rural areas. This altered the way China practiced contraception.

In a comprehensive survey done in China in 1983, 50% of married women between the ages of 15 and 49 used IUDs as their main method of family planning. 25% used tubal ligation, and 10% used vasectomies (male sterilization). Oral contraceptives, condoms, and other methods accounted for a minimal amount of contraception in China.[48] The one-child policy has not changed, which indicates that it is unlikely that the rates of contraceptive use will change in the foreseeable future. In a more recent study done among recently married couples in Shanghai, the main method of contraception is still the IUD. Among the couples surveyed, 70% used IUDs, 20% condoms, 5% hormonal methods, and few relied on sterilization.[49] The most interesting finding from this report was the increase in abortion as a form of contraception. Forty-three percent of the couples in the study conceived after they had already had one child, and 98% of those pregnancies ended in an induced abortion.[49]

Pacific Islands

Family planning in island culture is evolving from primitive preconceptions that there is no place for contraception to the gradual acceptance that some form of birth control may be appropriate in certain circumstances. There is still room for improvement, but the trends indicate that family planning is progressing in the Pacific Islands.

Traditionally men within island cultures have had control over when to have children and how many to have; however, recently, women have been included in those decisions, and women who knew almost nothing about contraception are beginning to practice it.[50] Among women in Samoa, 34% use some form of contraception. This rate is low, but contraceptive use typically does not begin until after a woman has had 2.9 children.[10,50] Depo-Provera is the most common form of birth control used. This is typically used when families want to delay having a child. When families are finished having children, they often choose to use tubal ligation.[51]

In Samoa, the next most common form of birth control is the rhythm method, followed by the pill, and then IUDs.[50] The rhythm method is a natural form of family planning. To use this form of contraception, couples abstain from sexual intercourse during the fertile time of the month. This method is not harmful to the woman or man in any way, but it is not the most effective form of contraception. The fact that many islanders are practicing contraception is an improvement, but the islands still need to address the issue of family planning in a way that makes it culturally acceptable and widely available.

Several of the cultural values inherent in island culture inhibit family planning. Many religious groups that are prevalent on the islands strongly discourage contraceptive use; thus, some clinics run by religious institutions refuse to dispense contraceptives, even if the person is not of the same faith.[51] Additionally, there is a strong tradition of abstinence before marriage and fidelity after. Because of this, in some areas, clinic workers will refuse to distribute contraceptives to singles or to someone they suspect is too young to be married or who may be having an affair. This is particularly common in small villages where the clinic workers know all the customers.[51] Cultural values may create health inequities that increase the likelihood of adverse reproductive health.

Latin America

Multiple factors affect the methods of contraception used by Latinos including tradition, religion, and wealth. Latino cultures, in general, are male dominated (the Argentine Civil Code of 1868 even sanctioned women's legal inferiority), and women have little control over the method of contraception used or whether contraception is used at all.[52,53] A study conducted by the University of California at San Francisco showed that conservative and traditional gender role beliefs in Latino men and women decrease the likelihood of condom use.[54]

Induced abortions have traditionally been used as a form of birth control in Latin America. Abortion may be induced by ingesting highly toxic plants, where the procedure is overseen by healers, herbalists, and sorcerers.[55] Today, these procedures are gradually being replaced by natural family planning methods (including the rhythm method); however, abortion-related complications remain the leading cause of maternal death in many Latin American countries.[52]

Religion has heavily influenced the acceptance of contraception in Latin America. The majority of those living in Latin America are connected to the Catholic Church in some way; this group discourages its members from using all forms of artificial contraception. As a result, natural family planning remains the predominant form of birth control practiced by Latin American women. As an example, access to modern contraception was denied to Argentine women until 2003 as a result of pressure from the Catholic Church on lawmakers. A law to create a national contraception program was passed in 2003; however, the law is only loosely enforced, and access continues to be fairly limited.[52] Similar restrictions exist in other Latin American counties. Brazil remains the only Latin American country open to modern forms of contraception.[53]

Economic factors also limit an individual's access to contraception. Women of the upper and middle classes have greater access and more available options; poorer women are more likely to continue the use of dangerous traditional or herbal methods.[52] As previously mentioned, women of lower socioeconomic status are more likely to participate in traditional induced abortions.

Latin America has the lowest rate of contraception use of any region in the world. On average, rates of contraception use are 17% lower than those in South and Southeast Asia (two regions that also experience low rates of contraceptive use). Latin America also shows the lowest rates of *modern* contraception use, with a significant gap existing between the middle and lower classes.[56]

Africa

Africa is plagued by many of the same problems mentioned earlier in association with other regions. Several factors are associated with a woman's utilization of contraception. These factors include a lack of availability of family planning services as well as previous births, lack of knowledge, cultural traditions, and socioeconomic status.[57] Religious affiliation and education were not found to have a significant impact on contraceptive use.[57] Ethnicity has been found to be a contributing factor to contraceptive use.[58]

Preferred methods of contraception differed among African nations. One Nigerian study showed that the most commonly used forms of modern contraception, in order of most used to least, were IUDs, oral contraceptives, and condoms. Rates of modern contraception use comprised only 18.8% of birth control measures used in Nigeria, despite programs to increase awareness and distribution, and the same study showed that 100% of Nigerian women were aware of modern birth control options. A similar study showed that 18% of women of childbearing age in Ghana use contraception.[57] More rural areas of Africa reported even lower rates of modern contraception awareness and use. A report from Ghana showed that nearly 80% of women had a preference for traditional family planning methods, including abstaining from sexual activity on certain days, breastfeeding amenorrhea, the hormonal contraceptive shot (22.1%), and oral hormonal contraceptives (4.5%).[59] In sub-Saharan Africa, less than 13% of the population uses contraception; of those that use contraception, less than 5% are using modern contraceptives (sterilization—male or female, the pill, injections, IUDs, condoms, others).[60]

Abortion is a common form of contraception in Africa. This procedure is used especially by adolescents, who cite fear of future infertility as the overriding factor in their decisions to rely on induced abortion rather than contraception. A majority of these procedures are not performed by trained medical professionals in a proper clinical setting and can lead to serious complications. As an example, an estimated 80% of all hospital administrations for teenage girls in sub-Saharan Africa are the result of complications resulting from incorrectly performed abortions.[61]

Gaps in contraceptive use between the poor and the averages in sub-Saharan Africa are high, although on average smaller by 15.8% than in Latin America and greater than in Southeast Asia by 4.2%. Sub-Saharan Africa still continues to exhibit the lowest national rates of use.[57]

After our comprehensive examination of contraception, a lack of knowledge is not the only barrier that prevents contraceptive use. Knowledge about contraception is just the first step in allowing women to control their reproductive lives. The lack of contraceptive use poses serious threats to nations and individuals. Individual lives and families can be damaged as women experience frequent, difficult, and complicated pregnancies. This affects the other members in the family and the community. It prevents women from being able to care for their families and homes. On a macro scale, the problems associated with uncontrolled population growth lead to poverty and great social inequity. The health, economic, and cultural problems related to contraception discussed in this paper must be addressed by the global community.

Conclusion

This chapter addressed issues associated with contraception for selected regions of the world. The five main categories of contraception were considered: sterilization, hormonal methods, barrier methods, IUDs, and traditional family planning methods. Health, economic, and cultural issues corresponding to birth control in general and for these selected categories of contraception were addressed.

Key Issues

1. Contraception (or birth control) is any strategy or device intended to reduce the chance of fertilization of an ovum by a spermatozoon.
2. Contraception falls into five main categories: sterilization, hormonal methods, barrier methods, IUDs, and traditional family planning methods.
3. Oral contraception is the most common form of contraception in North America, and it is most frequently used by younger White females with higher levels of education. The pill does not protect against sexually transmitted infections, but when properly used, it is a reliable source in preventing pregnancy. Women who are finished having children commonly choose sterilization to prevent future pregnancies.
4. Contraception use in Western Europe is similar to that found in the United States, but Western Europe has lower rates of female sterilization and higher rates of IUDs being used.
5. With Asia's fast-growing population, family planning is an issue that needs to be addressed but is challenged by cultural and social factors. Indian women are generally aware of modern forms of birth control but are often not allowed to practice it because of pressure from their husbands to bear children early and often. China's practices are unique because of its one

child per family policy; most Chinese females use IUDs to prevent further pregnancies.

6. Family planning methods are gaining acceptance in the Pacific Islands as more islanders realize that spacing or limiting births has a direct impact on a woman's health. The culture (including male leaders and religious groups) has long frowned on birth control of any form, but now women are helping to make family planning decisions, including receiving Depo-Provera shots and using the rhythm method to space out pregnancies.

7. Because of the strong influences of religion, traditional Latino gender roles, and economic status, Latin America has the lowest rate of contraceptive use in the world. Each of these factors limits women's access to birth control.

8. Education and awareness about modern birth control methods vary among African nations, but use is low in all areas. Unsafe induced abortions are common, especially among adolescents, and lead to other health complications.

Exercises

Key Terms

Define the following terms.
Barrier methods
Contraception   Sterilization
Depo-Provera   Traditional family planning methods
Hormonal methods
Intrauterine device

Study Questions

9.1 Explain the different forms of female sterilization. Include the benefits and risks of each.

9.2 Explain the patterns of contraception use in India.

9.3 What region of the world has the lowest rate of contraceptive use? Why?

9.4 Describe the benefits and risks of IUDs.

References

1. eMedicineHealth. Tubal sterilization. Available at: http://www.emedicinehealth.com/ tubal_sterilization/article_em.htm. Accessed February 12, 2009.
2. Mayo Clinic. Birth control. Available at: http://www.mayoclinic.com/health/birth-control/ BI99999/PAGE=BI00014. Accessed March 2, 2009.
3. Bioidentical Hormone MDs. Hormonal contraceptives. Available at: http://www.contracept .org/hormonal.php. Accessed February 12, 2009.
4. Calgary Sexual Health Center. Barrier methods of birth control. Available at: http:// www.cbca.ab.ca/Barrier%20Methods%20of%20Birth%20Control.htm. Accessed February 12, 2009.
5. Parr EL. Contraception with intrauterine devices. *BioScience.* 1973;23(5):281–286.
6. Wikipedia. Intrauterine device. Available at: http://en.wikipedia.org/wiki/Intrauterine_ device#cite_note-ined_2006-0. Accessed February 12, 2009.
7. Guttmacher Institute. Facts on contraceptive use. Available at: http://www.guttmacher .org/pubs/fb_contr_use.html. Accessed March 2, 2009.
8. Mosher WD, Martinez GM, Chandra A, et al. *Use of Contraception and Use of Family Planning Services in the United States: 1982–2002.* Atlanta, GA: National Center for Health Statistics, Centers for Disease Control and Prevention; 2004.
9. Bavo MJ. Natural family planning: the different methods. Available at: http://www .mjbovo.com/Contracept/Natural-What.htm. Accessed February 12, 2009.
10. Paterson J, Cowley ET, Percival T, Williams M. Pregnancy planning by mothers of Pacific infants recently delivered at Middlemore Hospital. *N Z Med J.* 2004;117(1188).
11. Margolis KL, Adami HO, Luo J, Ye W, Weiderpass E. A prospective study of oral contraceptive use and risk of myocardial infarction among Swedish women. *Fertil Steril.* 2007; 88(2):310–316.
12. Liu XF, van Melle G, Bogousslavsky J. Analysis of risk factors in 3901 patients with stroke. *Chin Med Sci J.* 2005;20(1):35–39.
13. Frye CA. An overview of oral contraceptives: mechanism of action and clinical use. *Neurology.* 2006;66(6 Suppl 3):S29–S36.
14. Lizarelli PM, Martins WP, Vieira CS, et al. Both a combined oral contraceptive and depot medroxyprogesterone acetate impair endothelial function in young women. *Contraception.* 2009;79(1):35–40.
15. Golden C, Katz L. The power of the pill: oral contraceptives and women's career and marriage decisions. *J Pol Econ.* 2002;110(4):730–770.
16. Hankinson SE, Colditz GA, Manson JE, et al. A prospective study of oral contraceptive use and risk of breast cancer (Nurses' Health Study, United States). *Cancer Causes Control.* 1997;8(1):65–72.
17. White E, Malone KE, Weiss NS, Daling JR. Breast cancer among young U.S. women in relation to oral contraceptive use. *J Natl Cancer Inst.* 1994;86(7):505–514.
18. Newcomb PA, Longnecker MP, Storer BE, et al. Recent oral contraceptive use and risk of breast cancer (United States). *Cancer Causes Control.* 1996;7(5):525–532.
19. McFarlane-Anderson N, Bazuaye PE, Jackson MD, Smikle M, Fletcher HM. Cervical dysplasia and cancer and the use of hormonal contraceptives in Jamaican women. *BMC Womens Health.* 2008;30:8–9.

20. Vanakankovit N, Taneepanichskul S. Effect of oral contraceptives on risk of cervical cancer. *J Med Assoc Thai.* 2008;91(1):7–12.
21. Hannaford PC, Selvaraj S, Elliott AM, Angus V, Iversen L, Lee AJ. Cancer risk among users of oral contraceptives: cohort data from the Royal College of General Practitioner's oral contraception study. *BMJ.* 2007;29;335(7621):651.
22. Smith JS, Green J, Berrington de Gonzalez A, et al. Cervical cancer and use of hormonal contraceptives: a systematic review. *Lancet.* 2003;361(9364):1159–1167.
23. International Collaboration of Epidemiological Studies of Cervical Cancer, Appleby P, Beral V, Berrington de González A, et al. Cervical cancer and hormonal contraceptives: collaborative reanalysis of individual data for 16,573 women with cervical cancer and 35,509 women without cervical cancer from 24 epidemiological studies. *Lancet.* 2007; 370(9599):1609–1621.
24. Rosenberg L. The risk of liver neoplasia in relation to combined oral contraceptive use. *Contraception.* 1991;43(6):643–652.
25. Scalori A, Tavani A, Gallus S, La Vecchia C, Colombo M. Oral contraceptives and the risk of focal nodular hyperplasia of the liver: a case-control study. *Am J Obstet Gynecol.* 2002; 186(2):195–197.
26. Gemer O, Moscovici O, Ben-Horin CL, Linov L, Peled R, Segal S. Oral contraceptives and liver hemangioma: a case-control study. *Acta Obstet Gynecol Scand.* 2004;83(12): 1199–1201.
27. Heinemann LA, Weimann A, Gerken G, Thiel C, Schlaud M, DoMinh T. Modern oral contraceptive use and benign liver tumors: the German Benign Liver Tumor Case-Control Study. *Eur J Contracept Reprod Health Care.* 1998;3(4):194–200.
28. Vessey M, Painter R. Oral contraceptive use and benign gallbladder disease: revisited. *Contraception.* 1994;50(2):167–173.
29. La Vecchia C, Negri E, D'Avanzo B, Parazzini F, Gentile A, Franceschi S. Oral contraceptives and non-contraceptive oestrogens in the risk of gallstone disease requiring surgery. *J Epidemiol Community Health.* 1992;46(3):234–236.
30. Stuart GS, Tang JH, Heartwell SF, Westhoff CL, QuickStart Study Group. A high cholecystectomy rate in a cohort of Mexican American women who are postpartum at the time of oral contraceptive pill initiation. *Contraception.* 2007;76(5):357–359.
31. Sivin I. Risks and benefits, advantages and disadvantages of levonorgestrel-releasing contraceptive implants. *Drug Saf.* 2003;26(5):303–335.
32. Dorjgochoo T, Shu XO, Li HL, et al. Use of oral contraceptives, intrauterine devices and tubal sterilization and cancer risk in a large prospective study, from 1996 to 2006. *Int J Cancer.* 2008 [Epub ahead of print].
33. Ness RB, Grisso JA, Vergona R, Klapper J, Morgan M, Wheeler J. Oral contraceptives, other methods of contraception, and risk reduction for ovarian cancer. *Epidemiology.* 2001;12(3):307–312.
34. Marsden J, Sturdee D. Cancer issues. *Best Pract Res Clin Obstet Gynaecol.* 2009;23 (1):87–107.
35. Huber JC, Bentz EK, Ott J, Tempfer CB. Non-contraceptive benefits of oral contraceptives. *Expert Opin Pharmacother.* 2008;9(13):2317–2325.
36. Gnagy S, Ming ES, Devesa SS, Hartge P, Whittemore AS. Declining ovarian cancer rates in U.S. women in relation to parity and oral contraceptive use. *Epidemiology.* 2000; 11(2):102–105.

37. Rodriguez CW, Tatham LM, Calle EE, et al. Infertility and risk of fatal ovarian cancer in a prospective cohort of US women. *Cancer Causes Control.* 1998;9(6):645–651.

38. Law SA. Sex discrimination and insurance for contraception. *Washington Law Rev.* 1998:73.

39. Finer L, Henshaw S. Abortion incidence and services in the United States in 2000. *Perspect Sex Reprod Health.* 2003;35(1):6–15.

40. Mayo Clinic. Estrogen and progestin oral contraceptives (oral route), 2003. Available at: http://www.mayoclinic.com/health/drug-information/DR602119. Accessed March 2, 2009.

41. Westhoff C, Davis A. Tubal sterilization: a focus on the US experience. *Fertil Steril.* 2000;73(5):913–922.

42. Siegler AM, Hulka J, Peretz A. Reversibility of female sterilization. *Fertil Steril.* 1985;43 (4):499–510.

43. Food and Drug Administration. Birth control guide. Food and Drug Administration, 2003. Available at October 2008, from www.fda.gov.

44. Ulrich RE. Most European women use contraceptives. *Population Reference Bureau.* Available at: http://www.prb.org/Articles/2001/MostEuropeanWomenUseContraceptives .aspx. Accessed May 5, 2009.

45. Central Intelligence Agency. *The World Factbook: India.* Available at: https://www.cia .gov/library/publications/the-world-factbook/geos/in.html#People. Accessed March 2, 2009.

46. Wilson-Williams L, Stephenson R, Juvekar S, Andes K. Domestic violence and contraceptive use in a rural Indian village. *Violence Against Women.* 2008;14(10):1181–1198.

47. Kumari C. Contraceptive practices of women living in rural areas of Bihar. *Br J Fam Plan.* 1998;24(2):75–77.

48. Qiu S. A survey of China's birth control among women of child-bearing age. *China Population Newsletter.* 1983;1(2):8–12, 17.

49. Che Y, Cleland J. Unintended pregnancy among newly married couples in Shanghai. *Int Fam Plan Perspect.* 2004;30(1):6–11.

50. Brewis A, McGarvey S, Tu'u'au-Potoi N. Structure of family planning. *Aust N Z J Pub Health.* 1998;22(4):424–427.

51. Kenyon M, Power J. *Family Planning in the Pacific Region: Getting the Basics Right.* Paper presented at the international symposium "Population Change in Asia and the Pacific: Implications for Development Policy," Australian National University, Canberra, Australia. June 2003.

52. Barrancos D. Problematic modernity: gender, sexuality, and reproduction in twentieth-century Argentina. *J Women Hist.* 2006;18(2):123–150.

53 Martin A. Emergency contraception in Latin America and the Caribbean (translated). *Revista Panam Salud Pub.* 2004;16(6):424–431.

54. Latino gender role-beliefs impede condom use. Education and prevention. *Sex Weekly Plus.* 1996;17. Available at: http://www.popline.org/docs/1162/116275.html. Accessed March 2, 2009.

55. Conway G, Slocumb J. Plants used as abortifacients and emmenagogues by Spanish New Mexicans. *J Ethnopharmacol.* 1979;1(3):241–261.

56. Gakidou E, Vayena E. Use of modern contraception by the poor is falling behind. *Pub Lib Sci Med.* 2007;4(2).

57. Orji E, Onwudiegwu U. Prevalence and determinants of contraceptive practice in a defined Nigerian population. *J Obstet Gynaecol.* 2002;22(5):540–543.
58. Addai I. Ethnicity and contraceptive use in sub-Saharan Africa: the case of Ghana. *J Biosoc Sci.* 1999;31(01):105–120.
59. Smit J, McFadyen L, Zuma K, Preston-Whyte E. Vaginal wetness: an underestimated problem experienced by progestogen injectable contraceptive users in South Africa. *Soc Sci Med.* 2002;55(9):1511–1522.
60. Bambra CS. Current status of reproductive behavior in Africa. *Hum Reprod Update.* 1999;5(1):1–20.
61. Fathella M. Women's health: an overview. *Int J Gynaecol Obstet.* 1994;46:105–118.

TEN

Mercury, Lead, Environmental Estrogens, and Reproductive Health

Learning Objectives

After completing this chapter, you should be able to:

1. Define mercury and methylmercury, identify sources of human exposure, and list reproductive health problems associated with exposure.
2. Define lead, identify sources of human exposure, and list reproductive health problems associated with exposure.
3. Define environmental exposure, identify sources of human exposure, and list reproductive health problems associated with exposure.
4. Describe and distinguish between organochlorines, organophosphates, and pyrethroids.
5. Discuss how selected pesticides, polychlorinated biphenyls, and bisphenol A may adversely affect human reproduction.

An important part of environmental epidemiology is the study of why and how environmental factors such as biological agents (pathogens), physical and chemical agents (e.g., radiation, lead, mercury, volatile organic compounds, and pesticides), and psychosocial influences (e.g., social networks and social support, neighborhoods, and communities) affect health. Environmental epidemiology seeks to clarify the association between environmental factors and human health.[1] Reproductive epidemiology includes the study of why and how environmental factors influence the reproductive system and the study of its functions and processes.

Although many environmental factors are essential to protecting and sustaining human life and reproductive health, some can adversely affect human reproduction. In Chapter 2, "Environments in Reproductive Epidemiology," several physical factors, chemicals, biological agents, and psychosocial conditions were identified that can adversely affect human reproduction. For example, reduced sperm count has been associated with ionizing radiation, heat, lead, and pesticides. Birth defects have been associated with ionizing radiation, rubella virus, mercury, and lead, and spontaneous abortion has been associated with ionizing radiation, lead, mercury, stress, and intense physical work.

Increasing industrialization and resulting environmental pollutants have resulted in greater use of synthetic chemicals and repeated exposure to hazardous compounds that adversely affect reproductive health. Some biohazardous compounds may act as endocrine disrupters and are increasingly being implicated in infertility, menstrual irregularities, spontaneous abortions, birth defects, endometriosis, and breast cancer.[2–4]

In this chapter, we further explore the relation between mercury, lead, and environmental estrogens and reproductive health problems.

Mercury and Reproductive Health Problems

Mercury is one of three heavy metals commonly cited as being associated with several adverse health effects. The other two metals are lead and cadmium. Mercury is a naturally occurring element in the environment that is found in air, water, and soil. It is odorless, colorless, and tasteless. Mercury is contained in many of the products we use, including thermometers, switches, fluorescent light bulbs, fungicides, paints, batteries, thimerosal-containing vaccines, and dental amalgams. People can be exposed to mercury through air, food, or water contaminated by mercury compounds.[5,6]

Mercury is released into the air from natural sources (e.g., volcanoes and off-gassing from the earth's crust and water). In the United States, coal-burning power plants are the primary human source of mercury emissions. Mercury is also released into the environment through improper treatment and disposal of products or wastes containing mercury, breaking mercury products, producing chlorine, and by medical waste incinerators.[7] Exposure to mercury may occur because of inappropriate handling or cleanup of spilled mercury, incinerators, and industries that burn mercury-containing fuels or mercury-contaminated workplace air. Inhaled mercury vapor easily crosses the pulmonary capillary membranes and accumulates in distal places in the body.[8]

Mercury in the air eventually settles on land or in water. Deposited mercury may combine with carbon to make organic mercury compounds. The most common is methylmercury, which is produced mainly by microscopic organisms in water and soil. **Methylmercury** is a highly toxic form of mercury that builds up in fish. Fish and shellfish are the primary sources of methylmercury in humans.[9] Studies have shown an association between maternal consumption of fish and high mercury concentrations in cord blood and hair of infants.[10-12] In a 7-year cohort study, an association was found between prenatal exposure to methylmercury through maternal consumption of fish and whale meat and cognitive deficit in children responsible for neuropsychological dysfunctions.[13] A 14-year cohort study showed that prenatal exposure to methylmercury from maternal seafood consumption increased the risk of impaired autonomic regulation of heart function and thus a decrease in ability to secure proper oxygen supply to the body.[14]

The effect of methylmercury for fetuses, infants, and children is primarily impaired neurological development. Exposure to the fetus can adversely affect the developing brain and nervous system. Some specific outcomes from methylmercury exposure in the womb include impaired cognitive thinking, memory, attention, language, and fine motor and visual spatial skills.[15-18] In addition, there is some evidence that it increases the risk of a preterm delivery.[19]

Exposure to mercury vapor has also been associated with increased risk of birth defects.[20] Several studies have shown that exposure to mercury vapor can increase the risk of menstrual cycle abnormalities, including changes in bleeding patterns and cycle length.[21-27] One study showed a decrease in fertility among female dental assistants exposed to mercury vapor.[28]

Biological monitoring of blood mercury levels by the Centers for Disease Control and Prevention has shown that most people in the United States have blood mercury levels below what can cause possible adverse health effects;[29,30] however, approximately 8% of women have blood concentrations of mercury higher than the U.S. Environmental Protection Agency's recommended reference dose of 5.8 µg/L.[31] In addition, women living in coastal areas in the Northeastern United States have been shown to have three to four times the risk of exceeding acceptable blood mercury levels compared with women residing in inland areas of the United States. Approximately one in five women living in the Northeast exceeded 3.5 micrograms per liter of mercury. In addition, Asian, Native American, Alaskan, Pacific Island, and Caribbean women were more likely to have elevated blood mercury levels.[32]

Lead and Reproductive Health Problems

Lead is a toxic metal that is harmful to human health if inhaled or swallowed. It is found naturally in the environment and in manufactured products. Historically, primary sources of lead emissions have come from motor vehicles and industrial sources, waste incinerators, utilities, and lead-acid battery manufacturers. Many building materials and other household items contain lead. In the United States, lead has been removed from gasoline, resulting in a dramatic decline of 91% of lead emissions between 1980 and 2007.[33] In 2002, industrial processes caused 43% of total emissions, while nonroad equipment caused 28%, electricity generation caused 13%, fossil fuel combustion caused 8%, waste disposal caused 7%, and solvent use caused 1%.[34]

The most common exposure to lead comes from swallowing or breathing in lead dust or paint chips. Lead poisoning may also occur from contact with lead-contaminated soil or exposure to drinking water containing lead. Although lead is rarely found in source water, it can enter tap water through corrosion of plumbing materials (lead pipes, fixtures, and solder). In the United States, considerable effort has been made in recent decades to remove lead from household materials and work sites.[35]

Regulations have also limited the use of lead in plumbing materials. Nevertheless, brass or chrome-plated brass faucets and fixtures may still leach significant amounts of lead into water.[34] In addition, lead remains in our environment at many levels, such as older buildings, near landfills, incinerators, mines, places of demolition, and waste or recycling plants.

A number of work and hobby environments expose people to lead. Occupational exposures also affect the families of the workers because lead particles can be transferred from clothes to persons. Occupations where lead poisoning is frequently reported include secondary smelting and refining of nonferrous metals; storage batteries; valve and pipe fittings; plumbing fixture fittings and trim (brass goods); brass or copper foundry; glass products; motor vehicle parts and accessories; firing range workers; chemicals and chemical preparations; bridges, tunnels, and elevated highway construction; automotive repair shops; industrial machinery and equipment; and inorganic pigments.[36] Furniture refinishing, making stained glass, making pottery, casting ammunition, burning lead-painted wood, having contact with fishing weights, doing home repairs, and remodeling may also result in lead exposure.[37] In the United States, the Occupational Safety and Health Administration General Industry Lead Standard governing lead exposures (29 CAR 1910.1026) has resulted in lower occupational lead exposure; however, some occupations are not covered by this regulation (e.g., workers in construction, lead abatement workers).[36] Construction workers have been shown to be at a particularly high risk of very high blood levels of lead.[38]

Tobacco smoking may also be a source of lead exposure. In one study, researchers found that long-term smoking led to higher levels of blood lead.[39]

Outside the United States, leaded gasoline continues to be widely used, contributing to elevated blood lead levels, especially in urban areas. Poorly glazed pottery may also result in high food lead levels, and such is the case in parts of Latin America. In several places in the world, point industrial sources of lead are not effectively regulated, such as in Eastern Europe. Furthermore, industries that recycle lead are often located near resident dwellings, such as in Central America and elsewhere.[36]

Lead serves no useful purpose in humans. Its toxicity can affect every organ system, regardless of exposure pathway. The mechanisms for toxicity include its ability to inhibit or mimic the action of calcium and interact with proteins.[40] Lead is generally stored in the bone, and during times of rebuilding (pregnancy), the lead is released into the bloodstream, raising blood lead levels. Lead levels are greatest in the first and last trimesters of pregnancy, resulting in the U-shaped pattern. Calcium intake is inversely associated with lead levels after 20 weeks of pregnancy.[41] Calcium may be thought of as a protective factor against lead.

Several health effects in humans have been associated with lead exposure, including adverse neurological effects, renal effects, hematological effects, endocrine effects, gastrointestinal effects, cardiovascular (hypertension) effects, developmental effects, and reproductive effects.[42–49] Decreased sperm count totals and increased abnormal sperm frequencies have been associated with elevated lead exposure.[50–55] Males who work with metals or who are otherwise exposed to high levels of lead are at greatest risk. Adverse effects on sperm may begin at blood lead levels of 40 μg/dL.[40] Diminished sperm concentrations, total sperm counts, and total sperm motility may also result from long-term lead exposure, independent of current levels of lead exposure.[50] The duration of these effects once lead exposure has ceased remains unclear.[35] The role of elevated blood lead levels and past lead exposure levels of female fertility remains unclear.[35]

Although the effect of low-level lead exposures on pregnancy outcomes remains unclear, higher level lead exposure (e.g., occupational) and adverse pregnancy outcomes have been observed. Women living near smelters are at increased risk for spontaneous abortions (miscarriages) and stillbirths.[56–59] Women with a blood lead level (BLL) of 5–9 μg/dL had a twofold to threefold increased risk of a spontaneous abortion compared with BLL less than 5 μg/dL.[57]

Cadmium and Reproductive Health Problems

Cadmium is a heavy metal found naturally in the earth's crust. Cadmium is found in rocks and soils, including coal and mineral fertilizers. It is rarely found in its pure form because it reacts readily with other elements such as oxygen, chlorine, and sulfur. It does not break down in the environment, but often changes forms. Some forms of cadmium dissolve easily in water (e.g., cadmium sulfates and cadmium chlorides). Cadmium binds strongly with soil particles. It enters soil, water, and air from industry, mining, coal burning, and household wastes.[60]

Cadmium and its compounds are very toxic, even in low concentrations, and have no value to the human body. Cadmium can enter the body through ingestion or inhalation. Uptake through the skin may also occur but is generally regarded as minimal.[61] Exposure to cadmium may occur through eating foods containing cadmium, with the highest levels in shellfish, liver, and kidney meats; smoking cigarettes or breathing secondhand smoke; breathing contaminated workplace air; drinking contaminated water; and living near industrial facilities that release cadmium into the air.[60] Cadmium is a major constituent of tobacco smoke that is absorbed more readily into the body than cadmium in food or water. With increased levels of phosphate fertilizers and sewage sludge applied to farm fields, food is a primary source of cadmium in nonsmokers. Roughly 2% to 6% of ingested cadmium is absorbed into the body compared with the about 30% to 64% of inhaled cadmium that is absorbed into the body in smokers.[62]

Uptake of cadmium in the body depends on the form of cadmium and the person's diet. A balanced diet that includes enough calcium, iron, protein, and zinc will help reduce the amount of cadmium that may be absorbed in the body.[63–65] One study found that iron deficiency during pregnancy is associated with increased cadmium absorption.[66]

Cadmium exposure has potentially serious consequences on human reproduction.[67,68] There is some evidence that cadmium levels in blood have a significant inverse association with sperm density and defective sperm.[69] A reduction in sperm count has also been observed in men with blood cadmium greater than 1.5 µg/L.[69] More recently, a significant inverse correlation was observed between cadmium and sperm density, as well as between cadmium and sperm number (per ejaculation).[70] Another study involving infertile men found a significant association between serum cadmium levels and abnormal sperm morphology and decreased sperm count, sperm motility, and sperm viability.[71] Reproductive risks associated with cadmium may also include premature birth and lower newborn size.[72–76]

To minimize exposure to cadmium, a proper diet with sufficient iron is important. People who work with cadmium should avoid carrying cadmium-containing dust home on clothes, skin, or hair and should use all safety precautions. In addition, tobacco smoke should be avoided, especially in enclosed spaces, and substances containing cadmium (e.g., nickel-cadmium batteries) should be stored safely and avoided during pregnancy.[60]

Environmental Estrogens and Reproductive Health Problems

The proper balance of natural estrogens in the human body is required for successful reproduction. **Estrogen** is a generic term for any substance, either natural or synthetic, that exerts biologic effects characteristic of estrogenic hormones. Estrogen is produced by the ovaries, placenta, testes, and possibly the adrenal cortex and by certain plants. It stimulates secondary sexual characteristics (e.g., puberty, menstruation, pregnancy) and exerts systemic effects in regulating growth of bones, skin, and other organs and tissues;[77] however, chemicals that "mimic" the body's natural estrogens are increasingly present in our environment. These environmental estrogens create reproductive problems as they confuse the body's estrogen receptors.[78]

In the early 1970s, scientists confirmed that Kepone was a weak estrogen, although its chemical structure has no resemblance to the natural hormone. Today, many synthetic compounds and plant products in the environment have been shown to have various effects on hormonal functions.[78–80] Those synthetic compounds and plant products that have estrogenic activity are labeled as **environmental estrogens**, ecoestrogens, estrogen mimics, or xenoestrogens (xeno means foreign). In addition to some being metabolites (breakdown products) generated from pesticides and **polychlorinated biphenyls** (PCBs), some are artifacts that arise during the manufacture of plastics and other synthetic materials.[78–80] Ecoestrogens produced naturally by plants are called phytoestrogens (*phyton* means plant).[81]

Environmental estrogens bind to estrogen receptors (within specialized cells) in a similar manner to estrogen itself. This sets the stage for potential havoc in the reproductive anatomy and physiology; therefore, environmental estrogens have been referred to as disruptors of endocrine function.[81] The **endocrine system** is the collective designation for those tissues capable of secreting hormones.[77] Interference with the healthy functioning of the endocrine system occurs by binding to hormone receptor sites and producing a number of unnatural responses. They may mimic natural hormones and increase the body's estrogenic level. They may also block natural hormones and alter the way in which hormones are produced, eliminated, and metabolized.[82]

Environmental estrogens appear in rainwater, well water, lakes, oceans, birds, fish, animals, and humans. They enter our food and drinking water in many ways, and as these chemicals move up the food chain, they become more concentrated, a process known as **bioaccumulation**. Hence, people on a vegetarian diet are protected somewhat from environmental estrogens.

Researchers believe that exposure to small amounts of different environmental estrogens may produce just as many negative results as an exposure to large amounts of one chemical.[83] They have now connected reproductive disorders to populations where the exposure to environmental estrogens is elevated. Globally researchers have compared exposure to certain chemicals with fertility rates in different geographic regions.

The increased incidence of reproductive disorders in males has been observed over the past 30 to 50 years. Testicular cancer, cryptorchidism, and urethral abnormalities have doubled during this time and sperm counts have fallen by roughly half.[84–88] Environmental estrogens affect the development of the Sertoli cells in the testes. These Sertoli cells secrete the masculine hormones, and disruption may result in a decrease in sperm counts. Several studies have suggested a link between environmental estrogens and decreased semen volume and sperm counts.[89–92] There is also some evidence that an increase in cryptorchidism (failure of the testes to descend) and hypospadias (opening of the urethra on the underside of the penis) may be associated with environmental estrogens;[91,93–96] however, there remains some uncertainty over this possible association.[97]

In females, exposure to the environmental estrogen diethylstilbestrol has been shown to increase the risk of breast cancer, endometriosis, ectopic pregnancy, preterm birth, and spontaneous abortion.[98–103]

Several diet-linked sources of increased estrogenic exposure to males in the womb have been established.[96,104] A diet low in fiber increases the levels of natural estrogen in women. Natural estrogens excreted in the bile have a greater tendency to be reabsorbed into the bloodstream if there is little dietary fiber in the lower intestine; therefore, a fetus may be exposed to higher levels of the mother's own natural estrogens if she has a diet low in fiber from whole grains, vegetables, and fruits. Fiber is absent in all meats, dairy products, and eggs.

Pesticides

Pesticides have a chemical structure of estrogen that can provoke a weak estrogenic effect on our systems. A **pesticide** is any substance or mixture of substances used to prevent, destroy, repel, or mitigate any pest (insects, mice, and other animals), weeds, fungi, bacteria, viruses, or parasites. Pesticides include insecticides, herbicides, fungicides, or any substance used to control pests. In addition, a pesticide includes a substance or substances used as a plant regulator, defoliant, or desiccant.[105]

Three general classes of insecticides are organochlorines, organophosphates, and **pyrethroids**. **Organochlorines** are man-made organic chemicals that are extremely persistent in the environment and in people's bodies. Most organochlorines are known or suspected endocrine toxicants (i.e., causing adverse effects on the endocrine system), with the best known being dichlorodiphenyltrichloroethane (DDT). Others include hexachlorobenzene, dichlorodiphenyltrichloroethylene (DDE), oxychlordane, trans-nonachlor, mirex, pentachlorophenol, 2,3,5-trichlorophenol, and 2,4,6-trichlorophenol. Although organochlorines are now strictly regulated and some are no longer used in the United States, they continue to be widely used in many parts of the world. In addition, as these chemicals vaporize and drift, much of the globe is exposed.

Human exposure to pesticides may result from ingestion, inhalation, and contact with skin or eyes in a number of settings (residential, community, agricultural, and occupational). Pesticide exposure may occur during various phases of the reproductive cycle: preconception (3 months before to 1 month after the last menstrual period), prenatal (in utero), and neonatal (breast-feeding).

Several studies have implicated organochlorines in adverse reproductive outcomes such as spontaneous abortions[106–109]; neural tube defects[110–114]; reduced sperm count and quality[115–118]; and low birth weight, shorter birth length, and smaller head circumference.[119–122] One study found that prenatal exposure to DDT, and to a lesser extent DDE, was associated with neurodevelopmental delays during early childhood.[123] Mothers can pass on high concentrations of fat-soluble chemicals such as PCBs and DDT to children through breast milk. For example, in the United States and Europe, "a six month old baby is fed five times the allowable daily levels of PCB set by international health standards for a 150 pound adult."[82] Yet, Eskenazi and colleagues (2006) concluded that breastfeeding was beneficial even in women with high levels of exposure.[123]

Organophosphates are insecticides that are less persistent in the environment than organochlorines. These chemicals stop a key enzyme in the insect's nervous system called acetylcholinesterase from working. There is currently no evidence that organophosphates cause reproductive problems.[124]

Pyrethroids are a group of synthetic forms of naturally occurring plant pesticides similar to the natural pesticide pyrethrum produced by chrysanthemum flowers. Those most commonly used in the United States include permethrin (Biomist), resmethrin (Scourge), and sumithrin (Anvil). They work by disrupting transmission of nerve impulses. They often only last 1 or 2 days in the environment and are considered less toxic. The EPA considers this latter type of insecticide as posing very little health risk to humans and the environment. Pyrethroids that enter the body are emitted quickly through the urine, feces, and exhalation. There is currently no evidence that pyrethroids cause reproductive problems.[125]

In the United States, the Environmental Protection Agency's Office of Pesticide Programs is responsible for regulating pesticides that are used by growers to protect crops, and they set limits on the amount of pesticides (called "tolerances") that can remain in or on foods. Established tolerance limits for each pesticide are based on the pesticide's risk to human health. Tolerances established for meat, poultry, and some egg products are enforced by the U.S. Department of Agriculture, whereas tolerances for other foods are enforced by the Food and Drug

Administration (FDA). The interested reader can read more about tolerance limits and assessment status elsewhere.[126,127] In addition, biologically based pesticides are gaining popularity and preference over traditional chemical pesticides.

PCBs

Polychlorinated biphenyls (PCBs) are mixtures of up to 209 chlorinated compounds. There are no known natural sources of PCBs. Commercial PCB mixtures in the United States are typically known by their trade name, Aroclor. PCBs have been used in various capacities (e.g., coolants and lubricants, transformers, capacitors, and other electrical equipment) because they are good insulators and do not burn easily. PCBs stopped being manufactured in the United States in 1977 because they are persistent and bioaccumulative in the environment and can adversely affect human life. PCBs enter the air, water, and soil from leaks or fires in products with PCBs, from accidental spills during transport, and during their use, manufacture, and disposal. They may also be released into the environment from hazardous waste sites, consumer products, waste incinerators, and leaks from old fluorescent lighting fixtures and appliances (e.g., television sets and refrigerators) made 30 or more years ago. Eating contaminated food, mainly fish, meat, and dairy products are also sources of exposure.[128]

PCBs can adversely affect the brain and nervous system, endocrine system, reproduction and fertility, and birth or development and have also been associated with cancer. In utero exposure to environmental levels of PCBs is associated with lower birth weight and smaller head circumference.[129,130] In utero exposure to environmental levels of PCBs has also been associated with poorer cognitive functioning in young children.[131–134] There is also evidence that spontaneous abortion and pregnancy loss are significantly associated with maternal exposure to PCBs.[135] There is not consistent evidence that exposure to PCBs affect male fertility or the female menstrual cycle.

Bisphenol A

Bisphenol A (BPA) was recognized as having estrogenic activity in 1936. Several years prior, it was used in forming polycarbonate plastic and resins in the early 1950s. Two primary mechanisms are believed to explain how BPA disrupts normal endocrine function. First, it may act as a weak estrogen in which it binds to the estrogen receptor. Second, it can block the effect of stronger natural estrogens, thereby inhibiting estrogen function.[136] Adverse health and reproductive effects have been associated with BPA exposure in numerous animals studies, as well as in some human studies, such as reduced fertility and mammary.[137,138] BPA has also been associated with an increased risk of spontaneous abortion in one study.[139]

Growth Hormones

Environmental estrogens can be found in many meats and dairy products in the form of chemicals and growth hormones that are given to the animals. Treatment with steroid hormones is a very cost-effective way to raise cattle as it has been shown to increase lean muscle growth and improve feed efficiency. The Joint Food and Agricultural Organization/World Health Organization's expert committee on food additives (JECFA) and the U.S. FDA stated in 1988 that residues found in meat are safe for human consumption. In the same year, the European Union showed their disagreement with the findings by banning the use of all hormone growth promoters in the production of beef.[140] A recent study re-evaluated the JECFA's findings and sided with the European Union's stance. The study focused primarily on exogenous estrogens in food and the resulting impact on human health and development, particularly in children. It concluded, "In light of recent progress in our understanding of estrogen levels in children, we conclude that possible adverse effects on human health by consumption of meat from estrogen treated animals cannot be excluded." It also pointed out that "the conclusions by JECFA concerning the safety of hormone residues in meat seem to be based on uncertain assumptions and inadequate scientific data."[141]

Another study looked at possible long-term risks from anabolic steroids and other xenobiotics in beef.[142] Researchers examined men's semen quality in light of their mother's beef consumption while pregnant. The results showed that maternal beef consumption was associated with lower sperm concentration and subfertility in their male offspring and that these associations may be related to the presence of anabolic steroids and other xenobiotics.

Conclusion

Mercury is a neurotoxin that is a naturally occurring element emitted by power plants and other sources. Bacteria can cause chemical changes that transform mercury into methylmercury in soil and water. Soil and water containing mercury can be sources of poisoning that can adversely affect reproductive health. Lead is a toxic metal that is harmful to human health if ingested. It is found naturally in the environment and in manufactured products. Several sources of lead exposure were presented. Lead accumulates in the bones, and maternal lead poisoning can be especially harmful to the developing brains of fetuses. Lead exposure can adversely affect fertility in men and the survival of the child in utero. Finally, environmental estrogens were described as chemicals that "mimic" the body's natural estrogens and confuse the body's estrogen receptors. Environmental estrogens have been associated with a number of reproductive health problems.

Key Issues

1. Prenatal exposure to methylmercury is associated with an increased risk of birth defects, impaired autonomic regulation of heart function, impaired development of the brain, and resulting neuropsychological dysfunction. In addition, there is increased risk of menstrual cycle abnormalities, preterm delivery, and a decrease in fertility. Women living in coastal areas are at increased risk of exposure to methylmercury.
2. Lead exposure is associated with lower sperm count, abnormal sperm frequency, and adverse pregnancy outcomes such as spontaneous abortions (miscarriages) and stillbirths.
3. Several studies have indicated a link between environmental estrogens and decreased semen volume and sperm counts. There is also some evidence that an increase in cryptorchidism (failure of the testes to descend) and hypospadias (opening of the urethra on the underside of the penis) may be associated with environmental estrogens. Exposure to diethylstilbestrol has been shown to increase the risk in women of breast cancer, endometriosis, ectopic pregnancy, preterm birth, and spontaneous abortion.
4. Organochlorine exposure increases the risk of spontaneous abortion, neural tube defects, reduced sperm count and quality, low birth weight, shorter birth length, and smaller head circumference. Prenatal exposure to DDT, and to a lesser extent DDE, is associated with neurodevelopmental delays during early childhood.
5. PCBs and BPA have also been implicated in reproductive disorders in humans.

Exercises

Key Terms

Define the following terms.

Bioaccumulation	Mercury
Bisphenol A	Methylmercury
Cadmium	Organochlorines
Endocrine system	Organophosphates
Environmental estrogens	Pesticides
Estrogen	Polychlorinated biphenyls
Lead	Pyrethroids

Study Questions

10.1 Describe the effects that lead exposure has on male fertility and female reproduction ability.

10.2 What types of fish most commonly contain high levels of methylmercury? What is the risk posed to Americans by eating them?

10.3 Explain the risk that hormone disruptors have on human health.

10.4 What are PCBs, and how have they been shown to affect reproductive health?

References

1. Merrill RM. *Environmental Epidemiology: Principles and Methods.* Sudbury, MA: Jones and Bartlett Publishers; 2008.
2. Bhatt RV. Environmental influence on reproductive health. *Int J Gynaecol Obstet.* 2000;70(1):69–75.
3. Kumar S. Occupational exposure associated with reproductive dysfunction. *J Occup Health.* 2004;46(1):1–19.
4. Sharpe RM, Irvine DS. How strong is the evidence of a link between environmental chemicals and adverse effects on human reproductive health? *BMJ.* 2004;328:447–451.
5. Agency for Toxic Substances and Disease Registry. National alert. a warning about continuing patterns of metallic mercury exposure. 1997. Available at: http://permanent .access.gpo.gov/lps21/970626.html. Accessed February 21, 2009.
6. Agency for Toxic Substances and Disease Registry. Toxicological profile for mercury. 1999. Available at: http://www.atsdr.cdc.gov/toxprofiles/tp46.pdf. Accessed February 14, 2009.
7. Wheeler M. Measuring mercury. *Environ Health Perspect.* 1998;106(3). Available at: http://www.ehponline.org/docs/1996/104-8/focus.html. Accessed February 18, 2009.

8. Magos L. Mercury blood interaction and mercury uptake by brain. *Environ Res.* 1967;1:323–337.

9. U.S. Environmental Protection Agency. Methylmercury (MeHg), 2008. Available at: http://www.epa.gov/iris/subst/0073.htm. Accessed February 18, 2009.

10. Grandjean P, Weihe P, Jorgensen PJ, Clarkson T, Cernichiari E, Videro T. Impact of maternal seafood diet on fetal exposure to mercury, selenium, and lead. *Arch Environ Health.* 1992;47:185–195.

11. Fok TF, Lam HS, Ng PC, et al. Fetal methylmercury exposure as measured by cord blood mercury concentrations in a mother-infant cohort in Hong Kong. *Environ Int.* 2007;33(1):84–92.

12. Ramón R, Murcia M, Ballester F, et al. Prenatal exposure to mercury in a prospective mother-infant cohort study in a Mediterranean area, Valencia, Spain. *Sci Total Environ.* 2008;392(1):69–78.

13. Grandjean P, Weihe P, White RF, Debes F, Araki S, Murata K. Cognitive deficit in 7-year-old children with prenatal exposure to methylmercury. *Neurotoxicology.* 1997;19: 417–428.

14. Grandjean P, Murata K, Budtz-Jorgensen E, Weihe P. Cardiac autonomic activity in methylmercury neurotoxicity. *J Pediatr.* 2004;144(2):169–176.

15. U.S. Environmental Protection Agency. Mercury: health effects, 2008. Available at: http://www.epa.gov/mercury/effects.htm. Accessed February 18, 2009.

16. Oken E, Bellinger DC. Fish consumption, methylmercury and child neurodevelopment. *Curr Opin Pediatr.* 2008;20(2):178–183.

17. Lederman SA, Jones RL, Caldwell KL, et al. Relation between cord blood mercury levels and early child development in a World Trade Center cohort. *Environ Health Perspect.* 2008;116(8):1085–1091.

18. Cohen JT, Bellinger DC, Shaywitz BA. A quantitative analysis of prenatal methyl mercury exposure and cognitive development. *Am J Prev Med.* 2005;29(4):353–365.

19. Xue F, Holzman C, Rahbar MH, Trosko K, Fischer L. Maternal fish consumption, mercury levels, and risk of preterm delivery. *Environ Health Perspect.* 2007;115(1):42–47.

20. Elghany NA, Stopford W, Bunn WB, Fleming LE. Occupational exposure to inorganic mercury vapour and reproductive outcomes. *Occup Med (Lond).* 1997;47(6):333–336.

21. Davis BJ, Price HC, O'Connor RW, Fernando R, Rowland AS, Morgan DL. Mercury vapor and female reproductive toxicity. *Toxicol Sci.* 2001;59(2):291–296.

22. De Rosis F, Anastasio SP, Selvaggi L, Beltrame A, Moriani G. Female reproductive health in two lamp factories: effects of exposure to inorganic mercury vapour and stress factors. *Br J Ind Med.* 1985;42:488–494.

23. Goncharuk GA. Problems relating to the occupational hygiene of women in production of mercury. *Gig Tr Prof Zabol.* 1977;5:17–20.

24. Marinova G, Chakarov O, Kaneva YA. A study of reproductive function of women working with mercury. *Probl Akush Ginekol.* 1973;1:75–77.

25. Mikhailova LM, Kobyets GP, Lyubomudrov VE, Braga GF. The influence of occupational factors on diseases of the female reproductive organs. *Pediatr Akush Ginekol.* 1971; 33:56–58.

26. Panova Z, Dimitrov G. The ovarian function in women with occupational exposure to metallic mercury. *Akush Ginekol.* 1974;13:29–34.

27. Sikorski R, Juszkiewicz T, Paszkowski T, Szprengier-Juszkiewicz T. Women in dental surgeries: reproductive hazards in occupational exposure to metallic mercury. *Int Arch Occup Environ Health.* 1987;59(6):551–557.

28. Rowland AS. The effect of occupational exposure to mercury vapor on the fertility of female dental assistants. *Occup Environ Med.* 1994;51:28–34.

29. Centers for Disease Control and Prevention. CDC's third national report on human exposure to environmental chemicals. Spotlight on mercury. 2005. Available at: http://www.cdc.gov/exposurereport/pdf/factsheet_mercury.pdf. Accessed February 18, 2009.

30. Jones RL, Sinks T, Schober SE, Pickett M. Blood mercury levels in young children and childbearing-aged women—United States, 1999–2002. *MMWR.* 2004;53(43):1018–1020.

31. Schober SE, Sinks TH, Jones RL, et al. Blood mercury levels in US children and women of childbearing age, 1999–2000. *JAMA.* 2003;289(13):1667–1674.

32. Mahaffey KR, Clickner RP, Jeffries RA. Adult women's blood mercury concentrations vary regionally in the United States: association with patterns of fish consumption (NHANES 1999-2004). *Environ Health Perpect.* 2009;117:47–53.

33. U.S. Environmental Protection Agency. Air trends: lead, 2008. Available at: http://epa.gov/air/airtrends/lead.html. Accessed February 18, 2009.

34. U.S. Environmental Protection Agency. Air emission sources: lead, 2008. Available at: http://epa.gov/air/emissions/pb.htm. Accessed February 18, 2009.

35. Agency for Toxic Substances & Disease Registry. *Lead Toxicity: What Are the Physiologic Effects of Lead Exposure?* Atlanta, GA: U.S. Department of Health and Human Services, Public Health Service, 2007. Available at: http://www.atsdr.cdc.gov/csem/lead/pbphysiologic_effects2.html. Accessed February 18, 2009.

36. National Center for Environmental Health. Preventing lead poisoning in young children. Available at: http://www.cdc.gov/nceh/lead/Publications/books/plpyc/tables.htm#Table%203-1. Accessed February 18, 2009.

37. Grandjean P, Bach E. Indirect exposures: the significance of bystanders at work and at home. *Am Ind Hyg Assoc J.* 1986;47:819–824.

38. Maizlish N, Rudolph L, Sutton P, Jones JR, Kizer KW. Elevated blood lead in California adults, 1987: results of a statewide surveillance program based on laboratory reports. *Am J Public Health.* 1990;80:931–934.

39. Benoff S, Centola GM, Millan C, Napolitano B, Marmar JL, Hurley IR. Increased seminal plasma lead levels adversely affect the fertility potential of sperm in IVF. *Hum Reprod.* 2003;18:374–383.

40. Agency for Toxic Substances and Disease Registry. *Toxicological Profile for Lead.* Atlanta, GA: U.S. Department of Health and Human Services, Public Health Service; 2005.

41. Hertz-Picciotto I, Schramm M, Watt-Morse M, Chantala K, Anderson J, Osterloh J. Patterns and determinants of blood lead during pregnancy *Am J Epidemiol.* 2000;152(9): 829–837.

42. Agency for Toxic Substances and Disease Registry. *Toxicological Profile for Lead.* Atlanta, GA: U.S. Department of Health and Human Services, Public Health Service; 1999.

43. Canfield RL, Henderson CR Jr, Cory-Slechta DA, Cox C, Jusko TA, Lanphear BP. Intellectual impairment in children with blood lead concentrations below 10 microg per deciliter. *N Engl J Med.* 2003;348(16):1517–1526.

44. Centers for Disease Control and Prevention. *Screening Young Children for Lead Poisoning: Guidance for State and Local Public Health Officials.* Atlanta, GA: U.S. Department of

Health and Human Services, Public Health Service, CDC Childhood Lead Poisoning Prevention Program; 1997.

45. Hu H, Aro A, Payton M, et al. The relationship of bone and blood lead to hypertension. The normative aging study. *JAMA.* 1996;275:1171–1176.

46. Korrick SA, Hunter DJ, Rotnitzky A, Hu H, Speizer FE. Lead and hypertension in a sample of middle-aged women. *Am J Public Health.* 1999;89(3):330–335.

47. Mendola P, Messer LC, Rappazzo K. Science linking environmental contaminant exposures with fertility and reproductive health impacts in the adult female. *Fertil Steril.* 2008;89(1):81–94.

48. Schwartz J. Lead, blood pressure, and cardiovascular disease in men. *Arch Environ Health.* 1995;50:31–37.

49. Victery W, Throler HA, Volpe R, et al. Summary of discussion sessions: symposium on lead blood pressure relationships. *Environ Health Perspect.* 1988;78:139–155.

50. Alexander H, Checkoway H, van Netten C, et al. Semen quality of men employed at a lead smelter. *Occup Environ Med.* 1996;53:411–416.

51. Gennart JP, Buchet JP, Roels H, Ghyselen P, Ceulemans E, Lauwerys R. Fertility of male workers exposed to cadmium, lead or manganese. *Am J Epidemiol.* 1992;135: 1208–1219.

52. Lerda D. Study of sperm characteristics in persons occupationally exposed to lead. *Am J Ind Med.* 1992;22:567–571.

53. Lin S, Hwang S, Marshall EG, Stone R, Chen J. Fertility rates among lead workers and professional bus drivers: a comparative study. *Ann Epidemiol.* 1996;6:201–208.

54. Telisman S, Cvitkovic P, Jurasovic J, Pizent A, Gavella M, Rocic B. Semen quality and reproductive endocrine function in relation to biomarkers of lead, cadmium, zinc, and copper in men. *Environ Health Perspect.* 2000;108:45–53.

55. Benoff S, Centola GM, Millan C, Napolitano B, Marmar JL, Hurley IR. Increased seminal plasma lead levels adversely affect the fertility potential of sperm in IVF. *Hum Reprod.* 2003;18:374–383.

56. Nordstrom S, Beckman L, Nordenson I. Occupational and environmental risks in and around a smelter in northern Sweden. V. Spontaneous abortion among female employees and decreased birth weight in their offspring. *Hereditas.* 1979; 90:291–296.

57. Borja-Aburto VH, Hertz-Picciotto I, Rojas Lopez M, Farias P, Rios C, Blanco J. Blood lead levels measured prospectively and risk of spontaneous abortion. *Am J Epidemiol.* 1999;150(6):590.

58. Baghurst PA, Robertson EF, McMichael AJ, Vimpani GV, Wigg NR, Roberts RR. The Port Pirie cohort study: lead effects on pregnancy outcome and early childhood development. *Neurotoxicology.* 1987;8:395–401.

59. McMichael AJ, Vimpani GV, Robertson EF, Baghurst PA, Clark PD. The Port Pirie cohort study: maternal blood lead and pregnancy outcome. *J Epidemiol Commun Health.* 1986;40:18–25.

60. Agency for toxic substances and disease registry. Division of toxicology and environmental medicine ToxFAQs™. Cadmium, 2008. Available at: http://www.atsdr.cdc.gov/tfacts5.pdf. Accessed February 18, 2008.

61. Lauwerys RR. *Health Maintenance of Workers Exposed to Cadmium.* New York: The Cadmium Council, Inc.; 1986.

62. World Health Organization. *Environmental Health Criteria 134—Cadmium International Programme on Chemical Safety (IPCS) Monograph.* Geneva, Switzerland: World Health Organization; 1992.

63. Agency for Toxic Substances and Disease Registry. *Toxicological Profile for Cadmium. Draft for Public Comment.* Atlanta, GA: U.S. Department of Health and Human Services; 1997.

64. Agency for Toxic Substances and Disease Registry. The Agency for Toxic Substances and Disease Registry, the U.S. Department of Health and Human Services. Prepared by Research Triangle Institute. *Toxicological Profile for Cadmium.* Atlanta, GA: U.S. Department of Health and Human Services; 1999.

65. Andersen O, Nielsen JB, Nordberg GF. Nutritional interactions in intestinal cadmium uptake: possibilities for risk reduction. *BioMetals.* 2004;17(5):543–547.

66. Henson MC, Chedrese PJ. Endocrine disruption by cadmium, a common environmental toxicant with paradoxical effects on reproduction. *Exp Biol Med.* 2004;229(5):383–392.

67. Akesson A, Berglund M, Schütz A, Bjellerup P, Bremme K, Vahter M. Cadmium exposure in pregnancy and lactation in relation to iron status. *Am J Public Health.* 2002;92(2): 284–287.

68. Thompson J, Bannigan J. Cadmium: toxic effects on the reproductive system and the embryo. *Reprod Toxicol.* 2008;25(3):304–315.

69. Xu B, Chia SE, Tsakok M, Ong CN. Trace elements in blood and seminal plasma and their relationship to sperm quality. *Reprod Toxicol.* 1993;7(6):613–618.

70. Xu DX, Shen HM, Zhu QX, et al. The associations among semen quality, oxidative DNA damage in human spermatozoa and concentrations of cadmium, lead and selenium in seminal plasma. *Mutat Res.* 2003;534(1–2):155–163.

71. Akinloye O, Arowojolu AO, Shittu OB, Anetor JI. Cadmium toxicity: a possible cause of male infertility in Nigeria. *Reprod Biol.* 2006;6(1):17–30.

72. Llanos MN, Ronco AM. Fetal growth restriction is related to placental levels of cadmium, lead and arsenic but not with antioxidant activities. *Reprod Toxicol.* 2009;27(1):88–92.

73. Nishijo M, Nakagawa H, Honda R, et al. Effects of maternal exposure to cadmium on pregnancy outcome and breast milk. *Occup Environ Med.* 2002;59(6):394–396; discussion 397.

74. Nishijo M, Tawara K, Honda R, Nakagawa H, Tanebe K, Saito S. Relationship between newborn size and mother's blood cadmium levels, Toyama, Japan. *Arch Environ Health.* 2004;59(1):22–25.

75. Odland JO, Nieboer E, Romanova N, Thomassen Y, Lund E. Blood lead and cadmium and birth weight among sub-arctic and arctic populations of Norway and Russia. *Acta Obstet Gynecol Scand.* 1999;78(10):852–860.

76. Salpietro CD, Gangemi S, Minciullo PL, et al. Cadmium concentration in maternal and cord blood and infant birth weight: a study on healthy non-smoking women. *J Perinat Med.* 2002;30(5):395–399.

77. Stedman TL. *Stedman's Medical Dictionary for the Health Professions and Nursing*, 5th ed. New York, NY: Lippincott, Williams & Wilkins; 2005.

78. Jobling S, Reynolds T, White R, Parker MG, Sumpter JP. A variety of environmentally persistent chemicals, including some phthalate plasticizers, are weakly estrogenic. *Environ Health Perspect.* 1995;103(6):582–587.

79. MacLusky NJ, Hajszan T, Leranth C. The environmental estrogen bisphenol A inhibits estradiol-induced hippocampal synaptogenesis. *Environ Health Perspect.* 2005;113(6):675–679.

80. Sonnenschein C, Soto AM. An updated review of environmental estrogen and androgen mimics and antagonists. *J Steroid Biochem Mol Biol.* 1998;65(1–6):143–150.

81. Trankina ML. The hazards of environmental estrogens, 2001. Available at: http://www.worldandi.com/public/2001/October/ee.html. Accessed February 14, 2009.

82. Blankespoor J. Our chemical world: Juliet Blankespoor explains environmental toxins' effects on women (and the rest of us). *New Life Journal.* 2006. Available at: http://www.accessmylibrary.com/coms2/summary_0286-32171221_ITM. Accessed February 21, 2009.

83. Barrett JR. Fertile grounds for inquiry, environmental effects on human reproduction. *Environ Health Perspect.* 2006;114(11):644–649.

84. Hutson JM, Williams MPL, Fallat ME, Attah A. Testicular descent: new insights into its hormonal control. In: Milligan SR, ed. *Oxford Reviews of Reproductive Biology.* Oxford, England: Oxford University Press; 1990:1–56.

85. Carlsen E, Giwercman A, Keiding N, Skakkebaek NE. Evidence for decreasing quality of semen during past 50 years. *BMJ.* 1992;305:609–613.

86. Giwercman A, Carlsen E, Keiding N, Skakkebaek NE. Evidence for increasing incidence of abnormalities of the human testis: a review. *Environ Health Perspect.* 1993;101(2):65–71.

87. Skakkebaek NE. Carcinoma-in-situ and cancer of the testis. *Int J Androl.* 1987;10:1–40.

88. Jensen TK, Toppari J, Keiding N, Skakkebaek NE. Do environmental estrogens contribute to the decline in male reproductive health? *Clin Chem.* 1995;41(12 Pt 2):1896–1901.

89. Abell A, Ernst E, Bonde JP. Semen quality and sexual hormones in greenhouse workers. *Scand J Work Environ Health.* 2000;26(6):492–500.

90. Hanke W, Jurewicz J. The risk of adverse reproductive and developmental disorders due to occupational pesticide exposure: an overview of current epidemiological evidence. *Int J Occup Med Environ Health.* 2004;17(2):223–243.

91. Sharpe RM, Skakkebaek NE. Are oestrogens involved in falling sperm counts and disorders of the male reproductive tract? *The Lancet.* 1993;341:1392–1395.

92. Swan SH, Kruse RL, Fan Liu Barr DB, et al. Semen quality in relation to biomarkers of pesticide exposure. *Environ Health Perspect.* 2003;111(12):1478.

93. Damgaard IN, Skakkebæk NE, Toppari J, et al. Persistent pesticides in human breast milk and cryptorchidism. *Environ Health Perspect.* 2006;114(7):133–138.

94. Andersen HR, Schmidt IM, Grandjean P, et al. Impaired reproductive development in sons of women occupationally exposed to pesticides during pregnancy. *Environ Health Perspect.* 2008;116(4):566–572.

95. Fernandez MF, Olmos B, Granada A, et al. Human exposure to endocrine-disrupting chemicals and prenatal risk factors for cryptorchidism and hypospadias: a nested case-control study. *Environ Health Perspect.* 2007;115(1):8–14.

96. Giordano F, Carbone P, Nori F, Mantovani A, Taruscio D, Figà-Talamanca I. Maternal diet and the risk of hypospadias and cryptorchidism in the offspring. *Paediatr Perinat Epidemiol.* 2008;22(3):249–260.

97. Safe S. Environmental estrogens: roles in male reproductive tract problems and in breast cancer. *Rev Environ Health.* 2002;17(4):253–262.

98. Palmer JR, Wise LA, Hatch EE, et al. Prenatal diethylstilbestrol exposure and risk of breast cancer. *Cancer Epidemiol Biomarkers Prev.* 2006;15(8):1509–1514.

99. Pavuk M, Cerhan JR, Lynch CF, Kocan A, Petrik J, Chovancova J. Case-control study of PCBs, other organochlorines and breast cancer in Eastern Slovakia. *J Expo Anal Environ Epidemiol.* 2003;13(4):267–275.

100. Kaufman RH, Adam E, Hatch EE, et al. Continued follow-up of pregnancy outcomes in diethylstilbestrol-exposed offspring. *Obstet Gynecol.* 2000;96(4):483–489.

101. Missmer SA, Hankinson SE, Spiegelman D, Barbieri RL, Michels KB, Hunter DJ. In utero exposures and the incidence of endometriosis. *Fertil Steril.* 2004;82(6):1501–1508.

102. Wolff MS, Toniolo PG, Lee EW, Rivera M, Dubin N. Blood levels of organochlorine residues and risk of breast cancer. *J Nat Can Inst.* 1993;85(8):648–652.

103. Wolff MS, Toniolo PG. Environmental organochlorine exposure as a potential etiologic factor in breast cancer. *Environ Health Perspect.* 1995;103(Suppl 7):141–145.

104. Sharpe RM. Declining sperm counts in men? Is there an endocrine cause? *J Endocrinol.* 1993;136:357–360.

105. U.S. Environmental Protection Agency. What is a pesticide? 1997. Available at: http://entweb.clemson.edu/pesticid/document/EPAdef.htm. Accessed February 18, 2009.

106. Arbuckle TE, Lin Z, Mery LS. An exploratory analysis of the effect of pesticide exposure on the risk of spontaneous abortion in an Ontario farm population. *Environ Health Perspect.* 2001;109(8):851–857.

107. Bretveld RW, Hooiveld M, Zielhuis GA, Pellegrino A, van Rooij IA, Roeleveld N. Reproductive disorders among male and female greenhouse workers. *Reprod Toxicol.* 2008;25(1):107–114.

108. Settimi L, Spinelli A, Lauria L, et al. Spontaneous abortion and maternal work in greenhouses. *Am J Ind Med.* 2008;51(4):290–295.

109. Shirangi A, Fritschi L, Holman CD. Maternal occupational exposures and risk of spontaneous abortion in veterinary practice. *Occup Environ Med.* 2008;65(11):719–725.

110. Garry VF, Harkins ME, Erickson LL, Long-Simpson LK, Holland SE, Burroughs BL. Birth defects, season of conception, and sex of children born to pesticide applicators living in the Red River Valley of Minnesota, USA. *Environ Health Perspect.* 2002; 110(3):441–449.

111. Lacasaña M, Vázquez-Grameix H, Borja-Aburto VH, et al. Maternal and paternal occupational exposure to agricultural work and the risk of anencephaly. *Occup Environ Med.* 2006;63(10):649–656.

112. Rull RP, Ritz B, Shaw GM. Neural tube defects and maternal residential proximity to agricultural pesticide applications. *Am J Epidemiol.* 2006;163(8):743–753.

113. Shaw GM, Wasserman CR, O'Malley CD, Nelson V, Jackson RJ. Maternal pesticide exposure from multiple sources and selected congenital anomalies. *Epidemiology.* 1999; 10(1):60–66.

114. Winchester PD, Huskins J, Ying J. Agrichemicals in surface water and birth defects in the United States. *Acta Paediatr.* 2009 [Epub ahead of print].

115. Garry VF, Holland SE, Erickson LL, Burroughs BL. Male reproductive hormones and thyroid function in pesticide applicators in the Red River Valley of Minnesota. *J Toxicol Environ Health A.* 2003;66(11):965–986.

116. Meeker JD, Barr DB, Hauser R. Human semen quality and sperm DNA damage in relation to urinary metabolites of pyrethroid insecticides. *Hum Reprod.* 2008;23(8):1932–1940.

117. Roeleveld N, Bretveld R. The impact of pesticides on male fertility. *Curr Opin Obstet Gynecol.* 2008;20(3):229–233.

118. Yucra S, Gasco M, Rubio J, Gonzales GF. Semen quality in Peruvian pesticide applicators: association between urinary organophosphate metabolites and semen parameters. *Environ Health.* 2008;17(7):59.

119. Kabanywanyi AM, Macarthur JR, Stolk WA, et al. Malaria in pregnant women in an area with sustained high coverage of insecticide-treated bed nets. *Malar J.* 2008;7:133.

120. Sagiv SK, Tolbert PE, Altshul LM, Korrick SA. Organochlorine exposures during pregnancy and infant size at birth. *Epidemiology.* 2007;18(1):120–129.

121. Tan J, Loganath A, Chong YS, Obbard JP. Exposure to persistent organic pollutants in utero and related maternal characteristics on birth outcomes: a multivariate data analysis approach. *Chemosphere.* 2009;74(3):428–433.

122. Wolff MS, Engel S, Berkowitz G, et al. Prenatal pesticide and PCB exposures and birth outcomes. *Pediatr Res.* 2007;61(2):243–250.

123. Eskenazi B, Marks AR, Bradman A, et al. In utero exposure to dichlorodiphenyltrichloroethane (DDT) and dichlorodiphenyl dichloroethylene (DDE) and neurodevelopment among young Mexican American children. *Pediatrics.* 2006;118(1):233–241.

124. U.S. Environmental Protection Agency. Common mechanism groups; cumulative exposure and risk assessment, 2008. Available at: http://www.epa.gov/pesticides/cumulative/common_mech_groups.htm#op. Accessed February 18, 2009.

125. U.S. Environmental Protection Agency. Permethrin, resmethrin, sumithrin: synthetic pyrethroids for mosquito control, 2002. Available at: http://www.epa.gov/pesticides/health/mosquitoes/pyrethroids4mosquitoes.htm. Accessed February 18, 2009.

126. U.S. Environmental Protection Agency. Accomplishments under the Food Quality Protection Act (FQPA), 2006. Available at: http://134.67.99.207/pesticides/regulating/laws/fqpa/fqpa_accomplishments.htm. Accessed February 18, 2009.

127. U.S. Environmental Protection Agency. Tolerance reassessment, 2009. Available at: http://www.epa.gov/oppsrrd1/tolerance/reassessment.htm. Accessed February 18, 2009.

128. Agency for Toxic Substances and Disease Registry. *ToxFAQs for Polychlorinated Biphenyls (PCBs).* Atlanta, GA: U.S. Department of Health and Human Services, Public Health Service. 2001. Available at: http://www.atsdr.cdc.gov/tfacts17.html#bookmark02. Accessed February 20, 2009.

129. Fein GG, Jacobson JL, Jacobson SW, Schwartz PM, Dowler JK. Prenatal exposure to polychlorinated biphenyls: effects on birth size and gestational age. *J Pediatr.* 1984;105(2):315–320.

130. Patandin S, Koopman-Esseboom C, de Ridder MA, Weisglas-Kuperus N, Sauer PJ. Effects of environmental exposure to polychlorinated biphenyls and dioxins on birth size and growth in Dutch children. *Pediatr Res.* 1998;44(4):538–545.

131. Patandin S, Lanting CI, Mulder PG, Boersma ER, Sauer PJ, Weisglas-Kuperus N. Effects of environmental exposure to polychlorinated biphenyls and dioxins on cognitive abilities in Dutch children at 42 months of age. *J Pediatr.* 1999;134(1):33–41.

132. Jacobson JL, Jacobson SW, Humphrey HE. Effects of in utero exposure to polychlorinated biphenyls and related contaminants on cognitive functioning in young children. *J Pediatr.* 1990;116(1):38–45.

133. Jacobson JL, Jacobson SW. Intellectual impairment in children exposed to polychlorinated biphenyls in utero. *N Engl J Med.* 1996;335(11):783–789.

134. Boersma ER, Lanting CI. Environmental exposure to polychlorinated biphenyls (PCBs) and dioxins. Consequences for long term neurological and cognitive development of the child lactation. *Adv Exp Med Biol.* 2000;478:271–287.

135. Tsukimori K, Tokunaga S, Shibata S, et al. Long-term effects of polychlorinated biphenyls and dioxins on pregnancy outcomes in women affected by the Yusho incident. *Environ Health Perspect.* 2008;116(5):626–630.

136. Environment and Human Health, Inc. Plastics that may be harmful to children and reproductive health. Available at: http://www.ehhi.org/reports/plastics/bpa_health_effects .shtml. Accessed February 20, 2009.

137. Maffini MV, Rubin BS, Sonnenschein C, Soto AM. Endocrine disruptors and reproductive health: the case of bisphenol-A. *Mol Cell Endocrinol.* 2006;254–255, 179–186.

138. vom Saal FS, Akingbemi BT, Belcher SM, et al. Chapel Hill bisphenol A expert panel consensus statement: Integration of mechanisms, effects in animals and potential to impact human health at current levels of exposure. *Reprod Toxicol.* 2007;24(2):131–138.

139. Sugiura-Ogasawara M, Ozaki Y, Sonta S, Makino T, Suzumori K. Exposure to bisphenol A is associated with recurrent miscarriage. *Hum Reprod.* 2005;20:2325–2329.

140. Wiener J, Rogers MD. Comparing precaution in the United States and Europe. *J Risk Res.* 2002;5(4):317–349.

141. Andersson A, Skakkebaek N. Exposure to exogenous estrogens in food: possible impact on human development and health. *Eur J Endocrinol.* 1999;140(6):477–485.

142. Swan SH, Liu F, Overstreet JW, Brazil C, Skakkebaek NE. Semen quality of fertile US males in relation to their mothers' beef consumption during pregnancy. *Hum Reprod.* 2007;22(6):1497–1502.

ELEVEN

Psychosocial Factors and Reproductive Health

Learning Objectives

After completing this chapter, you should be able to:

1. Describe major trends in marriage, cohabitation, and babies born to unmarried women.
2. Describe the association between marriage and physical and mental health.
3. Discuss potential social and health problems related to having children outside of marriage.
4. Describe some of the unique social and health problems experienced by pregnant teenagers.
5. Describe trends in legal abortions in the United States, England, and Wales and patterns of legal abortions worldwide.
6. Identify some of the potential social and physical health challenges associated with abortion.
7. Describe why many countries may still practice female circumcision.
8. Describe some of the health risks associated with female circumcision.

By its very nature, reproduction and the issues pertaining to it are an integral part of society, and the links between reproductive practices and society are many and varied. For example, social norms help to structure the way women view reproduction—these views can help determine the number and the spacing of children, which can have a considerable impact on maternal health. The use of contraceptives in family planning crosses religious and societal lines and societies grapple with illegal or unsanitary abortions. In addition, the world has had to consider ethical implications of genome research, genetic engineering, and cloning. A comprehensive list of societal concerns related to reproduction would be difficult to compile, simply because the social effects of reproduction are so all-encompassing. Hence, this chapter considers only the pressing issues of marriage, clinical abortion, and female circumcision, allowing for further, more comprehensive discussion elsewhere.

Marriage is a socially accepted practice worldwide, clinical abortions are gaining greater acceptance worldwide, and female circumcision is a social custom in developing African nations. These practices are all associated with health. The purpose of this chapter is to examine associations between marriage and health, clinical abortions and health, and female circumcision practices and health.

Marriage

Marital Trends

In the United States, the percentage of the male population aged 15 years and older who are married dropped from 68% in 1950 to 56% in 2007. Corresponding percentages for females are 66% and 54%, respectively. The percentage of people who never married increased from 26% to 33% for males and 20% to 26% for females during this same time period.[1] In addition, the estimated age at first marriage increased from 22.8 for males and 20.3 for females in 1950 to 27.5 for males and 25.6 for females in 2007 (see **Figure 11-1**).

Decreasing marriage prevalence in the United States is not unlike many selected places throughout the world (see **Table 11-1**).[2,3] In 2006, the lowest marriage rates were in Ireland, Italy, and Luxembourg, and the highest marriage rates were in Romania, the United States, and Russia. Countries with the greatest decrease in marriage rates were in Western, Eastern, and Southern Europe; however, increases in marriage rates were observed in Northern Europe. In all but 4 of the 27 countries, rates are falling.

FIGURE 11-1 *Estimated Median Age at First Marriage, by Gender: 1950–2007*

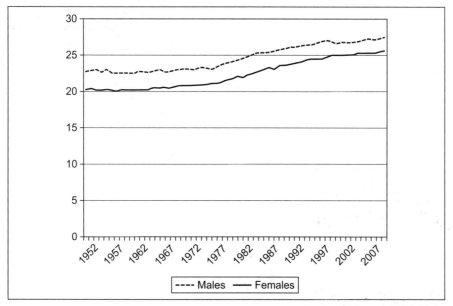

---- Males ——— Females

Source: U.S. Census Bureau, Current Population Survey, March and Annual Social and Economic Supplements, 2007 and earlier. Available at: http://www.census.gov/population/www/socdemo/hh-fam.html. Accessed February 15, 2009.

In England and Wales, the distribution of marriage across the age span changed noticeably between 1991 and 2005 (see **Figure 11-2**).[4] In 1991, 75% of all marriages that occurred were among people in the age groups up through 30 to 34 years. In contrast, in 2005 this percentage was 56%.

In many Western European nations, there have been dramatic increases in unmarried cohabitation and having children outside of marriage.[5] Cohabitation patterns across selected European nations are presented in **Table 11-2**. In many European nations, there is a large proportion of couple cohabitation, with cohabitation more common than marriage in many nations. Couples in the younger age group were much more likely to begin their first partnership by cohabitating. Partnerships in Italy were most likely to begin directly with marriage. On the other hand, partnerships in Sweden were least likely to begin directly with marriage. Age had the biggest impact on being married directly in Norway and France, but the smallest impact on being married directly was in Sweden, Spain,

TABLE 11-1	*Crude Marriage Rates Per 1,000 People for Selected Countries*			

	1990	1999	2006	Percent Change 1990 to 2006
Australia	6.9	6	5.4	–22%
Austria	5.8	4.8	4.5	–22%
Belgium	6.6	4.3	4.3	–35%
Bulgaria	6.7	4.2	4.3	–36%
Czech Republic	8.4	5.2	5.1	–39%
Denmark	6.1	6.6	6.7	10%
Finland	4.8	4.7	5.4	13%
France	5.1	—	4.4	–14%
Germany	6.5	5.2	4.5	–31%
Greece	5.8	6.4	5.2	–10%
Hungary	6.4	4.5	4.4	–31%
Ireland	5	4.9	4.1	–18%
Israel	7	5.9	5.9	–16%
Italy	5.4	—	4.1	–24%
Japan	5.8	6.3	5.8	0%
Luxembourg	6.2	4.9	4.1	–34%
Netherlands	6.4	5.6	4.4	–31%
New Zealand	7	5.3	5.1	–27%
Norway	5.2	5.3	4.7	–10%
Poland	6.7	5.7	5.9	–12%
Portugal	7.3	6.8	4.5	–38%
Romania	8.3	6.5	6.8	–18%
Russia	8.9	5.8	7.8	–12%
Sweden	4.7	4	5	6%
Switzerland	6.9	4.9	5.3	–23%
United Kingdom	6.8	5.1	5.1	–25%
United States	9.8	8.3	7.2	–27%

Source: United Nations, Monthly Bulletin of Statistics, April 2001. Available at: http://www.infoplease.com/ipa/A0004385.html. Accessed February 26, 2009. United Nations Statistics Division, Demographic Yearbook. Table 23. Available at: http://unstats.un.org/unsd/demographic/products/dyb/dyb2006.htm. Accessed February 26, 2009.

and Italy. Of those where cohabitation represented their first partnership, 48% resulted in marriage in the age group 25 to 29 years, and 62% resulted in marriage in the age group 35 to 39 years. The lowest percentage resulting in marriage was in East Germany and Spain. The highest percentage resulting in marriage was in Norway, Switzerland, and Italy.

FIGURE 11-2 *Marriage in England and Wales According to Age and Calendar Year*

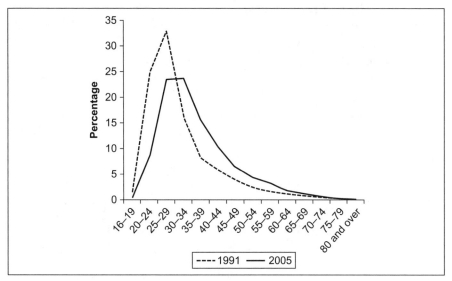

Source: National Statistics. UK snapshot neighbourhood economy census. Marriages: age at marriage by sex and previous marital status, 1991, 2001 and 2003–2005. Population trends 127. Available at: http://www.statistics.gov.uk/STATBASE/ssdataset.asp?vlnk=9599. Accessed February 26, 2009.

The risk of marital dissolution in a first marriage (or first partnership) in Western Europe for those aged 10 to 39 years is significantly greater in women who began the partnership by cohabitating compared with directly marrying. For example, the risk of marital dissolution among those whose first partnership began with cohabitation, after adjusting for age at first marriage, church attendance, and experience of parental divorce, was 58% greater in Sweden, 63% greater in France, 28% greater in Switzerland, 42% greater in West Germany, and 38% greater in East Germany.[5] The risk of dissolution of the partnership for women cohabitating compared with women who directly married, after adjusting for age at first marriage, church attendance, and experience of parental divorce, was 296% greater in Sweden, 392% greater in Norway, 244% greater in Finland, 504% greater in France, 208% greater in Austria, 384% greater in Switzerland, 207% greater in West Germany, and 55% greater in East Germany.

TABLE 11-2   *Type of First Partnership Among Women With a First Partnership According to Age Group at the Time of the Survey*

	Married Directly	Cohabited and Married	Cohabited	Married Directly	Cohabited and Married	Cohabited
	Ages 25–29 years			Ages 35–39 years		
Sweden	7	41	52	8	62	30
Norway	24	40	35	62	30	7
Finland	17	43	40	31	46	23
France	21	34	45	55	33	12
Great Britain	37	33	31	72	18	10
Austria	19	41	40	30	42	28
Switzerland	19	44	37	30	52	18
West Germany	16	38	46	38	33	29
East Germany	15	35	50	21	26	53
Spain	80	8	12	91	4	5
Italy	86	8	6	91	5	4

Source: Kiernan K. The rise of cohabitation and childbearing outside marriage in Western Europe. *Int J Law Policy Fam.* 2001;15:1–21.

Kiernan found that in Western European nations, those who had children within marriage were more likely to stay together (i.e., not separate) than those who had children within cohabiting unions.[6]

Bramlett and Mosher (2002) used data from Cycle 5 of the National Survey of Family Growth to calculate the probabilities of several specific events associated with marriage.[7] They found that non-Hispanic Black women had a lower probability of first marriage than other women. When compared with all women, the probability of an intact premarital cohabiting union turning into a marriage was higher for White women and lower for Black women. Black women had a higher probability of a premarital cohabiting union breaking up than White and Hispanic women. Asian women were less likely to experience first marital disruption, and Black women were more likely. White women were more likely than Black women to enter a new cohabiting union after the first marriage ended. White women who were separated were more likely to complete the legal divorce process than Black or Hispanic women who were separated. White divorced women had the highest probability of remarriage, whereas Black divorced women had the lowest probability. Second marriages were more likely to break up for Black women than for other women.

Trends in Births to Unmarried Women

As marriage rates decrease, a larger percentage of children being born outside of marriage might be expected. In the United States, for example, the percentage of births to unmarried women increased from 1975 to 2003 in all age groups (see **Figure 11-3**).[8] For all ages combined, there was a 76% increase. The increase was greater than 53% in all age groups, except under age 15 years, where the increase was 10%. The greatest increase was in women ages 25 to 29 years, with an increase of 80%. The increase in the percentage of all births to unmarried women has occurred with non-Hispanic Whites, non-Hispanic Blacks, and Hispanics. For example, between 1980 and 2005, percentages increased from 9.6%

FIGURE 11-3 *Percentage of Births to Unmarried Women in the United States by Age Group*

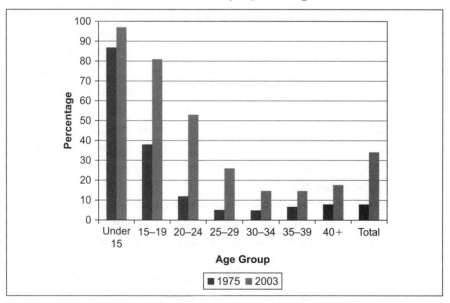

Source: National Health Marriage Resource Center. Trends in non-marital birth rates, 2005. Available at: http://www.healthymarriageinfo.org/docs/nonmaritalbirthrates.pdf. Accessed February 26, 2009.

to 25.4% (by 165%) for non-Hispanic Whites, 57.3% to 69.5% (by 21%) for non-Hispanic Blacks, and 23.6% to 47.9% (by 103%) for Hispanics.[9]

Using data from the 2002 National Survey of Family Growth, 14% of babies were born into cohabiting unions, and 21% were born to women who were neither married nor cohabiting. In addition, women ages 15 to 44 ever having cohabited was about 50% in 2002, up from the 41% in 1995. The percentage of women currently cohabiting had also increased from 7% in 1995 to 9% in 2002. Finally, the percentage of births to women 15 to 44 years of age that were unwanted at the time of conception in 2002 was about 14%, a 5% increase from 1995.

In the United States, Graefe and Litcher (2002) discovered that among women who had a nonmarital birth, 82% of White, 62% of Hispanic, and 59% of Black women had married by age 40.[10] These rates were higher among women who had not had a child before marriage: 89% of White, 93% of Hispanic, and 76% of Black women. The study also observed that the likelihood of divorce for unwed mothers who eventually marry was increased by nonmarital childbearing; however, the likelihood varies by race and ethnicity. Manning (2001) found that among women in cohabiting unions, Hispanic women were 77% more likely than White women to conceive a child.[11] Likewise, Black cohabiting women were 69% more likely than White cohabiting women to conceive. For women who became pregnant while cohabiting, Hispanic women were almost twice as likely and Black women were three times as likely as White women to remain cohabiting with their partner when their child was born. Furthermore, children born to cohabiting Hispanic women were 70% more likely to be intended than those born to cohabiting White women. Manning and Smock (1995) discovered that socioeconomic disadvantage during childhood reduced the odds of marriage for Black cohabiters, but not for White cohabiters.[12] Finally, the chance of cohabiters marrying their cohabiting partner, for both Blacks and Whites, was increased if the cohabiters had children together.[12]

Corresponding with an increase in cohabitation in European nations has been an increase in children born to nonmarried women (see **Figure 11-4**). In addition to there being a marked increase in nonmarital childbearing, there is also considerable variation according to European state. The Nordic countries show the greatest percentage of babies born to nonmarried women, whereas Italy and Greece show the smallest percentage of nonmarital childbearing. The greatest increase in babies born to nonmarried women occurred in the Netherlands, Ireland, Spain, and Belgium. The smallest increase in babies born to nonmarried women was in Sweden, West Germany, and Iceland.

FIGURE 11-4   *Extramarital Births Per 100 Births*

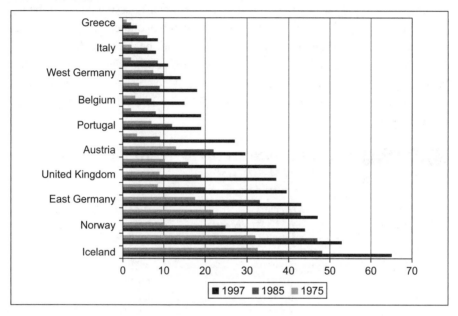

Source: Kiernan K. The rise of cohabitation and childbearing outside marriage in Western Europe. *Int J Law Policy Fam.* 2001;15:1–21.

Babies Born to Unmarried Mothers

Studies have shown that children born to unmarried mothers experience greater instability in their living arrangements as well as poverty and lower socio-economic status.[13–17] On average, they have a lower level of educational attainment, engage in sexual relationships at an earlier age, and have nonmarital births.[13,14] During adolescence and young adulthood, children born outside of marriage are less likely to be in school or employed, have lower occupational and income status, have more troubled marriages and divorces, and give birth outside of marriage more often.[18] Women who give birth outside of marriage have, on average, lower incomes and lower education levels and are more likely to receive welfare.[19–22] These economic disadvantages may also extend into old age. Mothers who were single for at least 10 years are more likely to be poor at ages 65 to 75 years.[23] They also have fewer marriage prospects compared with women without children.[24–26]

Marriage and Health

Several studies have found that marriage is significantly associated with better physical and mental health.[27–30] The extent to which healthier people self-select marriage versus marriage itself contributing to better health is not always clear. Nevertheless, married people tend to be healthier people. For example, on the basis of the U.S. Behavior Risk Factor Surveillance System survey, married people have better self-reported health[31] (see **Table 11-3**). This result was observed in each age group.

TABLE 11-3 *General Health Status by Age Group and Marital Status**

Age Group Health Status	Married No.	Percentage	Not Married No.	Percentage
Ages 18–49				
Excellent	73,897	26	41,405	21
Very good	108,333	37	66,458	33
Good	75,433	27	63,619	32
Fair	19,638	8	23,421	11
Poor	4,896	2	7,875	3
Unknown/Refused	579	0	563	0
Ages 50–69				
Excellent	48,998	19	25,467	15
Very good	86,602	32	45,560	25
Good	77,160	30	51,396	30
Fair	31,508	13	30,162	19
Poor	13,404	6	17,981	11
Unknown/refused	790	0	857	0
Ages 70+				
Excellent	9,367	11	11,536	9
Very good	22,690	26	30,117	23
Good	30,496	35	42,678	34
Fair	16,620	20	27,184	22
Poor	7,131	8	14,000	11
Unknown/Refused	513	0	1,201	1

Data source: Centers for Disease Control and Prevention. *Behavioral Risk Factor Surveillance System Survey Data*. Atlanta, Georgia: U.S. Department of Health and Human Services, Centers for Disease Control and Prevention, 2005, 2006, 2007. Available at: http://www.cdc.gov/ brfss/technical_infodata/surveydata.htm. Accessed July 21, 2008.
*Weighted estimates to yield U.S. estimates. Significant difference in self-reported health status by marital status within each age group, $P < 0.001$.

The U.S. Behavior Risk Factor Surveillance System survey data also indicates that married adults, ages 18 years and older, during 2005 to 2006 had fewer days during the past 30 days when their physical health was not good (9.7 [95% CI, 9.6–9.8] for married and 10.6 [95% CI, 10.4–10.7] for nonmarried), fewer days during the past 30 days when their mental health was not good (9.2 [95% CI, 9.1–9.3] for married and 10.8 [95% CI, 10.7–10.9] for nonmarried), and fewer days in the past 30 days when poor physical or mental health kept them from doing their usual activities, such as self-care, work, or recreation (9.8 [95% CI, 9.7–9.9] for married and 10.7 [95% CI, 10.5–10.8] for nonmarried).

Smith, Mercy, and Conn (1988) discovered that married persons in the United States had the lowest suicide rates for each marital status group, by age and gender.[32] In contrast, young, widowed males had the highest rates. Waldron, Hughes, and Brooks (1996) used data from the National Longitudinal Surveys of Young Women to study the effect of marriage on the health of women.[33] The study focused on women ages 24 to 34 years. Women were followed over two successive 5-year intervals, with married women having better health than unmarried women during each follow-up interval; however, women who had better health at the beginning of the survey were more likely to marry and less likely to experience marital dissolution. In another study, women who never married tended to have worse health (physical impairments and overall health problems) than divorced and separated women;[34] however, no differences were observed in psychosomatic symptoms between women who never married and divorced and separated women.

Trends in Teen Pregnancies

Historically, information on ways to avoid unwanted pregnancy and sexually transmitted diseases and having access to effective contraceptive protection is much greater among adults than teens. This may help explain why roughly half of the new cases of HIV infections occur in people aged 15 to 24 years. Higher rates are generally associated with marginalized young people, such as street children.[35] In addition, some argue that higher rates of HIV, syphilis, gonorrhea, and chlamydia, and lower use of contraception or condoms in the United States compared with the Netherlands, Germany, and France is because there is less access to sexual health information and services and less comfort with sexuality in the United States.[36]

Efforts to reduce teen pregnancy in the United States have been encouraging. For example, the pregnancy rate per 1,000 teenage women aged 15 to 19 years dropped from 111.0 in 1980 to 75.4 in 2002 (−32%). Over this same time period, the birth rate dropped from 53.2 to 43.0 (−21%), and the abortion rate dropped 42.8 to 21.7 (−49%);[37] however, rates of teen pregnancy in the United States remain high relative to many other countries. For example, the teen pregnancy rate per 1,000 women aged 15 to 19 in 2004 was 72.2 in the United States. Corresponding rates in France, Germany, and the Netherlands were 22.6, 16.3, and 12.8, respectively (Wijsen & van Lee, 2006; Ventura et al., 2008;[38,39] personal communication with Henshaw, Guttmacher Institute, 2007; as cited by Advocates for Youth, 2009[36]).

In the United States, there have been steep declines since the 1960s in the percentage of premaritally pregnant women aged 15 to 19 years marrying before the birth of their first child. From the early 1960s to the mid-1990s, the marriage rate for pregnant teens dropped from 69.4% to 19.3% for Whites and from 36.0% to 6.7% for Blacks.[21,40] Marriage stability is directly associated with age at marriage. For example, approximately 50% of teen marriages involving women aged 18 to 19 years end in divorce within 15 years compared with about 33% of marriages involving older women.[40] Nevertheless, marrying prior to the birth of a child can result in greater paternal support (e.g., financial, emotional), even if the couple eventually divorces.[41]

Health Risks Associated With Teen Pregnancies

There are several reasons why reducing teen pregnancy is important, including teens being less able to take care of a child and more likely to be economically disadvantaged, pregnancy among teens being more dangerous and traumatic, a large percentage of teen pregnancies ending in abortions, limited educational opportunities for teen mothers, and almost all teen pregnancies being unintended.[21,40] One report indicated that pregnant teenagers had a higher risk of developing anemia and preeclampsia and maternal mortality compared with the rest of the maternal population.[42] A study conducted in the United States found that teenage mothers had higher rates of depression than teenage girls in general with 40% of teenage mothers experiencing an episode of depression within one year of giving birth.[43]

Teens may also be less responsible or careful during pregnancy. For example, some disturbing health practices and trends among teenage mothers in England

and Wales that could have negative impacts on their health and the health of their unborn children were identified in a national survey to assess infant feeding practices.[44] Among other things, they reported substance abuse practices. Over 80% of teenage mothers in 1995 drank alcohol before pregnancy and 56% drank alcohol during pregnancy. In addition, two thirds of teenage mothers smoked before pregnancy and almost half smoked during pregnancy.

Clinical Abortion

World Abortion Rates and Selected Trends

An **abortion** is the removal or expulsion of an embryo or fetus from the uterus. The word *abortion* is typically used to reflect intentional termination of pregnancy. The intentional termination of pregnancy could result from a doctor, a lay person, or the woman herself. In contrast, the word **miscarriage** generally refers to a pregnancy that ended unintentionally. A miscarriage is also sometimes referred to as a **spontaneous abortion**. The percentage of pregnancies ending in legal abortions varies considerably throughout the world, with the highest levels in Russia and Greenland (see **Table 11-4**). In both Russia and Greenland, the percentage of pregnancies ending in legal abortions exceeds 50% compared with the United States, where it is about 23%.[45] Historically, the percentage of pregnancies ending in legal abortions in the United States peaked in the late 1970s and early 1980s at above 30%, but has decreased steadily since that time (see **Figure 11-5**). In contrast, in England and Wales the percentages have steadily increased in the past three decades and are now at about 22%.[46]

Abortion in a Modern Context

Few aspects of reproductive health are as publicly contested as abortion. Since the landmark Supreme Court decision of *Roe vs. Wade* in 1973, abortion, along with its moral, ethical, and legal implications, has occupied an important place in the realm of U.S. and world politics. A 2007 national poll of U.S. voters found that 22% of those surveyed would not vote for a candidate whose views on abortion differed from their own.[47] Public opinion, then, can have a huge impact on political decisions concerning abortion and can, therefore, affect individual health outcomes on a grand scale.

In the United States, the flurry of rhetoric surrounding abortion is charged on both sides. Those who support the *Roe vs. Wade* decision hold that barring abortion

TABLE 11-4 *Percentage of Pregnancies Ending in Legal Abortions*

Country	Year	%	Country	Year	%
Russia	2006	52.0	Singapore	2006	23.9
Greenland	2005	50.3	Reunion	2006	23.8
Romania	2006	40.6	French	2006	23.4
Guadeloupe	2006	39.1	Guiana		
Hungary	2006	38.9	Lithuania	2006	23.4
Estonia	2006	38.7	New	2006	23.3
Belarus	2006	37.7	Zealand		
Latvia	2006	34.7	Vietnam	2005	23.3
Cuba	2005	34.1	Slovenia	2006	23
Bulgaria	2006	33.5	Armenia	2006	22.8
Ukraine	2006	33.3	United	2005	22.6
Kazakhstan	2006	31.9	States		
China (PRC)	2006	31.5	Canada	2005	22.1
Georgia	2006	30.7	Albania	2006	21.8
Moldova	2006	29.5	United	2006	21.8
Cocos	1978	28.6	Kingdom		
Islands			Macedonia	2006	21.4
Belize	1996	28	Australia	2006	21.3
Czech	2006	27.4	France	2005	21.0
Republic			Guyana	2003	20.9
Serbia	2006	26.6	Mongolia	2006	20.4
Slovakia	2006	26.1	Japan	2006	20.2
Korea,	1999	25.6	Hong	2005	19.9
South (ROK)			Kong		
Sweden	2007	25.4	Croatia	2006	19.7
New	1998	25.2	Italy	2004	19.6
Caledonia			Norway	2006	19.5

Country	Year	%	Country	Year	%
Denmark	2006	18.8	Turks and	2005	9.1
Iceland	2005	16.8	Caicos		
Spain	2005	16.1	Islands		
Finland	2006	15.1	Tajikistan	2006	8.6
Germany	2006	15.3	Tunisia	2001	8.4
Channel	2004	13.8	Ireland	2006	7.3
Islands			Saint	1990	7.1
Dominican	2005	13.7	Helena		
Republic			Faeroe	2006	5.8
Netherlands	2006	13.3	Islands		
Belgium	2005	13.2	Kosovo	2006	4.6
Greece	2003	13.1	Bosnia and	2001	3.2
Andorra	1995	13.0	Herzegovina		
Taiwan	1999	13.0	Austria	2000	3
(ROC)			Suriname	1994	3
Switzerland	2005	12.9	India	2000	2.7
Isle of Man	2007	12.8	Gibraltar	2005	1.9
Azerbaijan	2006	12.3	Malta	2006	1.4
Israel	2006	11.8	Qatar	2005	1.3
Puerto Rico	2005	11.7	Portugal	2005	0.8
Bahrain	2002	11.4	Venezuela	1968	0.8
Anguilla	2005	11.2	Poland	2006	0.09
Barbados	1995	10.3	Mexico	2005	0.07
Costa Rica	2005	10	Botswana	1984	0.04
Bermuda	1984	9.9	Chile	1991	0.02
South	2005	9.2	Luxembourg	1997	0.02
Africa			Panama	2000	0.02

Source: Johnston WR. Global abortion summary, 2008. Available at: http://www
.johnstonsarchive.net/policy/abortion/wrjp333pd.html. Accessed February 26, 2009.

FIGURE 11-5 *Abortions as a Percentage of Pregnancies (Excluding Fetal Deaths/Miscarriages) in the United States and in England and Wales Over Selected Calendar Years*

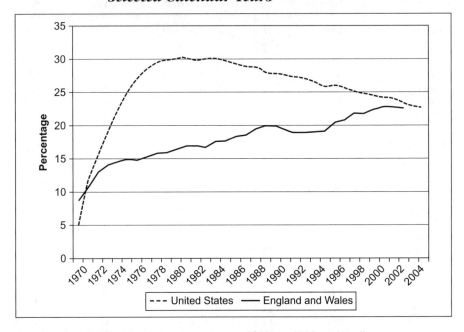

Source: Johnston WR. Global abortion summary. 2008. Available at: http://www
.johnstonsarchive.net/policy/abortion/#CM. Accessed February 26, 2009.

is both an invasion of privacy under the 9th and 14th amendments and that it poses a substantial threat to the health and even the life of mothers to whom pregnancy poses substantial danger. In this view, mothers have the unalienable right to make their own reproductive decisions, including the decision to abort a pregnancy. Alternatively, pro-life proponents hold moral and ethical considerations as paramount over these legal barriers—their claim is that the fetus or unborn child has a right to live, on which the mother should not be able to infringe.

Caught in the middle of this debate are the women and the fetuses, whose relative rights are so closely scrutinized. In 2003, there were 241 legal abortions performed for every 1,000 live births, amounting to a total of 848,163 legal induced abortions nationwide.[48] A 2004 national study found that 13% of mothers claim concerns for the health of the fetus influenced their decision, whereas 12% of mothers cite concerns for their own health as a factor that influenced their decision to have an abortion. Only 1% of the sample said they were victims of rape.[49] A national opinion poll conducted in September 2008 by NBC News and the *Wall Street Journal* found that 37% of respondents, the highest percentage going to a single category, thought abortion should be illegal with a few exceptions.[50] These statistics indicate that the majority of abortions are performed for reasons that most Americans do not deem acceptable.

Psychological and Health Impact of Abortion

Faced with what some authors have called a "social stigma" against abortion, women choose to cope with abortion in a variety of ways. Research suggests that "the personality resources that a woman brings with her to the abortion context shape her cognitive appraisals of the abortion prior to its occurrence (how threatening it is and how well she expects to cope with it), which in turn shape the coping strategies she engages in subsequent to the abortion."[51] This evaluation also concludes that certain nonquantifiable characteristics such as self-esteem, perceived control, and optimism have a large impact on the way that a woman copes with the social and mental pressures that come with having an abortion.

This framework could explain the conflicting results obtained by other studies attempting to measure the impact of abortion on a woman's social, mental, and physical health. A 1992 study found "no evidence of widespread post abortion trauma,"[52] suggesting that abortion's mental effect on subsequent life and reproductive practices operated solely through its influence on fertility and access to coping resources. In contrast, a 2006 cohort study found that women who had experienced an abortion showed a higher likelihood of depression, anxiety, and suicidal behavior, which is the direct opposite of the 1992 finding.[53]

It is clear that the ability of women to cope with the psychological stresses of abortion depends on a variety of factors. It is possible that the maternal response could also depend on the physical repercussions of abortion. Early research indicates that unless infection or abnormal consequences arise after an abortion, the abortion has no significant effect on later fertility, although the risk of premature delivery in a subsequent pregnancy may be slightly higher for women who have had a previous abortion, but this effect was found to be small.[54]

Societal Effects of Abortion Legislation

Since *Roe vs. Wade*, over 20 million abortions have been performed in the United States alone. This number represents 20 million children who could have been born, attended school, paid taxes, received welfare payments, committed crimes, or had children of their own. The demographic impact that abortion has had on the United States is massive, and it has affected society in rather unexpected ways.

Economists John Donohue and Steven Levitt found in 2001 that as much as 50% of the 1990's nationwide reduction in crime, usually attributed to increased police activity, was actually a consequence of an increase in abortions about 18 years previous. According to Donohue and Levitt (2001), the increase in abortions was disproportionately concentrated among low-income women, whose children, were they carried to term, would have become a disproportionately large portion of the criminals.[55]

Other studies have shown that, as a consequence of the abortion reforms in the 1970s, labor participation and schooling among Black women saw a dramatic increase, whereas out-of-wedlock fertility and teen marriage among both Black and White women saw a dramatic decline. Furthermore, the increase in schooling and labor participation among Black women can be attributed to the decrease in out-of-wedlock fertility and teen marriage.

Female Circumcision

Background and Prevalence

Female circumcision refers to a process by which female external reproductive tissues are altered for nonmedical purposes. In contrast to the widespread hygienic practice of male circumcision, female circumcision has several negative health consequences. The practice occurs mostly in African females, with ages ranging from infancy to 15 years. Currently, 130 million women worldwide have undergone female circumcision.[56] The prevalence of the procedure varies depending on the region. In Egypt, Somalia, Ethiopia, Eritrea, and Sudan, prevalence ranges from 80% to 100%; in Mali, Chad, and Liberia, prevalence ranges from 51% to 79%; 50% in Nigeria and Kenya; and 20% or less in Senegal, Tanzania, Zaire, and Uganda.[57] The World Health Organization (WHO) states that approximately 3 million girls live with the risk for female circumcision annually.[58]

The WHO classifies female circumcision, or female genital cutting (FGC), into four categories.[58,59] Type I involves the total or partial removal of the clitoris or prepuce (clitoridectomy). Type II is the partial or total removal of the clitoris and labia minora, with or without removal of the labia majora (excision). Type III is the narrowing of the vaginal opening by creating a seal by cutting and positioning the labia minora and/or the labia majora with or without removal of the clitoris (infibulations). Type IV is classified as all other harmful procedures to female genitalia for nonmedical purposes. This includes burning, stretching, or other cutting of genital tissues.

Reasons for female genital cutting stem from a mix of social, cultural, and religious roots. The underlying assumption of these societies is that women are highly sexual, promiscuous beings; therefore, there is good reason to control or remove the body parts that contribute to sexual promiscuity. The clitoris and labia are considered unclean sexual body parts. Their removal symbolizes the emergence of a clean and chaste woman; therefore, female circumcision is used to achieve a society's ideal of beauty, femininity, and modesty. Removal of the unclean genitalia is also seen as a way to reduce a woman's libido, thereby ensuring her virginity and her fidelity to her husband.[60] Societies, therefore, view the procedure as a girl's initiation into womanhood, a way to prepare her for marriage, and a method to maintain marital fidelity.[58] Religious leaders vary on their stance toward female genital cutting. Some leaders endorse the practice, whereas others seek to eliminate it.

Physiological Effects

Genital cutting has no medical benefits for women. The procedure itself is dangerous and often carried out under unsanitary conditions. Although medical circumcisions are available, midwives, older women, healers, birth attendants, or barbers are more commonly used to perform the circumcision. The instruments used include knives, razor blades, scissors, pieces of glass, or other instruments.[61] The most common complications that occur are shock, hemorrhage, infection, urinary retention, sepsis, and death. Hemorrhage is the most common complication, as amputation of the clitoris often cuts the clitoral artery. Prolonged bleeding may lead to anemia, affecting the child's growth. The procedure is also incredibly painful because the excised tissues are highly innervated and thus, highly sensitive.[62] The lack of sanitary measures during the procedure also contributes to infections of the wound. Stitching the wound reduces the size of the openings of the urethra and vagina. This causes urine, vaginal fluid, and menstrual fluid retention within the scar tissue. The retention of these fluids makes the women more susceptible to chronic urethral and vaginal infections. Urinary and kidney stones can also develop due to the chronic urinary tract infections. Scarring, cyst, and keloid formation are also common.

Female circumcision poses many negative effects on female reproduction. Trends show increased infertility rates as high as 25% to 30% in circumcised women.[63] Women also have complications in labor and delivery. Circumcised women have higher rates of caesarean section and higher postpartum blood loss than women who did not undergo FGC.[64]

A multicountry study done by the WHO showed the adverse effects of female circumcision on newborns. Despite access to hospital care during labor and delivery, circumcised women had more postpartum hemorrhages, longer hospital stays, and higher rates of perineal tearing than uncircumcised women. The study also concluded that the overall rate of infants needing resuscitation immediately after birth increased in mothers who were circumcised.[64] Infant death rates during and immediately after birth were also higher in circumcised women. Women with type I had a 15% higher rate of infant death, with 32% higher for type II, and 55% higher for type III circumcision.[64] Childbirth is especially risky for infibulated (type III) women. If deinfibulation is not performed, strong labor contractions combined with the exit of the fetal head causes perineal tears in the mother. If contractions are weak and delivery of the fetus is delayed, death of the child and necrosis of the fetus can occur, leading to infection and incontinence in the mother.[62]

The added risk of female circumcision on child and maternal health is of special concern because the nations in which female genital cutting is performed already have a background of high maternal and infant death rate. The risk of maternal death is 1 in 35 in Ghana and 1 in 12 in Burkina Faso. The estimated perinatal mortality rate of the infant is 44 for every 1,000 births in Sudan and 88 to every 1,000 births in Nigeria.

Conclusion

This chapter illustrates that the association between reproductive practices and society are many and varied. This chapter considered marriage, clinical abortion, and female circumcision and their implications on health. Marriage rates are decreasing in the United States, Europe, and many other places in the world, and an increase in cohabitation has been observed. The percentage of births out of wedlock is also increasing in these and other regions of the world. Children born to unmarried mothers tend to have a greater chance of experiencing adverse health and social consequences. Pregnant teenagers tend to experience greater health problems than older pregnant women. Abortion rates are high in many places of the world, representing the majority of pregnancies in Russia and Greenland. Finally, female circumcision continues to adversely affect many women worldwide, mostly in African nations.

Key Issues

1. Social customs have wide ranging repercussions in maternal and child health. Social norms influence marriage rates, age of marriage and pregnancy, and family planning, all of which can influence maternal and child health.

2. A decrease in marriage and an increase in cohabitation are occurring throughout the United States, Europe, and elsewhere.

3. The percentage of births to nonmarried women is increasing in the United States, Europe, and elsewhere.

4. Children born to unmarried mothers tend to experience greater instability in their living arrangements, poverty, and socioeconomic status; attain lower levels of educational; engage in sexual relationships at an earlier age; and go on to have nonmarital births.

5. There is a positive association between marriage and physical and mental health.

6. Pregnant teenagers have a higher risk of developing anemia and pre-eclampsia and maternal mortality compared with the rest of the maternal population and higher rates of depression than teenage girls in general.

7. The percentage of pregnancies ending in legal abortions varies considerably throughout the world, with more than 50% occurring in Russia and Greenland and about 23% in the United States, England, and Wales.

8. The ability of women to cope with the psychological stresses of abortion depends on a variety of factors, including physical repercussions of abortion.

9. There are currently 130 million women worldwide that have undergone female circumcision, with the prevalence of the procedure depending on the region. In Egypt, Somalia, Ethiopia, Eritrea, and Sudan, prevalence ranges from 80% to 100%; in Mali, Chad, and Liberia, prevalence ranges

from 51% to 79%; 50% in Nigeria and Kenya; and 20% or less in Senegal, Tanzania, Zaire, and Uganda. The WHO estimates that roughly 3 million girls live with the risk for female circumcision annually.

10. Reasons for female genital cutting stem from a mix of social, cultural, and religious roots but have no medical benefits for women. The procedure itself is dangerous and often carried out under unsanitary conditions. Trends show increased infertility rates as high as 25% to 30% in circumcised women, complications in labor and delivery, and higher rates of caesarean section and higher postpartum blood loss.

Exercises

Key Terms

Define the following terms.

Abortion

Female circumcision

Miscarriage

Spontaneous abortion

Study Questions

11.1 Explain the four types of female genital cutting.

11.2 Explain the opposing viewpoints of supporters and critics of the 1973 *Roe vs. Wade* decision.

11.3 What factors have been shown to be elements of a woman's coping strategy when dealing with abortion?

11.4 What are the health effects of teenage pregnancy on the mother?

11.5 Describe the evidence for the protective and selective effects of marriage on women's health.

References

1. U.S. Census Bureau. Current population survey, March and annual social and economic supplements, 2007 and earlier. Available at: http://www.census.gov/population/www/socdemo/hh-fam.html. Accessed February 15, 2009.

2. United Nations, Monthly Bulletin of Statistics, April 2001. Available at: http://www.info lease.com/ipa/A0004385.html. Accessed February 26, 2009.

3. United Nations Statistics Division, Demographic Yearbook, Table 23. Available at: http://unstats.un.org/unsd/demographic/products/dyb/dyb2006.htm. Accessed February 26, 2009.

4. National Statistics. UK Snapshot Neighbourhood Economy Census. Marriages: age at marriage by sex and previous marital status, 1991, 2001 and 2003–2005. Population Trends 127. Available at: http://www.statistics.gov.uk/STATBASE/ssdataset.asp?vlnk= 9599. Accessed February 26, 2009.

5. Kiernan K. The rise of cohabitation and childbearing outside marriage in Western Europe. *Int J Law Policy Fam*. 2001;15:1–21.

6. Kiernan K. Childbearing outside marriage in Western Europe. *Pop Trends*. 1999;(98): 11–20.

7. Bramlett MD, Mosher WD. Cohabitation, marriage, divorce, and remarriage in the United States. *Vital Health Stat*. 2002;23(22).

8. National Health Marriage Resource Center. Trends in non-marital birth rates, 2005. Available at: http://www.healthymarriageinfo.org/docs/nonmaritalbirthrates.pdf. Accessed February 26, 2009.

9. Child Trends DataBank. Percentage of births to unmarried women, 2005. Available at: http://www.childtrendsdatabank.org/indicators/75UnmarriedBirths.cfm. Accessed February 25, 2009.

10. Graefe DR, Litcher DT. Marriage among unwed mothers: Whites, Blacks and Hispanics compared. *Perspect Sex Reprod Health*. 2002;34(6):286–293.

11. Manning WD. Childbearing in cohabiting unions: racial and ethnic differences. *Fam Plan Perspect*. 2001;33(5):217–223.

12. Manning WD, Smock PJ. Why marry? Race and the transition to marriage among cohabitors. *Demography*. 1995;32(4):509–520.

13. McLanahan S, Sandefur G. *Growing Up with a Single Parent: What Hurts, What Helps*. Cambridge, MA: Harvard University Press; 1994.

14. Aquilino WS. The life course of children born to unmarried mothers: childhood living arrangements and young adult outcomes. *J Marr Fam*. 1996;58(2):293–310.

15. Bumpass L, Lu HH. Trends in cohabitation and implications for children's family contexts in the United States. *Pop Stud*. 2000;54(1):29–41.

16. Demo D, Cox M. Families with young children: a review of research in the 1990s. *J Marr Fam*. 2000;62(4):876–895.

17. Haveman R, Wolfe B, Pence K. Intergenerational effects of nonmarital and early childbearing. In Wu LL, Wolfe B, eds. *Out of Wedlock: Causes and Consequences of Nonmarital Fertility*. New York, NY: Russell Sage Foundation; 2001.

18. Amato Paul. The impact of family formation change on the cognitive, social, and emotional well-being of the next generation. *Future Child*. 2005:15(2). Available at: http://www.futureofchildren.org/usr_doc/05_FOC_15-2_fall05_Amato.pdf. Accessed February 26, 2009.

19. Driscoll AK, Hearn GK, Evans VJ, Moore KA, Sugland BW, Call V. Nonmarital childbearing among adult women. *J Marr Fam*. 1999;61:178–187.

20. Moore KA. *Executive Summary: Report to Congress on Out-of-Wedlock Childbearing*. (Full report available from DHHS Publication No. 95-1257-1.) Washington, DC: U.S. Government Printing Office. 1995. Available at: http://www.cdc.gov/nchs/data/misc/wedlock.pdf. Accessed February 26, 2009.

21. Terry-Humen E, Manlove J, Moore KA. Births outside of marriage: perceptions vs. reality. In *Child Trends Research Brief*. Washington, DC: Child Trends; 2001. Available at: http://www.childtrends.org/Files/rb_032601.pdf. Accessed February 26, 2009.

22. Lichter D, Graefe D, Brown J. Is marriage a panacea? Union formation among economically disadvantaged unwed mothers. *Social Prob.* 2003;50:60–86.
23. Johnson R, Favreault M. *Economic Status in Later Life Among Women Who Raised Children Outside of Marriage.* Washington, DC: The Urban Institute; 2004.
24. Lichter D, Graefe D. Finding a mate: the marital and cohabitation histories of unwed mothers. In Wu L, Wolf B, eds. *Out of Wedlock: Causes and Consequences of Nonmarital Fertility.* New York, NY: Russell Sage Foundation; 2001:317–343.
25. Upchurch D, Lillard L, Panis C. The impact of non-marital childbearing on subsequent marital formation and dissolution. In Wu L, Wolf B, eds. *Out of wedlock: Causes and Consequences of Nonmarital Fertility.* New York, NY: Russell Sage Foundation: 2001;344–380.
26. Bennett NG, Bloom DE, Miller CK. The influence of nonmarital childbearing on the formation of first marriages. *Demography.* 1995;32(1):47–62.
27. Gallo LC, Troxel WM, Kuller LH, Sutton-Tyrrell K, Edmundowicz D, Matthews KA. Marital status, marital quality, and atherosclerotic burden in postmenopausal women. *Psychosom Med.* 2003;65(6):952–962.
28. Gallo LC, Troxel WM, Matthews KA, Kuller LH. Marital status and quality in middle-aged women: associations with levels and trajectories of cardiovascular risk factors. *Health Psychol.* 2003;22(5):453–463.
29. Ikeda A, Iso H, Toyoshima H, et al. JACC Study Group. Marital status and mortality among Japanese men and women: the Japan Collaborative Cohort Study. *BMC Public Health.* 2007;7:73.
30. Manzoli L, Villari PM, Pirone G, Boccia A. Marital status and mortality in the elderly: a systematic review and meta-analysis. *Soc Sci Med.* 2007;64(1):77–94.
31. Centers for Disease Control and Prevention. *Behavioral Risk Factor Surveillance System Survey Data.* Atlanta, Georgia: U.S. Department of Health and Human Services, Centers for Disease Control and Prevention, 2005, 2006, 2007. Available at: http://www.cdc.gov/brfss/technical_infodata/surveydata.htm. Accessed July 21, 2008.
32. Smith JC, Mercy JA, Conn JM. Marital status and the risk of suicide. *Am J Public Health.* 1988;78(1):78–80.
33. Waldron I, Hughes ME, Brooks TL. Marriage protection and marriage selection—Prospective evidence for reciprocal effects of marital status and health. *Soc Sci Med.* 1996;43(1):113–123.
34. Waldron I, Weiss CC, Hughes ME. Marital status effects on health: are there differences between never married women and divorced and separated women? *Soc Sci Med.* 1997;45(9):1387–1397.
35. Guttmacher Institute. Into a new world: young women's sexual and reproductive lives, 1998. Available at: http://www.guttmacher.org/pubs/new_world_engl.html. Accessed February 26, 2009.
36. Advocates for youth. Adolescent sexual health in Europe and the U.S.—why the difference? 2009. Available at: http://www.advocatesforyouth.org/PUBLICATIONS/factsheet/fsest.htm. Accessed February 25, 2009.
37. Guttmacher Institute. U.S. teenage pregnancy statistics national and state trends and trends by race and ethnicity, 2006. Available at: http://www.guttmacher.org/pubs/2006/09/12/USTPstats.pdf. Accessed February 26, 2009.
38. Wijsen C, van Lee L. *National Abortion Registration, 2005.* Utrecht, Netherlands: Rutgers Nisso Groep, 2006.

39. Ventura SJ, Abma JC, Mosher WD, et al. Estimated pregnancy rates by outcome for the United States, 1990-2004. *Nat Vital Stat Rep*. 2008;56(15):1–24.

40. Center for Law and Social Policy. Is teen marriage a solution? 2002. Available at: http://www.clasp.org/publications/teenmariage02-20.pdf. Accessed February 25, 2009.

41. Hanson T, Garfinkel I, McLanahan S, Miller C. Trends in child support outcomes. *Demography*. 1996;33(4):483.

42. Irvine H, Bradley T, Cupples M, Buhan M. The implications of teenage pregnancy and motherhood for primary health care: unresolved issues. *Br J Gen Pract*. 1997;47(418): 323–326.

43. Wilson J. Maternity policy: Caroline: a case of a pregnant teenager. *Prof Care Mother Child*. 1995;5(5):139–142.

44. Foster K, Lader D, Cheesborough S. *Infant Feeding Survey 1995*. London: The Stationary Office, 1997.

45. Johnston WR. Global abortion summary, 2008. Available at: http://www.johnstonsarchive .net/policy/abortion/wrjp333pd.html. Accessed February 26, 2009.

46. Johnston WR. Global abortion summary, 2008. Available at: http://www.johnstonsarchive .net/policy/abortion/#CM. Accessed February 26, 2009.

47. Quinnipiac University Poll. April 25-May 1, 2007. Abortion and birth control. Retrieved October 14, 2008, from http://www.pollingreport.com/abortion.htm. Corroborated by other polls: Time July 31–Aug, 4 2008 (20%) and June 18–25, 2008 (23%).

48. Centers for Disease Control and Prevention. Abortion surveillance—United States, 2002. Surveillance Summaries. *MMWR*. 2005;54(SS-7).

49. Finer L, Frohwirth LF, Dauphinee LA, Singh S, Moore AM. Reasons why US women have abortions: a quantitative and qualitative approach. *Perspect Sex Reprod Health*. 2005;37(3):110–118.

50. *NBC News/Wall Street Journal Poll*. September 6–8, 2008. Abortion and birth control. Available at: http://www.pollingreport.com/abortion.htm. Retrieved October 14, 2008.

51. Major B, Richards C, Cooper ML, Cozzarelli C, Zubek J. Personal resilience, cognitive appraisals, and coping: an integrative model of adjustment to abortion. *J Personal Soc Psychol*. 1998;74(3):735–752.

52. Russo NF, Zierk KL. Abortion, childbearing, and women's well being. *Prof Psychol Res Pract*. 1992;23(4):269–280.

53. Fergusson DM, Horwood LJ, Ridder EM. Abortion in young women and subsequent mental health. *J Child Psychol Psychiatry*. 2006;47(1):16–24.

54. Atrash HK, Hoque CJ. The effect of pregnancy termination on future fertility. *Baill Clin Obstet Gynaecol*. 1990;4(2):391–405.

55. Donohue JJ, Levitt SD. The impact of legalized abortion on crime. *Q J Econ*. 2001; 116(2):379–420.

56. Donohoe M. Female genital cutting: epidemiology, consequences, and female empowerment as a means of cultural change. *Medscape Obstet Gynecol Women Health*. 2006;11(2). Available at: http://www.medscape.com/viewarticle/546497. Retrieved October 14, 2008.

57. Jones S, Ehiri J, Anyanwu E. Female genital mutilation in developing countries: an agenda for public health response. *Eur J Obstet Gynecol*. 2004;116(2):144–151.

58. World Health Organization. Fact sheet: female genital mutilation, 2008. Available at: http://www.who.int/mediacentre/factsheets/fs241/en/index.html. Retrieved October 14, 2008.

59. World Health Organization. Classification of female genital mutilation, 2008. Available at: from http://www.who.int/reproductive-health/fgm/terminology.htm. Retrieved October 14, 2008.
60. Morris RI. Female genital mutilation: perspectives, risks, and complications. *Urol Nurs.* 1999;19(1):13–19.
61. Little CM. Female genital circumcision: medical and cultural considerations. *J Cult Divers.* 2003;10(1):30–34.
62. Toubia N. Female circumcision as a public health issue. *N Engl J Med.* 1994;331(11): 712–716.
63. Nour N. Female circumcision and genital mutilation: a practical and sensitive approach. *Contemp Obstet Gynecol.* 2000;45(3):50–55.
64. World Health Organization. Female genital mutilation and obstetric outcome: WHO collaborative prospective study in six African countries. *Lancet.* 2006;367(9525):1835–1841.

TWELVE

Early Childbearing: Trends and Consequences

Learning Objectives

After completing this chapter, you should be able to:

1. Describe selected patterns and trends in early age at first birth.
2. Discuss the physical, mental, and social consequences of early age at childbirth, including who is affected and other factors that may contribute to the consequences.
3. Describe some of the underlying factors that contribute to early age at first birth.

Several studies have explored the acute and long-term health and social consequences of pregnancy among women giving birth at a very young age. In considering these consequences, prevention programs often encourage women, especially adolescents, to delay the onset of sexual activity and to use effective methods of contraception.[1] Consequently, the mean age at first birth has increased in many places throughout the world. For example, in 2002, the mean age at first birth for women in the United States was 25.1 years, representing a 3.7-year increase from 1970.[2] Mothers living in the northeastern United States are the oldest at first birth, whereas mothers living in Arkansas, Louisiana, Mississippi, New Mexico, Oklahoma, and Wyoming are the youngest.[3] *The World Fertility Report 2003* indicates that the mean age at first birth rose in both developing and developed countries, although increases have been more dramatic in developed countries. In three quarters of these developed countries, the mean age at first birth rose 1.7 years from the 1970s to the 1990s;[4] however, despite these positive trends, a large number of women continue to give birth at a young age. On a global scale, adolescent childbearing represents approximately 1 of every 10 births.[5] The fertility rate (annual number of live births per 1,000) for girls aged 15 to 19 years is estimated to be 50 per 1,000 worldwide from the period 2000 to 2005.[6] Family planning is the most important factor in determining maternal age at first birth. The woman's education level and type of occupation also strongly influence the choice of the time of first birth.

The purpose of this chapter is to present maternal health, social, and economic consequences associated with early age at first birth.

Definition and Methods

Early age at first birth, as used in various literature sources, generally pertains to first full-term delivery under the age of 19 years. Individuals under the age of 19 are consistently referred to as "adolescents." The World Health Organization defines adolescent or early pregnancy and delivery to be between 10 and 19 years of age;[1] however, the United Nations Children Fund defines adolescent fertility as the incidence among girls aged 15 to 19 years.[6] Considering the absence of a standard age classification for early age at first birth, we define early age at first birth to mean first full-term delivery in adolescent women ages 12 to 19 years.

Articles cited in this chapter were located by searching electronic databases (i.e., MEDLINE, Web of Science, and Academic Search Premier) using such Boolean expressions as "age at first birth," "teen pregnancy," "implications," "complications," and "consequences." Reference lists were explored from electronically identified articles in an attempt to cull materials that were not electronically referenced. Articles were excluded if they did not fit the early age at first birth definition outlined previously. Twenty-seven national and international research studies were identified that specifically addressed the physical, mental, and social implications of early age at first birth.

Physical Health Consequences

Research indicates that there are a number of health implications for adolescents who give birth (Appendix IIIa). Around the world, these short-term physical complications in pregnancy and childbirth claim the lives of approximately 70,000 adolescent girls every year, with the greatest risk to these young girls and babies coming from countries in sub-Saharan Africa.[5] Obstructed labor is common and can result in painful and often humiliating disabilities such as the inability to control bladder or bowel function.[5] Research conducted for the *State of the World's Mothers 2006* report indicates that adolescents around the world are twice as likely to die during childbirth or pregnancy compared with older mothers.[7] One study examined the cause of death among a sample of 460,434 Swedish women between 1990 and 1995 and concluded that teenage mothers were at increased risk for premature death.[8] Controlling for socioeconomic background, these researchers reported that the teenage mothers were 1.6 times more likely to die prematurely (95% confidence interval [CI], 1.4 to 1.9) compared with older mothers. Research conducted in the United States confirms the increased risk for mortality among first-time adolescent mothers and concludes that the relative death hazard steadily decreases with increasing age at first birth, particularly in women older than 18.9 years of age.[9] In addition, health problems declined as first birth was delayed from early adolescence until about the age of 34 years, after which time health problems began to increase, especially after the age of 40 years.[9]

Although the risk of mortality is higher among mothers giving birth during adolescence, there is evidence showing increased risk of other physical complications to the mother and fetus. Retrospective research among 398 Bulgarian adolescent mothers showed substantially higher numbers of complications such as anemia, premature rupture of the membranes, preeclampsia, and preterm labor as compared with a control group of older mothers.[10] Similarly, one retrospective study of adolescent mothers in Turkey during 1990 to 1994 found a higher incidence of preeclampsia, low birth weight infants, and preterm delivery among adolescent mothers.[11] In a retrospective case-control study conducted during 1992–1993 among 80 adolescent mothers from India, pregnancy-related complications were found to be significantly higher than in the control group. Complications included pregnancy-related anemia (27.5%), pregnancy-induced hypertension

(15%), and intrauterine growth retardation. In addition, the incidence of forceps delivery was significantly higher (17.4%).[12]

Not only are the physical consequences of early age at first birth detrimental to the mother, research conducted for the *State of the World's Mothers 2006* report indicates that babies born to adolescent mothers have a 50% higher risk of mortality compared with babies born to mothers in their 20s.[7] Many of these deaths are attributed to lack of prenatal care, as many adolescent mothers do not seek prenatal care or wait until pregnancy is well advanced.[11,13] Babies born to adolescent mothers also run a higher risk of low birth weight and serious long-term disabilities and are more likely to be undernourished than children born to older mothers.[6] The incidence of sudden infant death syndrome in the babies of adolescents is six times greater than in children of mothers 10 years older. Other risks to the baby include infection, accidents, violence, low birth weight, prematurity, and developmental problems. Low birth weight is associated with lower socioeconomic status, smoking, alcohol, drugs, poor nutrition, and inadequate prenatal care. In addition, babies born to adolescent mothers are less likely to be immunized, receive regular medical care, and be breastfed and are more likely to be overfed or underfed.[14]

Some studies indicate there may be long-term physical consequences to women who give birth during adolescents. One study involving Black women in the United States revealed increasing risk of coronary heart disease with decreasing age at first birth and parity (number of births).[15] Similarly, among 858 cases in Massachusetts, the relative risk estimate for myocardial infarction for first birth under the age of 20 was 1.7 (95% CI, 1.1–2.6) when compared with later age at first birth.[16] Among 169 women under the age of 60 years, the relative risk for coronary heart disease for women whose age at first birth was less than 20 years was 1.9 (95% CI, 0.7–5.6) with relative risk decreasing to 1.8 (95% CI, 1.1–3.3) for women whose age at first birth was 20–24.[17]

Research shows important short- and long-term physical consequences to both the mother and fetus. Indeed, much of the risk to the physical health of both the mother and fetus may be the result of incomplete development of the reproductive system and/or poor preparation for motherhood.[9] Conditions such as these are also linked to lower socioeconomic class, poor personal habits regarding nutrition, drug and alcohol use, and inadequate prenatal care.[14]

Increased maternal cervical and endometrial cancer risk has been associated with early maternal age at first birth.[18]

Mental Health Consequences

Generally, depression among women of all ages is common both during and after pregnancy. A meta-analysis containing 21 studies indicates that prevalence rates for depression during pregnancy were 7.4%, 12.8%, and 12.0% for the first, second, and third trimesters, respectively.[19] Research has also shown that 10% to 15% of White middle-class women[20] and as high as 30% of non-White indigent women[21] experience postpartum depression.

Despite the common occurrence of postpartum depression for all new mothers, the age at first birth has been found to be an important risk factor for depression. Indeed, studies have shown higher rates of depression among adolescent mothers as well as among young adults who were adolescent mothers (Appendix IIIb). Analysis of the 1988 National Maternal and Infant Health Survey indicated that adolescent mothers who were 15 to 17 years old were more than twice as likely to be depressed as adult mothers.[22] These depressive symptoms appear to extend into adulthood for unmarried adolescent mothers. The United States National Longitudinal Survey of Youth was used to examine the influence of marital status and age at first birth on later-life psychological health. Results revealed that the psychological health of married teenage mothers in later life was similar to that of married adult mothers, but that unmarried teenage mothers and unmarried adult mothers had similarly poor psychological health.[23] The results of this study suggest that not being married at the time of first birth rather than age at first birth is associated with depressive symptoms later in life.

Evidence shows that becoming a parent at an early age and leaving school erodes emotional well-being. In 1987, researchers in Great Britain found that depressed mothers reported more often than nondepressed mothers that they had truanted extensively from school (38% and 7%, respectively) and had their first child at an early age (61% and 15%, respectively).[24] A longitudinal study of women in Dunedin, New Zealand, from 1975 to 1994 explored the relationship between mental health, level of education, and age at first birth among 807 women. Findings revealed that women reported greater depressive symptoms if they had their first child before the age of 21 years and had dropped out of school.[25]

A cross-sectional study of 2,595 adults aged 18 to 95 years found that males and females who became parents before the age of 23 had increased feelings and signs of depression compared with nonparents. Emotional well-being steadily improved for males as age at first birth increased, although for females, depressive signs and symptoms only improved until first birth, around age 30 years, after which time depression began to increase;[26] therefore, the association between age at first birth and depression appears to be parabolic for females.

There is less evidence that early age at first birth contributes to other psychiatric conditions. One prospective study of two British birth cohorts (1946 and 1958) was used to explore the effects of adolescent childbearing and mental health problems later in life. Significantly more adolescent mothers reported psychiatric morbidity (depression, anxiety, and phobias) in their mid-30s as compared with mothers in the comparison cohort who had their first child after adolescence.[27]

Social Health Consequences

A number of studies have addressed the social health implications of early age at first birth (Appendix IIIc). These social implications tend to compound, producing adverse long-term consequences. For example, early age at first birth may be associated with an early marriage, which often ends in divorce, interrupted education, and decreased earning potential. The combination of teen pregnancy, failed marriage, low education, and poverty is addressed in this section.

Isolation and Loneliness

A study of 100 Black, White, and Hispanic mothers aged 16 to 19 years at the time of delivery reported problems with isolation and loneliness.[28] For many of these new mothers, isolation was the result of an inability to reconnect with former peers and friends after delivery. This isolation was not restricted to single mothers and provided a major void in the mother's social support system. The lack of such a system "contributed to the probability of child abuse and neglect, depression, suicide and marital stress."[28] Reducing day-to-day stressors through social support from others was not possible for the mothers in this study, thus contributing to isolation and feeling lonely.

Educational Attainment

Failure to obtain an education is another potential problem associated with an early age at first birth. Analysis of 1969 to 1994 natality data from the National Center for Health Statistics revealed that age at first birth was positively associated with level of education achieved. For example, among 1,994 participants, 17.9 was the median age at first birth for women completing the 8th grade, 22.9 was the median age at first birth for those completing high school, and 29.5 was the median age at first birth for those having 16 or more years of education. Researchers suggest that the median age at first birth varies little for those with fewer than 12 years of education, but age at first birth distribution is significantly higher as educational attainment increases. These results indicate that "among women without a high school diploma, early childbirth may interfere with educational attainment, and low educational aspirations may result in early childbearing; the two are inextricable."[29]

In a study involving 120 inner-city African American and Puerto Rican postpartum women in the United States, aged 14 to 19 years, 33% attended school during their pregnancy and graduated within 28 to 36 months; 19% did not attend school during their pregnancy but returned and graduated within 28 to 36 months of giving birth; 12% dropped out of school before becoming pregnant and did not return; and the remaining 36% left school during their pregnancy and did not return.[30] In a quasi-experimental study of 216 African American adolescents in the United States, age at first birth was associated with subsequent graduation from high school.[31] In this case, the younger the age at first birth the less likely individuals completed high school. Similarly, one study found that women with an age at first birth before 21 years are far less likely to proceed with education.[25]

In a 1984 Canadian study of 2,083 women aged 35 to 49 years old, researchers explored the relationship between education, age at first birth, and lifetime fertility.[32] Results indicated that for women giving birth during adolescence, the percentage completing 8 or less, 9 to 11, 12 to 13, and 14 or more years of schooling was 32.6%, 24.8%, 12.2%, and 4.6%, respectively. In this study, the timing of first birth rather than number of children was more closely related to educational attainment. A longitudinal study compared 404 mostly Black urban women who were adolescent mothers with their firstborn children.[33] Those firstborn children who later also became adolescent mothers experienced greater difficulty in school. Fifty-seven percent of these daughters compared with 33% of mothers reported having failed a grade. On the other hand, adolescent daughters who did not have a teenage birth were more likely to finish high school (82%) compared with their mothers who did have a teenage birth (45%). In addition, adolescent daughters who did not have a teenage birth were more likely to want additional education (88%) compared with their mothers who did have a teenage birth (37%).

Relationships

Pregnancy among adolescent women often compels early marriage, and the younger the age of the mother at first birth, the higher the probability of marital instability, based on data from the United States National Survey of Family Growth.[34] According to a sample of 9,797 women, 68% of those who conceived under the age of 20 were married by the time the baby was born. Of those with an age at first birth from 14 to 17 years who married, 20.5% were separated within 5 years of the marriage and 43.6% within 15 years of the marriage. These percentages declined as age at first birth increased. For example, of those who had their first child at age 18 or 19 years, 12.6% were separated within 5 years of the marriage, with 28.8% separated within 15 years of marriage.

Research based on data from the National Longitudinal Study and the Panel Study of Income Dynamics indicated that early age at first birth is strongly associated with less stable marriages.[35] In a longitudinal cohort study of 807 women conducted in New Zealand beginning in 1975, 8.2% of the women who had their first baby before the age of 21 years initially reported being separated from the father of the child compared with 6.4% of the women who had their first child after the age of 21 years.[25] For women who had their first child before age 21 years, compared with women at an older age, the number and percentage separated from their father grew consistently higher over a 19-year period.

In a 1997 prospective study, two British birth cohorts (1946 and 1958) were examined to determine the psychosocial risks of teenage motherhood.[27] Results of this study found that for those adults who were teenage mothers, 40.8% of the 1946 cohort and 49.0% of the 1958 cohort experienced separation or divorce in their relationships. For those mothers whose first birth was after the age of 20 years, marital breakdowns were 16.3% of the 1946 cohort and 24.3% of the 1958 cohort. In another British study, data from the National Child Development Study revealed that women who became mothers in their teens had the greatest chance of negative outcomes at the age of 33 years.[36] In fact, 53.0% of women who were teen mothers reported that they had been a lone mother at some point up to the age of 33 years compared with 13.6% of women who had their first child after the age of 23 years. Approximately 34.5% of women who were teen mothers reported their first child was born outside of marriage compared with 10.4% of women who had their first child after the age of 23 years.

Married women with their spouses present were identified as being more likely to have had their first child at an older age, based on data from the National

Longitudinal Survey of Labor Market Experience.[37] In Indian society, a woman's age at marriage is also positively associated with her age at first birth.[38]

Earning Potential

Lower levels of educational attainment and single parenthood experienced by adolescent mothers often directly impact subsequent earning potential. Research indicates that a strong association exists between early childbearing and poverty at the age of 27 years.[39] This is consistent with results from a longitudinal study involving 300 urban Black women residing in Baltimore, Maryland, which found that adolescent childbearing increased the risk of low economic success and was associated with higher parity.[33] Two national surveys conducted in the United States in 1968, one sampling 5,000 young women aged 14 to 24 years and the other sampling 5,000 households, found early age at first birth and subsequent high fertility to be associated, after adjusting for factors such as religion, education, and parental status.[35] Subsequent high fertility and costs associated with supporting a larger family explain how an early age at first birth can hinder economic success later in life.

Data from the World Fertility Surveys and Demographic and Health Surveys showed that a higher socioeconomic status was an indicator of a later age at first birth.[40] A later age at first birth was also associated with lower risk of prolonged unemployment and lack of money for household necessities.[41]

Discussion

Despite positive trends in the mean age of first birth for women in the United States and in developing countries, a large number of women continue to give birth at a young age. Worldwide, 1 of every 10 children are born to adolescent mothers,[5] with the highest maternal risk for health problems and mortality occurring with first birth under the age of 22.[9] This literature review identifies a number of adverse physical, mental, and social health outcomes associated with women having their first child during adolescence. These outcomes include but are not limited to preterm labor and delivery, mortality, depression, lower educational attainment, relationship disruption, and decreased earning potential.

A consideration of the maternal health consequences naturally leads to a consideration of the underlying reasons. These reasons are important for health professionals who are interested in implementing programming aimed at delaying early age at first birth and improving health among adolescent women. Several intrapersonal and social/cultural risk factors have been identified that contribute as antecedents to early age at first birth among adolescents. Individually, a woman's age at menarche is directly related to age at first birth and suggests the importance of implementing age-appropriate prevention activities as soon as possible.[42,43] In general, adolescent women with more education have a later age at first birth,[38,44] and the current trend in the United States toward older age at first birth is primarily associated with women who finish high school.[29] Additionally, health professionals engaged in prevention efforts should consider evidence that mental health problems (i.e., anxiety, affective, addictive, or conduct disorders) contribute to an earlier age at first birth,[45] whereas the use of contraceptives delays the age at first birth.[46]

Evidence also suggests that social and cultural factors also impact early age at first birth among adolescents. These findings provide valuable evidence in support of an ecological prevention framework for early age at first birth. For example, the association between age of menarche and first birth varies across cultures[47] and is directly related to malnutrition in impoverished areas.[48] Additionally, early age at first birth among Blacks is associated with having more siblings, being raised by single parents, and early menstruation.[39] For Hispanic women, early age at first birth is also associated with being raised by single parents, whereas for Whites, early childbearing is associated with coming from a large family.[39] Family background appears to play a more significant role among Blacks than Whites in determining age at first birth, whereas circumstances of poverty contribute to increased risk of adolescent pregnancy among all racial/ethnic groups.[37,49] For example, working conditions in Norway have been shown to significantly influence age at first birth, whereas in China, urban dwellers have a greater tendency to delay childbirth than their rural counterparts.[50,51] Other contributing factors include peer influence and school disengagement and dropout.[52,53]

Conclusion

Maternal health consequences of early age at first birth among adolescents are numerous and well documented in the literature. Unfortunately, early first pregnancies contribute to a high percentage (57%) of unwanted pregnancies that ultimately end in abortion.[54] Greater understanding of the maternal health consequences of early age at first birth among adolescents can help health professionals at all levels better assist women in delaying age at first birth. Prevention efforts should include careful attention to not only intrapersonal risk factors, but also important social/cultural considerations that interact with the intrapersonal and provide justification for ecological health promotion approaches.

Key Issues

1. Early age at first birth is defined in this chapter as first full-term delivery in adolescent women ages 12 to 19 years.
2. Adolescents around the world are twice as likely to die during childbirth or during pregnancy compared with older mothers.
3. Death hazard steadily decreases with increasing age at first birth. Adolescent mothers have substantially higher numbers of complications such as anemia, pregnancy-induced hypertension, intrauterine growth retardation, premature rupture of the membranes, preeclampsia, preterm labor, low birth weight, developmental problems, and long-term disability as compared with older mothers.
4. Babies born to adolescent mothers are less likely to be immunized, receive regular medical care, and be breastfed and are more likely to be overfed or underfed.
5. An increased maternal cervical and endometrial cancer risk has been associated with early maternal age at first birth.
6. Age at first birth has been found to be an important risk factor for depression. Becoming a parent at an early age and leaving school erodes emotional well-being. Social consequences of first birth at a young age include isolation and loneliness, neglect, depression, suicide, and marital stress.
7. Women younger than 21 years of age at first birth are far less likely to proceed with education. Timing of first birth rather than number of children is more closely related to educational attainment.
8. Pregnancy among adolescent women often compels early marriage, and the younger the age of the mother at first birth, the higher the probability of marital instability. Married women with their spouses present are more likely to have had their first child at an older age.
9. Often lower levels of educational attainment and single parenthood experienced by adolescent mothers negatively impacts subsequent earning potential.

Exercises

Key Terms

Define the following terms.

Adolescent fertility   Early age at first birth

Study Questions

12.1 Identify and discuss complications to both mother and infant due to a young age of a mother at first birth.

12.2 Discuss the mental health complications to mother and others due to a young age at first birth.

12.3 Identify factors associated with social health consequences of young age at first birth, and discuss the various implications of these factors.

12.4 Identify one example from within the chapter, and describe epidemiologically how we know that mothers who were young at first birth are at higher risk for that specific complication/consequence.

12.5 Discuss some of the cultural differences associated with those at risk for being young at first birth (i.e., factors unique among Blacks, Hispanics, and Whites).

References

1. World Health Organization. World health day safe motherhood. 1998. Available at: http://www.who.int/docstore/world-health-day/en/whday1998.html. Retrieved April 6, 2006.
2. Martin JA, Hamilton BE, Ventura SJ, Menacker F, Park MM, Sutton PD. Births: final data for 2001. *Nat Vital Stat Rep.* 2002;51(2):1–102.
3. Centers for Disease Control. QuickStats: Average age at first birth, by state—United States. *MMWR.* 2002;54(19):488.
4. United Nations. *World Fertility Report 2003.* Available at: http://www.un.org/esa/population/publications/worldfertility/World_Fertility_Report.htm. Retrieved April 6, 2006.
5. Ahmad K. Pregnancy complications kill 70000 teenagers a year. *Lancet.* 2004;363 (9421):1616.
6. UNICEF. Fertility and contraceptive use, 2006. Available at: http://www.childinfo.org/eddb/fertility/. Retrieved November 17, 2006.
7. Save the Children. *State of the World's Mothers 2006.* 2006. Available at: http://www.savethechildren.org/publications/mothers/2006/SOWM_2006_final.pdf. Retrieved May 7, 2009.

8. Otterblad O, Haglund B, Ringback Weitoft G, Cnattingius S. Premature death among teenage mothers. *Int J Obstet Gynecol.* 2004;111(8):793–799.
9. Mirowsky J. Age at first birth, health and mortality. *J Health Social Behav.* 2005; 46(1):32–50.
10. Zhekova K, Rachev E, Asparukhova E, et al. [Pregnancy, delivery and perinatal outcome in adolescent pregnancy]. *Akush Ginekol (Sofiia).* 2001;40(3):19–23.
11. Bozkaya H, Mocan H, Usluca H, Beser E, Gumustekin D. A retrospective analysis of adolescent pregnancies. *Gynecol Obstet Invest.* 1996;42(3):146–150.
12. Pal A, Gupta KB, Randhawa I. Adolescent pregnancy: a high risk group. *J Ind Med Assoc.* 1997;95(5):127–128.
13. Patch LK. Adolescent pregnancy: psychosocial issues. *Indiana Med.* 1990;83(1):30–33.
14. Hechtman L. Teenage mothers and their children: risks and problems: a review. *Can J Psych.* 1989;34(6):569–575.
15. Rosenberg L, Palmer JR, Rao RS, Adams-Campbell LL. Risk factors for coronary heart disease in African American women. *Am J Epidemiol.* 1999;150(9):904–909.
16. Palmer JR, Rosenberg L, Shapiro S. Reproductive factors and risk of myocardial infarction. *Am J Epidemiol.* 1992;136(4):408–416.
17. Beard CM, Fuster V, Annegers JF. Reproductive history in women with coronary heart disease: a case-control study. *Am J Epidemiol.* 1984;120(1):108–114.
18. Merrill RM, Fugal S, Novilla LB, Raphael MC. Cancer risk associated with early and late maternal age at first birth. *Gynecol Oncol.* 2005;96:583–593.
19. Bennett HA, Einarson A, Taddio A, Koren G, Einarson TR. Prevalence of depression during pregnancy: systematic review. *Obstet Gynecol.* 2004;103(4):698–709.
20. Beck CT, Gable RK. Postpartum Depression Screening Scale: development and psychometric testing. *Nurs Res.* 2000;49(5):272–282.
21. Fergerson S, Jamieson D, Lindsay M. Diagnosing postpartum depression: can we do better? *Am J Obstet Gynecol.* 2002;186(5):899–902.
22. Deal LW, Holt VL. Young maternal age and depressive symptoms: results from the 1988 National Maternal and Infant Health Survey. *Am J Public Health.* 1998;88(2):266–270.
23. Kalil A, Kunz J. Teenage childbearing, marital status, and depressive symptoms in later life. *Child Dev.* 2002;73(6):1748–1760.
24. Cox AD, Puckering C, Pound A, Mills M. The impact of maternal depression in young children. *J Child Psychol Psychiatry Allied Discipl.* 1987;28(6):917–928.
25. Williams S, McGee R, Olaman S, Knight R. Level of education, age of bearing children and mental health of women. *Social Sci Med.* 1997;45(6):827–836.
26. Mirowsky J, Ross CE. Depression, parenthood, and age at first birth. *Social Sci Med.* 2002;54(8):1281.
27. Maughan B, Lindelow M. Secular change in psychosocial risks: the case of teenage motherhood. *Psychol Med.* 1997;27(5):1129–1144.
28. Cannon-Bonventre K, Kahn J. Interviews with adolescent parents: looking at their needs. *Child Today.* 1979;8(5):17–19, 41.
29. Heck KE, Schoendorf KC, Ventura SJ, Kiely JL. Delayed childbearing by education level in the United States, 1969–1994. *Matern Child Health J.* 1997;1(2):81–88.
30. Leadbeater BJ. School outcomes for minority-group adolescent mothers at 28 to 36 months postpartum: a longitudinal follow-up. *J Res Adolesc.* 1996;6(4):629–648.

31. Jones ME, Mondy LW. Lessons for prevention and intervention in adolescent pregnancy: a five-year comparison of outcomes of two programs for school-aged pregnant adolescents. *J Pediatr Health Care.* 1994;8(4):152–159.

32. Grindstaff C, Blakrishnan T, Dewit D. Education attainment, age at first birth and lifetime fertility: an analysis of Canadian fertility survey data. *Cancer Rev Social Anthropol.* 2001;28:324–339.

33. Furstenberg FF Jr, Brooks-Gunn J, Morgan SP. Adolescent mothers and their children in later life. *Fam Plan Perspect.* 1987;19(4):142–151.

34. McCarthy J, Menken J. Marriage, remarriage, marital disruption and age at first birth. *Fam Plan Perspect.* 1979;11(1):21–23, 27–30.

35. Moore KA, Hofferth SL, Wertheimer R II. Teenage motherhood: its social and economic costs. *Child Today.* 1979;8(5):12–16.

36. Hobcraft J, Kiernan K. Childhood poverty, early motherhood and adult social exclusion. *Br J Sociol.* 2001;52(3):495–517.

37. Maxwell NL. Influences on the timing of first childbearing. *Contemp Policy Issues.* 1987;5(2):113–122.

38. Nath DC, Land KC, Goswami G. Effects of the status of women on the first-birth interval in Indian urban society. *J Biosocial Sci.* 1999;31(1):55–69.

39. Moore KA, Myers DE, Morrison DR, Nord CW, Brown B, Edmonston B. Age at first childbirth and later poverty. *J Res Adolesc.* 1993;3(4):393–422.

40. dos Santos Silva I, Beral V. Socioeconomic differences in reproductive behaviour. *IARC Sci Pub.* 1997;138:285–308.

41. World Health Organization. Early sex: early motherhood: facing the challenge. *Safe Motherhood Newsletter.* 1996;22(3):4–8.

42. Presser HB. Age at menarche, socio-sexual behavior, and fertility. *Social Biol.* 1978; 25(2):94–101.

43. Sandler DP, Wilcox AJ, Horney LF. Age at menarche and subsequent reproductive events. *Am J Epidemiol.* 1984;119(5):765–774.

44. Bloom DE, Trussell J. What are the determinants of delayed childbearing and permanent childlessness in the United States? *Demography.* 1984;21(4):591–611.

45. Kessler RC, Berglund PA, Foster CL, Saunders WB, Stang PE, Walters EE. Social consequences of psychiatric disorders, II: teenage parenthood. *Am J Psychiatry.* 1997; 154(10):1405–1411.

46. Khoo SE, Krishnamoorthy S. Changes in the timing of births in Melbourne, Australia. *J Biosocial Sci.* 1985;17(2):235–247.

47. Udry JR, Cliquet RL. A cross-cultural examination of the relationship between ages at menarche, marriage, and first birth. *Demography.* 1982;19(1):53–63.

48. Komlos J. The age at menarche and age at first birth in an undernourished population. *Ann Hum Biol.* 1989;16(5):463–466.

49. McCrate E. Labor market segmentation and relative Black/White teenage birth rates. *Rev Black Pol Econ.* 1990;18(4):37–53.

50. Strand K, Wergeland E, Bjerkedal T. Fertility patterns according to occupational grouping in Norway, 1989. *Scand J Social Med.* 1996;24(1):50–54.

51. Zheng Z. Social-demographic influence on first birth interval in China, 1980–1992. *J Biosocial Sci.* 2000;32(3):315–327.

52. Bearman P, Bruckner H. *Power in Numbers: Peer Effects on Adolescent Girls Sexual Debut and Pregnancy.* Washington, DC: National Campaign to Prevent Teen Pregnancy; 1999.

53. Manlove J. The influence of high school dropout and school disengagement on the risk of school-age pregnancy. *J Res Adolesc.* 1998;8(2):187–220.

54. Creatsas G, Elsheikh A. Adolescent pregnancy and its consequences. *Eur J Contracept Rep.* 2002;7(3):167–172.

THIRTEEN

Cancer Risk Associated With Early and Late Maternal Age at First Birth

Learning Objectives

After completing this chapter, you should be able to:

1. Discuss the various definitions for young age at first birth.
2. Identify types of cancer that are associated with early and/or late maternal age at first birth, and discuss other risk factors for each of the cancers.
3. Discuss why age at first birth may be associated with cancer.
4. Use epidemiologic literature to explore associations between reproductive health factors, such as age at first birth, and health outcomes, such as cancer.

In recent years, several studies have explored the association between maternal age at first birth and cancer risk. Both young and old ages at first maternal birth have shown an increased risk for certain cancers. The rationale for investigating this association is that it might provide information that can be useful in family planning. It may also serve as a guide in establishing and reorienting existing healthcare services to better meet the needs of specific age groups.

In a review article by Merrill and colleagues,[1] late maternal age at first birth was associated with an increased risk of breast and brain cancers but a decreased risk of cervical and endometrial cancers. There was an unclear correlation between maternal age at first birth and ovarian, colorectal, thyroid, pancreatic, and kidney cancers. This chapter presents the article by Merrill et al.,[1] with the inclusion of a few references that have come out since the paper was published.

Early and Late Age at First Birth

There has been a lack of consistency among public health organizations in defining "young" and "old" age at first birth. A large population-based study ($n = 768,029$) consisting of 1995 U.S. birth certificate data concluded that the definition for early adolescent childbearing should include all females giving birth at age 15 or younger.[2] The basis of this definition stems from better birth outcomes when the maternal age was 16 years and older. When reporting national vital statistics information, the Center for Disease Control and Prevention (CDC) and the National Center for Health Statistics (NCHS) categorize maternal age into the following age groups: 10 to 14, 15 to 17, 18 to 19, 20 to 24, 25 to 29, 30 to 34, and 35 to 44.[3] Studies focusing mainly on the risks of teenage childbearing typically define teenage mothers as females between the ages of 15 and 19. This group may be further broken down into smaller subgroups to examine risks associated with younger and older teenage ages. For example, the National Vital Statistics Report for 1991–2000 of teenage births in the United States examines subgroups of teenage mothers: young teens (15–17 years) and older teens (18–19 years).[4] In looking at adverse labor and birth outcomes in older women, many studies use larger age categories. In a study conducted by the Texas Department of Health, researchers used broader 10-year age categories (10 to 19 years, 20 to 29 years, 30 to 39 years, and 40+ years) to assess maternal or fetal risks, with delayed childbearing defined as first birth in women aged 40 years and older.[5]

Although the CDC and the NCHS consistently use their own established maternal age categories when reporting national vital statistics information, other studies examining maternal age inconsistently use age categories based on their data. Although there are currently no standardized maternal age categories, there is a tendency to refer to young age at first birth as maternal age of 19 years or younger. First full-term births to women 35 years of age and older are generally considered to reflect older age at first birth. This age group has been used by many agencies, including the CDC, because of the increased risk of pregnancy-related mortality after 35 years of age.[6]

Maternal Age at First Birth and Breast Cancer

Certain reproductive variables strongly influence a woman's risk for developing breast cancer in her lifetime. Some of these reproductive factors include the timing of menarche and menopause, **parity** (the condition of having given birth), **nulliparity** (never having a child), and age at first birth.[7–9] The relationship between maternal age at first full-term birth and breast cancer risk is consistent across several studies. Research indicates older age at first birth is directly related to increased breast cancer risk. On the basis of data from the National Health and Nutrition Examination Survey (NHANES I) Epidemiology Follow-up Study (NHEFS) examining breast cancer risk, the population attributable risk for older women at first birth or nulliparity was 30.1% for the NHEFS cohort and 29.5% for the U.S. population.[10] In other words, roughly 30% of breast cancer cases in U.S. women were attributed to later age at first birth and/or nulliparity.

Many studies on breast cancer etiology have reached a similar conclusion regarding older age at first birth and increased breast cancer risk. In a study examining the risk factors for breast cancer and benign breast disease, the only variable that discriminated breast cancer from benign breast disease was early age at first birth.[9] Researchers of this study concluded that women with benign breast disease may be offered substantial protection from malignant breast cancer if their first full-term pregnancy occurred at an earlier age.[9] Researchers in a study examining the combined effect of childbearing, menstrual events, and body size on age-specific breast cancer risk discovered the effects of later age at menarche and earlier age at first full-term birth were more protective against breast cancer in premenopausal than postmenopausal women.[11] Researchers of a study examining breast cancer risk based on median age at first birth revealed a 3.7 (95% confidence interval [CI], 1.30–10.52) times higher relative risk in women with a median age of 41 at first birth when compared with a median age of 23 at first birth.[12] In a 14-year prospective investigation of 91,523 women participating in the Nurses' Health Study, both age at first birth and age at subsequent births had long-term influences on breast cancer incidence. Researchers found that the cumulative incidence (up to age 70) of breast cancer among women who first gave birth at age 20 was 20% lower than nulliparous women, and women whose age at first birth was 25 had a 10% reduced cumulative incidence.[13] Women who were 35 years old at their first birth had a 5% increased risk of breast cancer when compared with nulliparous women. For parous women, age at subsequent birth was protective against breast cancer for both premenopausal and postmenopausal women, regardless of age at first birth.

Many studies designed to examine breast cancer risk consider both parity and age at first birth, allowing investigators to examine their separate and combined effects. In a case-control study of histologically confirmed breast cancer cases (184 community controls and 184 hospitalized patients in Spain) breast cancer risk for women with an age at first full-term birth after 30 years had an **odds ratio** of 3.5 (95% CI, 1.41–9.83) in comparison with women whose first birth was before the age of 21.[14] In this study, multiple logistic regression was used to analyze the individual influence of parity, age at first full-term birth, and lactation and the risk of breast cancer among parous women. The study concluded that parity is an independent risk factor for breast cancer and women with an older age at first full-term birth comprise a high-risk group for breast cancer.[15]

Another study consisted of a cohort of 86,978 grand multipara women, women having at least five full-term pregnancies, extracted from the Population Register of Finland. This large cohort was linked with the population-based Finnish Cancer Registry to ascertain the effects of parity, age at first birth, and average birth interval on breast cancer risk. Results of this study indicate that women whose first full-term delivery occurred after age 30 have nearly twice the risk of breast cancer than those younger than age 20 at first birth. Additional results indicate women with eight or nine deliveries had a 30% lower breast cancer risk than women with five deliveries.[15] Researchers discovered after adjusting for study variables that young age at first birth and an increasing number of births are independent protective factors for breast cancer from the fifth child onward.

In a recent case-control study, women who gave birth before age 25 years were 36% less likely to develop breast cancer compared with women who started their families at an older age.[16] This protective effect occurred only in estrogen receptor–progesterone receptor-positive breast cancer. Later age at first birth increased the risk of estrogen receptor/progesterone receptor (ER/PR)-negative cancers. Multiple births reduced the risk of ER/PR-positive cancers among women with first birth at an early age and in women who breastfed. For women with late age at first birth who never breastfed, having multiple children increased the risk of breast cancer.

The cellular changes that occur in the breast and lead to the progression of breast cancer are thought to be a result of a combination of multiple changes rather than a simple, orderly progression.[7] The loss of normal regulation of cell number is one of the first recognizable alterations, resulting in an abnormal increase in epithelial cells. This is followed by genetic instability resulting in the abnormal growth and multiplication of cells (atypical ductal hyperplasia) that advances into an in situ, invasive, and eventually a metastatic carcinoma.[17] Breast cancer is characterized by cellular changes such as the stimulation of oncogenes (e.g., c-*erb-B2*, *Her2/neu*, *INT2*, c-*ras*, and c-*myc*), a reduction in function or expression of tumor-suppressor genes (e.g., *NM23*, *p53*, and *RB*), structural changes in cells, loss of cell adhesion, and an increased expression of cell cycle proteins, angiogenic factors, and proteases.[8]

There have been two predominant hypotheses on the causal mechanisms of breast cancer. One study believes that hormonal changes in early pregnancy result in molecular changes that stabilize *p53*, a tumor suppressor gene that promotes cell cycle arrest. With *p53* stabilized, it remains functionally active longer to repair cumulative DNA damage and to prevent cellular proliferation induced by **carcinogens**.[7]

Another theory of the mechanism for the development of breast cancer is that it is primarily caused by exposure to excessive endogenous estrogens.[7] Researchers have extensively studied the impact of endogenous hormones on breast cancer risk. A recent study supports the hypothesis that in utero exposures reflective of higher endogenous hormone levels could affect the risk for development of breast cancer in adulthood.[18] Much of the present evidence implicates an underlying hormonal mechanism involving estrogens, progesterone, prolactin, testosterone, and IGF-1 that may exert their effects by stimulating terminal differentiation of mammary gland stem cells.[9] Terminal differentiation occurs as mammary gland cells are permanently transformed to prepare for lactation. Cellular differentiation renders the breast epithelium resistant to carcinogenesis.[19] Lagiou et al. suggest that mammary gland differentiation has not been fully attained among women who have a propensity for breast cancer development.[9] Another study that concurred with Lagiou et al. postulated that breast cancer results from the interaction of a carcinogen with undifferentiated breast tissue.[19] Most likely, the protection offered during pregnancy at an early age at first birth is what exerts the inhibitory effect on breast tissue via the human chorionic gonadotropin, which results in the protective differentiation of breast tissue that is increased with each subsequent pregnancy.[20]

Maternal Age at First Birth and Cervical Cancer

Cervical cancer risk has also been linked to maternal age at first birth, but in a different way than breast cancer—it is higher in women who had an earlier first pregnancy and delivery. In a case-control study conducted in northern Italy, researchers examined certain reproductive variables and their association with development of certain cancers, including parity, age at first birth, and number of induced and spontaneous abortions. The risk of cervical cancer increased in women who reported their first birth before age 25 and decreased in women whose first birth occurred at age 25 or older.[21] A large prospective cohort study in Norway involving over 62,000 women also found that older age at first birth was associated with a decreased risk of cervical cancer.[21] The estimated odds ratio for women with first birth at 35 years and older was 0.18 (95% CI, 0.10–0.31) when compared with their younger counterparts whose first birth occurred at age 19 years or younger.[22] Similarly, a Swedish cohort study involving over 40,000 women found that older age at first birth prevented cervical cancer but increased the risk for breast, endometrial, and ovarian cancers.[23] In a study that correlated cervical cancer mortality rates with reproductive indices and other selected factors in 65 rural Chinese counties, cervical cancer mortality rates were also negatively associated with age at first birth.[24] The Norwegian Cancer Registry and Census Data found a 48% reduction in squamous cell carcinomas of the cervix in women who had their first birth after age 27 in comparison with those whose age at first birth was less than 20 years.[25]

A young age at first birth and the corresponding increase in cervical cancer risk are related to an early age at first intercourse. Researchers of a study examining cervical cancer risk and reproductive factors postulated that early age at first birth may stand as a proxy for early age at first intercourse, which is likewise linked to having multiple sexual partners and higher parity.[24,26] Studies on cervical cancer have shown that early sexual activity among adolescents renders the immature cervical epithelium vulnerable to carcinogens (e.g., human papillomavirus). In addition, pregnancy and delivery, particularly at a younger age, may cause cervical erosions that increase exposure to potential carcinogens.

In a study conducted among rural Indian women with established lower rates of sexual promiscuity, researchers linked early age at first intercourse and extramarital sexual relationships with increased risk of cervical cancer. In this study, 84% of cervical cancer patients experienced their first intercourse before the age of 16, and their risk of cervical cancer increased significantly with decreasing age at first coitus.[26] In a case-control study consisting of 366 cervical cancer patients and 323 control subjects, a relative risk of 2.4 (95% CI, 1.1–5.3) was identified for cervical intraepithelial neoplasia (severe dysplasia or carcinoma in situ) among women who had coitus before the age of 18 as compared with women who reported no intercourse or first intercourse after age 22.[27]

Maternal Age at First Birth and Endometrial Cancer

Studies have identified that older age at first birth protects against endometrial cancer. In a large cohort study in Norway, researchers investigated the effects of childbearing on mortality from endometrial cancer among 431,604 married women between the ages of 45 and 74. Women whose first birth occurred at age 35 or older had a relative risk of 0.53 (95% CI, 0.34–0.83) as compared with women less than 20 years of age.[28] This study found that high parity has a protective effect against endometrial cancer. Women with 8 to 11 children carried a relative risk of 0.35 (95% CI, 0.14–0.85) compared with nulliparous women.[27] The study concluded that high parity and delayed childbearing may reduce death associated with endometrial cancer. Researchers investigating risk factors among young women with endometrial cancer discovered a decreased risk in women who had an induced abortion, used oral contraceptives for 1 to 5 years, or delayed childbearing, which was the most significant protective factor.[29] In a cohort study of grand multiparous women giving birth to five or more children, those women whose first birth occurred at or after age 30 had a lower risk of endometrial cancer, with a risk ratio of 0.58 (95% CI, 0.34–0.97), than women giving birth before age 20.[30] In the same study, longer birth periods (the time between first and last births) of 20 years or more significantly decreased the risk of endometrial cancer. Women with birth periods of 20 years or more had a risk ratio of 0.57 (95% CI, 0.34–0.96) compared with women with birth periods less than 10 years. A case-control study in Italy also observed that later age at first birth decreased endometrial cancer risk when compared with nulliparous women.[31] A study in Sweden reported an increased risk for endometrial cancer among nulliparous women, while later age at last birth among women with two or more children significantly decreased the risk.[32] The authors of this Swedish study suggested that childbirth provides a protective effect by promoting the mechanical shedding of cells in the endometrial lining that may have undergone a malignant transformation, where these cells tend to increase with age.[32]

There are a small number of studies that found no statistical association between endometrial cancer and age at first birth. One study found an increasing risk of endometrial cancer with later age at first birth, which contradicts previously cited research;[23] however, the accuracy of the results may have been compromised by failing to adjust for confounding factors such as oral contraceptive use, estrogen replacement therapy without supplementation with progesterone, and age at menopause.[23] In a case-control study involving five different areas in the United States, no relationship was found between age at first birth and endometrial cancer risk after adjusting for other reproductive variables.[33]

Like other reproductive cancers, endometrial cancer is considered a hormone-dependent cancer. Long-term unopposed exposure to endogenous estrogen, decreased progesterone secretion, and anovulatory cycles are believed to result in malignant changes in the endometrium.[30] Unopposed estrogen (estrogen exposure without progesterone) promotes an increased rate of endometrial cell division and potential carcinogenic changes. The endometrial layer of the uterus is continually exposed to high levels of estrogen. During pregnancy when progesterone production is high, it reduces the length of time that the endometrium is exposed to estrogen alone. This may explain the increased risk of endometrial cancer among nulliparous women. Researchers of another study suggested that infertility contributes to an increased risk for endometrial cancer secondary to exposure to exogenous estrogen among women receiving hormone replacement therapy for either infertility or premenopausal symptoms.[31]

Maternal Age at First Birth and Ovarian Cancer

The relationship between age at first birth and ovarian cancer risk remains unclear because of contradictory findings in published studies. Some studies report an increased risk with an older maternal age at first birth[23,34] or a younger age at first birth,[35,36] whereas other investigations conclude that there is no risk correlation between age at first birth and ovarian cancer.[37–42] Studies that report a decreasing risk with an older maternal age may be confounded by difficulty of conception which is linked to an increased risk for ovarian cancer.[37] On the other hand, it is also possible that those who are older at the time of their first delivery may also represent a subgroup of women with healthier ovaries and can therefore conceive longer and at a later age and with a theoretically lower risk for ovarian cancer.[35]

Most of the factors associated with lower ovarian cancer risk, such as pregnancy and oral contraceptives, cause a suppression of ovulation though in different ways.[43] Currently, two main hypotheses relate risk factors to increased risk of ovarian cancer: incessant ovulation and exposure to high levels of gonadotropins. A few decades ago, Fathalla developed the "incessant ovulation" theory, in which ovarian cancer stems from the continual cycle of ovulation and constant delivery of estrogen on the epithelium of the ovary.[44] Ovulation subjects the ovary to microtrauma with the release of an ovum and exposes the ovarian epithelium to estrogen-rich follicular fluid, thus increasing the risk of ovarian cancer.[45] This hypothesis explains the protective effects of pregnancy but does not explain why young age at first birth is not protective. In addition, the potential cancer protection from pregnancy may be confounded by parity because multiparous women generally begin reproductive life earlier.[34]

Exposure to a high concentration of gonadotropins released from the pituitary gland parallels the idea of incessant ovulation. Pregnancy, and thus parity, suppresses the release of gonadotropins from the pituitary for temporary periods of time. An increasing number of full-term pregnancies (multiparity) consistently lowers the risk of ovarian cancer, whereas nulliparity increases ovarian cancer risk.[34,35,37,38,40–43,46]

Maternal Age at First Birth and Colorectal Cancer

The correlation between age at first birth and colorectal cancer risk is neither strong nor consistent. Colorectal cancer risk was associated with increasing maternal age at first birth in three studies,[47–49] whereas the majority of studies did not find a statistically significant association.[50–54] Further investigation of colorectal cancer risk and maternal age at first birth will need to clarify associated risk. Of the significant reproductive factors, higher parity is more consistently associated with decreased risk of colorectal cancer.[53,55–57]

There are a few theories on mechanisms relating colorectal cancer development with maternal age at first birth. The possibility of childbearing being protective against colorectal cancer has not been completely explored. One of the earliest theories proposed by Bjelke addresses the issues of immunological stimulation by ABO-incompatible fetal antigens.[58] More recently, attention has been turned to the idea that pregnancy reduces the excretion of bile acid, thus reducing colorectal cancer risk.[59] This reduction in the exposure of the colon and rectum to potentially harmful bile acids is hormonally controlled by a pregnancy, thus solidifying the association between higher parity and reduced colorectal cancer risk. Peters et al. suggested that a growing fetus or a delivery may cause injury to the large bowel, resulting in the promotion of carcinogenesis.[60] Further investigations may reveal more clear and consistent mechanisms resulting in colorectal cancer development.

Maternal Age at First Birth and Other Cancers

Some researchers theorize that hormonal factors may modify the cancer risk in men and women and that hormonal differences may explain the varying malignancy rates between genders.[61] A case-control study in Iowa examined the effect of parity and age at first birth on the risk for brain, colon, rectal, kidney, and pancreatic cancers.[62] With the exception of brain cancer, no associations were identified between age at first birth and these cancer sites. The risk for brain cancer was observed to be slightly higher in women whose first delivery occurred at age 25 years or older. Compared with women younger than age 20, the study reported odds ratios for brain cancer of 1.3, 1.9, and 1.3 for ages 20–24, 25–29, and 30 and above, respectively. In a multicenter case-control study, early age at first birth was associated with reduced risk of glioma.[62]

The correlation between thyroid cancer and maternal age at first birth is unclear. A study of 379 women in Italy found that older age at first birth increased the risk of thyroid cancer. The relative risk was 2.4 (95% CI, 1.2–5.0), between women who gave birth at age 28 or older and women who gave birth at 21 years or younger.[63] In a pooled analysis of 14 case-control studies from North America, Europe, and Asia, younger age at first birth (defined in this study as prior to age 25) was the only significant reproductive risk factor that showed decreased risk of thyroid cancer.[64] In one study that involving the Norwegian Cancer Registry and the Central Population Register of Norway, researchers examined individual records from all 1.1 million Norwegian women for risk of thyroid cancer. Researchers found no correlation between maternal age at first birth and thyroid cancer risk.[65]

Pancreatic cancer risk also has an unclear association with maternal age at first birth. A study conducted in Shanghai examined 451 diagnosed cases of pancreatic cancer and 1,552 controls. After adjusting for confounding factors such as age, income, and history of smoking, the authors found only a modest increase in pancreatic cancer risk due to young age at first birth.[66] Conversely, in a case-control study of 500 women conducted in Italy, researchers found the strongest protection against pancreatic cancer in their study to be young maternal age at first birth (25 years or less) with an odds ratio of 0.5 (95% CI, 0.3–0.9).[67] Researchers involved in the Nurses' Health Study, a large prospective cohort study involving 121,701 nurses aged 30 to 55, found that women who gave birth to their first child prior to age 30 experienced a small increased risk of pancreatic cancer (relative risk, 1.43; 95% CI, 0.87–2.35), although the risk was not statistically significant.[68]

The relationship between bladder cancer risk and maternal age at first birth has not been thoroughly researched. One study identified bladder cancer cases from the Iowa Health Registry consisting of 317 cases of female bladder cancer and 833 population controls. The data suggest a decreasing bladder cancer risk with increasing age at first birth, although the trend is not statistically significant.[69]

Causal mechanisms have not been proposed in the literature for the cancers in this section.

Conclusion

Various studies have shown that age at first birth, early or late, can impact the risk for both reproductive and nonreproductive cancers. A woman experiencing her first childbirth at age 35 or older may be at increased risk for breast and brain cancers. On the other hand, a first birth occurring at age 19 or younger may increase the risk for cervical and endometrial cancers. There is insufficient statistical evidence to link age at first birth with site-specific malignancies such as ovarian, colorectal, thyroid, pancreatic, and kidney cancers. A summary of articles exploring potential associations between early and late age at first birth and cancer risk is presented in Appendix IV.

Various mechanisms have been offered by different researchers that may explain the possible pathways between maternal age at first birth and cancer risk. In breast and ovarian cancers, it is theorized that the timing of a woman's first birth and the associated changes in hormonal levels that trigger multiple changes, rather than a single alteration at the cellular level, limit exposure to excessive estrogen and gonadotropins that promote carcinogenesis. For cervical cancer, it is proposed that mechanical trauma from an early onset of sexual activity may render the immature cervical epithelium susceptible to carcinogens. On the other hand, long-term unopposed exposure to endogenous estrogen, decreased progesterone secretion, and anovulatory cycles have been implicated in endometrial cancer. Because the association between age at first birth and other cancers is less clear, identifying plausible biological mechanisms is not currently warranted.

Key Issues

1. First childbirth at age 35 or older may be at increased risk for breast and brain cancers.
2. Births occurring at maternal age 19 or younger may increase the risk for cervical and endometrial cancers.
3. There are many theories as to why age at first birth is associated with various forms of cancer. It can be associated with changes in hormonal levels, damage to epithelial cells, and other factors.
4. Epidemiologic research reveals associations and risks between age at first birth and cancer. Understanding the literature and how to access it is critical.
5. This research provides information that can be useful in family planning and can serve as a guide in establishing and reorienting existing healthcare services in order to better meet the needs of specific age groups.

Exercises

Key Terms

Define the following terms.

Carcinogens   Odds ratio
Nulliparity   Parity

Study Questions

13.1 Discuss the various definitions for young age at first birth, why there are different definitions, and which one you would establish as a standard.
13.2 Discuss the connection between breast cancer and age at first birth.
13.3 Select one of the two prominent hypotheses of the causal mechanisms of breast cancer, and discuss how maternal age at first birth could influence the mechanism.

13.4 Select one of the cancers discussed in the chapter (other than breast cancer). Discuss the association between the cancer and age at first birth. Interpret the findings from the literature, what the findings tell us, and how significant those findings are.

13.5 Select an article from the table presented in Appendix IV, and discuss the findings in context of age at first birth and cancer risk.

References

1. Merrill RM, Fugal S, Novilla LB, Raphael MC. Cancer risk associated with early and late maternal age at first birth. *Gynecol Oncol.* 2005;96:583–593.
2. Phipps MG, Sowers M. Defining early adolescent childbearing. *Am J Public Health.* 2002;92:125–128.
3. Martin JA, Hamilton BE, Sutton PD, Ventura SJ, Menacker F, Munson ML. Births: final data for 2002. *Natl Vital Stat Rep.* 2003;52:1–113.
4. Ventura SJ, Matthews TJ, Hamilton BE. Teenage births in the United States: state trends, 1991–2000, an update. *Natl Vital Stat Rep.* 2002;50:1–4.
5. Smoot M. Delayed childbearing: increased maternal age at first birth and its association with labor and delivery outcomes [online]. 1997 [cited 2004, March 5]. Available from: http://www.tdh.state.tx.us/bvs/reports/sreport2.pdf. Accessed February 24, 2009.
6. Center for Disease Control. Fact sheet: pregnancy related mortality surveillance—United States 1991–1999 [online]. 2003 [cited 2004, July 6]. Available from: http://www.cdc.gov/od/oc/media/pressrel/fs030220.htm. Accessed February 24, 2009.
7. Sivaraman L, Conneely OM, Medina D, O'Malley BW. P53 is a potential mediator of pregnancy and hormone-induced resistance to mammary carcinogenesis. *Proc Natl Acad Sci USA.* 2001;98:12379–12384.
8. Lester SC, Cotran RS. The breast. In: Cotran RS, Kumar V, Collins T, eds. *Robbins Pathologic Basis of Disease.* Philadelphia: WB Saunders; 1999:1104–1107.
9. Lagiou A, Lagiou P, Vassilarou DS, Stoikidou M, Trichopoulos D. Comparison of age at first full-term pregnancy between women with breast cancer and women with benign breast diseases. *Int J Cancer.* 2003;107:817–821.
10. Madigan MP, Ziegler RG, Benichou J, Byrne C, Hoover RN. Proportion of breast cancer cases in the United States explained by well-established risk factors. *J Natl Cancer Inst.* 1995;87:1681–1685.
11. Kampert JB, Whittemore AS, Paffenbarger RS Jr. Combined effect of childbearing, menstrual events, and body size on age-specific breast cancer risk. *Am J Epidemiol.* 1988;128: 962–979.
12. Lee SH, Akuette K, Fulton J, Chelmow D, Chung MA, Cady B. An increased risk of breast cancer after delayed first parity. *Am J Surg.* 2003;186:409–412.
13. Rosner B, Colditz GA, Willet WC. Reproductive risk factors in a prospective study of breast cancer: the Nurses' Health Study. *Am J Epidemiol.* 1994;139:819–835.
14. Ramon JM, Escriba JM, Casas I, et al. Age at first full-term pregnancy, lactation and parity and risk of breast cancer: a case-control study in Spain. *Eur J Epidemiol.* 1996; 12:449–453.

15. Hinkula M, Pukkala E, Kyyronen P, Kauppila A. Grand multiparity and the risk of breast cancer: population-based study in Finland. *Cancer Causes Control.* 2001;12:491–500.
16. Lord SJ, Bernstein L, Johnson KA, et al. Breast cancer risk and hormone receptor status in older women by parity, age of first birth, and breastfeeding: a case-control study. *Cancer Epidemiol Biomarkers Prev.* 2008;17(7):1723–1730.
17. Russo J, Russo IH. The pathway of neoplastic transformation of human breast epithelial cells. *Radiat Res.* 2001;155:151–154.
18. Park SK, Kang D, McGlynn KA, Garcia-Closas M, Kim Y, Yoo KY, Brinton LA. Intrauterine environments and breast cancer risk: meta-analysis and systematic review. *Breast Cancer Res.* 2008;10(1):R8.
19. Russo J, Hu YF, Silva ID, Russo IH. Cancer risk related to mammary gland structure and development. *Microsc Res Tech.* 2001;52:204–223.
20. Russo J, Lynch H, Russo IH. Mammary gland architecture as a determining factor in the susceptibility of the human breast to cancer. *Breast J.* 2001;7:278–291.
21. La Vecchia C, Negri E, Franceschi S, Parazzini F. Long-term impact of reproductive factors on cancer risk. *Int J Cancer.* 1993;53:215–219.
22. Kvale G, Heuch I, Nilssen S. Reproductive factors and risk of cervical cancer by cell type. A prospective study. *Br J Cancer.* 1988;58:820–824.
23. Mogren I, Stenlund H, Hogberg U. Long-term impact of reproductive factors on the risk of cervical, endometrial, ovarian and breast cancer. *Acta Oncol.* 2001;40:849–854.
24. Guo WD, Hsing AW, Li JY, Chen JS, Chow WH, Blot WJ. Correlation of cervical cancer mortality with reproductive and dietary factors, and serum markers in China. *Int J Epidemiol.* 1994;23:1127–1132.
25. Bjorge T, Kravdal O. Reproductive variables and risk of uterine cervical cancer in Norwegian registry data. *Cancer Causes Control.* 1996;7:351–357.
26. Biswas LN, Manna B, Maiti PK, Sengupta S. Sexual risk factors for cervical cancer among rural Indian women: a case-control study. *Int J Epidemiol.* 1997;26:491–495.
27. Parazzini F, La Vecchia C, Negri E, Fedele L, Franceschi S, Gallotta L. Risk factors for cervical intraepithelial neoplasia. *Cancer.* 1992;69:2276–2282.
28. Lochen ML, Lund E. Childbearing and mortality from cancer of the corpus uteri. *Acta Obstet Gynecol Scand.* 1997;76:373–377.
29. Parslov M, Lidegaard O, Klintorp S, et al. Risk factors among young women with endometrial cancer: a Danish case-control study. *Am J Obstet Gynecol.* 2000;182:23–29.
30. Hinkula M, Pukkala E, Kyyronen P, Kauppila A. Grand multiparity and incidence of endometrial cancer: a population-based study in Finland. *Int J Cancer.* 2002;98:912–915.
31. Parazzini F, La Vecchia C, Negri E, Fedele L, Balotta F. Reproductive factors and risk of endometrial cancer. *Am J Obstet Gynecol.* 1991;164:522–527.
32. Lambe M, Wuu J, Weiderpass E, Hsieh CC. Childbearing at older age and endometrial cancer risk (Sweden). *Cancer Causes Control.* 1999;10:43–49.
33. Brinton LA, Berman ML, Mortel R, et al. Reproductive, menstrual, and medical risk factors for endometrial cancer: results from a case-control study. *Am J Obstet Gynecol.* 1992;167:1317–1325.
34. Greggi S, Parazzini F, Paratore MP, et al. Risk factors for ovarian cancer in central Italy. *Gynecol Oncol.* 2000;79:50–54.
35. Adami HO, Hsieh CC, Lambe M, et al. Parity, age at first childbirth, and risk of ovarian cancer. *Lancet.* 1994;344:1250–1254.

36. Whiteman DC, Siskind V, Purdie DM, Green AC. Timing of pregnancy and the risk of epithelial ovarian cancer. *Cancer Epidemiol Biomarkers Prev.* 2003;12:42–46.

37. Whittemore AS, Harris R, Itnyre J. Characteristics relating to ovarian cancer risk: collaborative analysis of 12 US case-control studies. II. Invasive epithelial ovarian cancers in White women. Collaborative Ovarian Cancer Group. *Am J Epidemiol.* 1992;136:1184–1203.

38. Lund E. Mortality from ovarian cancer among women with many children. *Int J Epidemiol.* 1992;21:872–876.

39. Nandakumar A, Anantha N, Dhar M, et al. A case-control investigation on cancer of the ovary in Bangalore, India. *Int J Cancer.* 1995;63:361–365.

40. Hankinson SE, Colditz GA, Hunter DJ, et al. A prospective study of reproductive factors and risk of epithelial ovarian cancer. *Cancer.* 1995;76:284–290.

41. Riman T, Dickman PW, Nilsson S, et al. Risk factors for epithelial borderline ovarian tumors: results of a Swedish case-control study. *Gynecol Oncol.* 2001;83:575–585.

42. Kvale G, Heuch I, Nilssen S. Reproductive factors cancers of the breast and genital organs—are the different cancer sites similarly affected? *Cancer Detect Prev.* 1991;15:369–377.

43. Franceschi S. Reproductive factors and cancers of the breast, ovary and endometrium. *Eur J Cancer Clin Oncol.* 1989;25:1933–1943.

44. Fathalla MF. Incessant ovulation—a factor for ovarian neoplasia? *Lancet.* 1971;2:163.

45. Casagrande JT, Louie EW, Pike MC, Roy S, Ross RK, Hendersen BE. "Incessant ovulation" and ovarian cancer. *Lancet.* 1979;2:170–173.

46. Albrektsen G, Heuch I, Kvale G. Reproductive factors and incidence of epithelial ovarian cancer: a Norwegian prospective study. *Cancer Causes Control.* 1996;7:421–427.

47. Potter JD, McMichael AJ. Large bowel cancer in women in relation to reproductive and hormonal factors: a case-control study. *J Natl Cancer Inst.* 1983;71:703–709.

48. Howe GR, Craib KJ, Miller AB. Age at first pregnancy and risk of colorectal cancer: a case-control study. *J Natl Cancer Inst.* 1985;74:1155–1159.

49. Kune GA, Kune S, Watson LF. Children, age at first birth, and colorectal cancer risk: data from the Melbourne Colorectal Cancer Study. *Am J Epidemiol.* 1989;129:533–542.

50. Kvale G., Heuch I. Is the incidence of colorectal cancer related to reproduction? A prospective study of 63,000 women. *Int J Cancer.* 1991;47:390–395.

51. Troisi R, Schairer C, Chow WH, Schatzkin A, Brinton LA, Fraumeni JF Jr. Reproductive factors, oral contraceptive use, and risk of colorectal cancer. *Epidemiology.* 1997;8:75–79.

52. Negri E, La Vecchia C, Parazzini F, et al. Reproductive and menstrual factors and risk of colorectal cancer. *Cancer Res.* 1989;49:7158–7161.

53. Broeders MJ, Lambe M, Baron JA, Leon DA. History of childbearing and colorectal cancer risk in women aged less than 60: an analysis of Swedish routine registry data 1960–1984. *Int J Cancer.* 1996;66:170–175.

54. Chute CG, Willett WC, Colditz GA, Stampfer MJ, Rosner B, Speizer FE. A prospective study of reproductive history and exogenous estrogens on the risk of colorectal cancer in women. *Epidemiology.* 1991;2:201–207.

55. Marcus PM, Newcomb PA, Young T, Storer BE. The association of reproductive and menstrual characteristics and colon and rectal cancer risk in Wisconsin women. *Ann Epidemiol.* 1995;5:303–309.

56. Slattery ML, Mineau GP, Kerber RA. Reproductive factors and colon cancer: the influence of age, tumor site, and family history on risk (Utah, United States). *Cancer Causes Control.* 1995;6:332–338.

57. Talamini R, Franceschi S, Dal Maso L, et al. The influence of reproductive and hormonal factors on the risk of colon and rectal cancer in women. *Eur J Cancer.* 1998;34: 1070–1076.

58. Bjelke E. Colorectal cancer: clues from epidemiology. International Cancer Congress Series, 354, *Excerpta Med.* 1973;6.

59. McMichael JA, Potter JD. Reproduction, endogenous and exogenous sex hormones, and colon cancer: a review and hypothesis. *J Nat Cancer Inst.* 1980;65:1201–1207.

60. Peters RK, Pike MC, Chang WWL, Mack TM. Reproductive factors and colon cancers. *Br J Cancer.* 1990;61:741–748.

61. Cantor KP, Lynch CF, Johnson D. Reproductive factors and risk of brain, colon, and other malignancies in Iowa (United States). *Cancer Causes Control.* 1993;4:505–511.

62. Hatch EE, Linet MS, Zhang, J, et al. Reproductive and hormonal factors and risk of brain tumors in adult females. *Int J Cancer.* 2005;114:797–805.

63. Franceschi S, Fassina A, Talamini R, et al. The influence of reproductive and hormonal factors on thyroid cancer in women. *Rev Epidemiol Sante Pub.* 1990;38:27–34.

64. Negri E, Ron E, Franceschi S, et al. Risk factors for medullary thyroid carcinoma: a pooled analysis. *Cancer Causes Control.* 2002;13:365–372.

65. Kravdal O, Glattre E, Haldorsen. Positive correlation between parity and incidence of thyroid cancer: new evidence based on complete Norwegian birth cohorts. *Int J Cancer.* 1991;49:831–836.

66. Ji BT, Hatch MC, Chow WH, et al. Anthropometric and reproductive factors and the risk of pancreatic cancer: a case-control study in Shanghai, China. *Int J Cancer.* 1996; 66:432–437.

67. Fernandez E, La Vecchia C, D'Avanzo B, Negri E. Menstrual and reproductive factors and pancreatic cancer risk in women. *Int J Cancer.* 1995;62:11–14.

68. Skinner HG, Michael DS, Colditz GA, et al. Parity, reproductive factors, and the risk of pancreatic cancer in women. *Cancer Epidemiol Biomarkers Prev.* 2003;12:433–438.

69. Cantor KP, Lynch CF, Johnson D. Bladder cancer, parity, and age at first birth. *Cancer Causes Control.* 1992;3:57–62.

APPENDIX I

Classification of Selected Measures of Association and Statistical Tests According to Variable Type

Appropriate measures and statistical tests of association depend on the type of outcome and exposure variables under consideration. The health outcome variable of interest is a consequence or an end result. In reproductive epidemiology, the outcome variable indicates the status of a given health-related state or event; it reflects the presence of a particular adverse reproductive health outcome under investigation. The presence of the outcome may be measured on a nominal, ordinal, discrete, or continuous scale. In this appendix, a selected list of measures and tests of association are presented for various types of outcome and exposure data.

Appendix Ia

Outcome Data: Nominal With Two Categories (Dichotomous)

Exposure Variable	Measures of Association	Test Statistics
Continuous, normally distributed	Logistic regression	−2 Log L, AIC, SC* Wald chi-square
Continuous, not normally distributed, or ordinal with more than two categories	Logistic regression	−2 Log L, AIC, SC Wald chi-square
Nominal with more than categories (multichotomous)	Logistic regression Contingency table	2 Log L, AIC, SC Wald chi-square Pearson's chi-square Likelihood ratio test
Nominal with two categories (dichotomous)	Logistic regression Contingency table Risk ratio Rate ratio Odds ratio Prevalence proportion	2 Log L, AIC, SC Wald chi-square Paired data Sign test McNemar's test Confidence intervals Nonpaired data Fisher's exact test Pearson's chi-square test Likelihood ratio test Z for comparing two proportions Confidence intervals CMH stratified

*Akaike Information Criterion (AIC) and Schwarz Criterion (SC) are deviants of negative two times the Log-Likelihood (−2 Log L), where L stands for Likelihood.

Appendix Ib

Outcome Data: Nominal With More Than Two Categories (Multichotomous)

Exposure Variable	Measures of Association	Test Statistics
Continuous, normally distributed	ANOVA (treating the exposure as the dependent variable)	F test
Continuous, not normally distributed, or ordinal with more than categories		Kruskall-Wallis (treating the exposure as the dependent variable) Mantel-Haenszel chi-square (trend test), if ordinal exposure variable
Nominal with more than categories (multichotomous)	Contingency table	Pearson's chi-square test
Nominal with two categories (dichotomous)	Contingency table	Pearson's chi-square test

Appendix Ic

Outcome Data: Continuous, Not Normally Distributed, or Ordinal With More Than Two Categories

Exposure Variable	Measures of Association	Test Statistics
Continuous, normally distributed	Spearman rank correlation	T test
Continuous, not normally distributed, or ordinal with more than categories	Spearman rank correlation	T test Mantel-Haenszel chi-square (trend test), if ordinal outcome and exposure variables
Nominal with more than categories (multichotomous)		Kruskall-Wallis Mantel-Haenszel chi-square (trend test), if ordinal outcome variable
Nominal with two categories (dichotomous)	Polytomous logistic regression Rank ANOVA	−2 Log L, AIC, SC Wald chi-square CMH statistic Wilcoxon rank sum Mantel-Haenszel chi-square (trend test), if ordinal outcome and exposure variables

Appendix Id

Outcome Data: Continuous, Normally Distributed

Exposure Variable	Measures of Association	Test Statistics
Continuous, normally distributed	Correlation coefficient Linear regression	T test F test
Continuous, not normally distributed, or ordinal with more than categories	Spearman rank correlation	T test
Nominal with more than categories (multichotomous)	Analysis of variance	F test
Nominal with two categories (dichotomous)	Comparison of means	T test Wilcoxon rank sum test

APPENDIX II

Selected Reproductive Health Indicators

Some of the many health indicators commonly considered in reproductive epidemiology are presented here.

Reproductive Health Indicators

1. Antenatal care coverage (%)
2. Births attended by skilled health personnel (%)
3. Availability of basic essential obstetric care (per 500,000)
4. Availability of comprehensive essential obstetric care (per 500,000)
5. Low birth weight prevalence (%)
6. Perinatal mortality rate (per 1,000)
7. Maternal mortality ratio
8. Number of maternal deaths
9. Lifetime risk of maternal death (1 in)
10. Proportion of maternal deaths (%)
11. Total fertility rate
12. Prevalence of infertility in women (15–49) (%)
13. Contraceptive prevalence
14. Prevalence of positive syphilis serology in pregnant women (15–24) (%)
15. Reported incidence of urethritis in men (15–49) (%)
16. Proportion of adults (15–49) living with HIV/AIDS (%)
17. HIV prevalence in pregnant women (15–24) (%)

(continues)

Reproductive Health Indicators (*continued*)

18. Percentage of men/women aged 15–24 with comprehensive correct knowledge of HIV/AIDS
19. Reported prevalence of women with female genital mutilation (%)
20. Prevalence of anemia in women (15–49) (%)
21. Percentage of obstetric and gynecological admissions caused by abortion (%)

Socioeconomic and Demographic Indicators

1. Total population (× 1,000)
2. Population growth rate (%)
3. Urban population (%)
4. Gender ratio (males per 100 females)
5. Crude birth rate (per 1,000)
6. Crude death rate (per 1,000)
7. Fertility rate (per 1,000)
8. Infant mortality rate (per 1,000)
9. Neonatal morality rate (per 1,000)
10. Postneonatal mortality rate (per 1,000)
11. Perinatal mortality rate (per 1,000)
12. Fetal death rate (per 1,000)
13. Abortion rate (per 1,000)
14. Child mortality under 5 years, male (per 1,000)
15. Child mortality under 5 years, female (per 1,000)
16. Maternal mortality rate (per 100,000)
17. Life expectancy at birth, male (years)
18. Life expectancy at birth, female (years)
19. Net primary school enrollment rate, male (%)
20. Net primary school enrollment rate, female (%)

Sources: WHO. *Reproductive Health Indicators for Global Monitoring. Report of the Second Interagency Meeting.* Geneva, Switzerland: World Health Organization, 2001; WHO. *Reproductive Health Indicators: Guidelines for their generation, interpretation, and analysis for global monitoring.* Geneva, Switzerland: World Health Organization, 2006; WHO. Definition of indicators and data sources. Available at: http://www.who.int/reproductive_indicators/definitionofindicators.asp. Accessed December 5, 2008.

APPENDIX III

Maternal Health Consequences of Early Age at First Birth

Appendix IIIa

Maternal Physical Health Consequences of Early Age at First Birth

Reference	Study Design	Study Period	Geographic Area	Population	Age at First Birth
Pregnancy-related anemia					
Zhekova et al., 2001[10]	Case-control		Bulgaria	398 adolescent mothers up to 15 years of age and between 16 and 18 years of age. Control group included 398 mothers 20–24 years of age.	≤15, 16–18
Pal et al., 1997[12]	Case-control	June 1992 to July 1993	India	Department of obstetric and gynecology of Indira Gandhi Medical College, Shimla. Women less than or equal to 19 years of age who were pregnant. Control group not pregnant.	≤19
Pregnancy-induced hypertension					
Pal et al., 1997[12]	Case-control	June 1992 to July 1993	India	Department of obstetric and gynecology of Indira Gandhi Medical College, Shimla. Women less than or equal to 19 years of age who were pregnant. Control group not pregnant.	≤19

Preeclampsia

Study	Design	Years	Location	Description	Age
Zhekova et al., 2001[10]	Case-control		Bulgaria	398 adolescent mothers up to 15 years of age and between 16 and 18 years of age. Control group included 398 mothers 20–24 years of age.	≤15, 16–18
Bozkaya et al., 1996[11]	Case-control	1990–1994	Trabzon, Turkey	Adolescent women giving birth at the Department of Gynecology and Obstetrics of the Black Sea Technical University ($n = 562$). Control group formed from patients 20–30 years giving birth sequentially following the delivery of an adolescent mother ($n = 525$).	≤18

Cesarean section

Study	Design	Years	Location	Description	Age
Bozkaya et al., 1996[11]	Case-control	1990–1994	Trabzon, Turkey	Adolescent women giving birth at the Department of Gynecology and Obstetrics of the Black Sea Technical University ($n = 562$). Control group formed from patients 20–30 years giving birth sequentially following the delivery of an adolescent mother ($n = 525$).	≤18

(continues)

Maternal Physical Health Consequences of Early Age at First Birth (continued)

Reference	Study Design	Geographic Study Period	Area	Population	Age at First Birth
Intrauterine growth retardation					
Pal et al., 1997[12]	Case-control	June 1992 to July 1993	India	Department of obstetric and gynecology of Indira Gandhi Medical College, Shimla. Women less than or equal to 19 years of age who were pregnant. Control group not pregnant.	≤19
Mortality and long-term health problems					
Otterblad et al., 2004[8]		Followed up on women who died December 1, 1990, to December 31, 1995	Sweden	460,434 Swedish women who were born between 1950 and 1964	Thirteen percent were ≤19
Mirowsky, 2005[9]		1986 with 8-year mortality follow-up	United States	2,215 women ages 25–95 years drawn from 52 standard metropolitan statistical areas and 18 nonmetropolitan areas.	≥14

Rosenberg et al., 1995[15]	Case-control	1995	64,530 Black women ages 21–69 years. A total of 167 reported having coronary heart disease (cases) and were frequency matched on age with 509 controls.	≤19
Palmer et al., 1992[16]	Case-control	1986–1990	A total of 858 women ages 45–69 who had their first myocardial infarction (cases) were aged matched with controls from the same area of residence.	≤19
Beard et al., 1984[17]	Case-control	1960–1976	Cases included 169 women under the age of 60 who had been diagnosed with coronary heart disease.	≤19

Please note that the reference numbers in Appendix IIIa correspond to the references in Chapter 13.

Appendix IIIb
Maternal Mental Health Consequences of Early Age at First Birth

Reference	Study Design	Study Period	Geographic Area	Population	Age at First Birth
Depression					
Deal et al., 1998[22]	Cross-sectional	1988	United States	447 women 15–17 years old, 479 women 18–19 years old, and 870 adult women 25–34 years old. National Center for Health Statistics 1988 National Maternal and Infant Health Survey.	≤19
Kalil and Kunz, 2002[23]	Prospective cohort study	Initial = 1979–1980; follow-up = 1992	United States	990 married and unmarried teenage childbearers 14–16 years old. Follow-up 27–29 years old. National Longitudinal Survey of Youth.	≤19
Cox et al., 1987[24]		—	Great Britain	An urban working class sample of depressed mothers with 2-year-olds was compared with a control group of nondepressed mothers using	≤20

Study	Study design	Years	Location	Description	Age
Williams et al., 1997[25]	Prospective cohort study	1975–1994	New Zealand	maternal interviews, home observations, and developmental assessments of the children. 49 depressed and 27 controls. Women residents of Dunedin and their children who were all born at Queen Mary Hospital. Began with 1,037 children and 1,025 mothers.	≤20
Mirowsky et al., 2002[26]	Cross-sectional	1995	United States	2,592 U.S. adults 18–95 years old. Data collected in 1995 survey of aging, status, and the sense of control.	≤23
Depression, anxiety, and phobias					
Maughan and Lindelow, 1997[27]	Prospective cohort study	1946–1993	England, Scotland, and Wales	Two different cohorts were selected, 12 years apart, and followed. Teenage mothers. National Survey of Health and Development Study.	≤19

Please note that the reference numbers in Appendix IIIb correspond to the references in Chapter 13.

Appendix IIIc
Social Health Consequences of Early Age at First Birth

Reference	Study Design	Study Period	Geographic Area	Population	Age at First Birth
Isolation and Loneliness					
Cannon-Bonventre et al., 1979[28]	Cross-sectional		United States	100 Black, White, and Hispanic women 16 to 19 at delivery. Also interviewed service providers.	16–19
Educational Attainment					
Heck et al., 1997[29]	Cross-sectional	1969–1994	United States	Women who had first birth between 1969 and 1994 in 36 states. National Center for Health Statistics.	>15
Leadbeater, 1996[30]	Prospective longitudinal cohort study	1987–1991	United States	14–19 year olds with 3- to 4-week-old baby. 53.1% African American, 42% Puerto Rican.	14–19
Jones and Mondy, 1994[31]	Quasi-experimental		United States	African American, single, and younger than 18 years of age at the time of first birth. All participants were of low socioeconomic status.	≤18

Reference	Study design	Years	Country	Description	Age
Williams et al., 1997[25]	Prospective longitudinal cohort study	1975–1994	New Zealand	Women residents of Dunedin and their children who were all born at Queen Mary Hospital. Began with 1,037 children and 1,025 mothers.	≤20
Grindstaff et al., 2001[32]	Cross-sectional	1984	Canada	Canadian National Fertility Survey of 1984 ($N = 2,083$).	≤19
Furstenberg et al., 1987[33]	Longitudinal study	1966–1988	United States	404 primarily urban Black women who gave birth as adolescents in the middle to late 1960s.	≤18

Relationships

Reference	Study design	Years	Country	Description	Age
McCarthy and Menken, 1979[34]	Retrospective cohort study	1973	United States	National Survey of Family Growth. 9,797 women who were either ever-married or who were single and had at least one of their children living with them at the time of the survey.	≤19
Williams et al., 1997[25]	Prospective cohort study	1975–1994	New Zealand	Women residents of Dunedin and their children who were all born at Queen Mary Hospital. Began with 1,037 children and 1,025 mothers.	≤20

(continues)

Social Health Consequences of Early Age at First Birth (continued)

Reference	Study Design	Study Period	Geographic Area	Population	Age at First Birth
Maughan and Lindelow, 1997[27]	Prospective cohort study	1946–1993	England, Scotland, and Wales	National Survey of Health Development Study. Two different cohorts were selected, 12 years apart and followed. Teenage mothers.	≤19
Hobcraft and Kiernan, 2001[36]	Prospective cohort study	1958–1991	England	National Child Development Study. A longitudinal study of children born in March 1958.	≤22
Earning Potential					
Furstenberg et al., 1987[33]	Prospective cohort study	1966–1988	United States	404 primarily urban Black women who gave birth as adolescents in the middle to late 1960s.	≤18
Moore et al., 1979[35]	Prospective cohort study	NLS: 1968–1973 PSID: 1968–1978	United States	National Longitudinal Study (NLS) sampled 5,000 young women. Follow-up interviews were made annually. The Panel Study of Income Dynamics (PSID) interviews 5,000 families annually.	14–24

Please note that the reference numbers in Appendix IIIc correspond to the references in Chapter 13.

APPENDIX IV

Summary of Papers Examining the Potential Relation Between Early and Late Age at First Birth (AFB) and Cancer Risk

Appendix IV

Study, Year, and Reference Number	Study Design	Study Period	Geographic Area	Population	Age in Years	Risk Associated With Early AFB	Risk Associated With Late AFB
Breast Cancer							
Lagiou et al., 2003[9]	Case-control	Oct. 2001 to Dec. 2002	Athens, Greece	174 breast cancer, 116 benign breast disease; Caucasian	≥30	No	Yes
Madigan et al., 1995[10]	Cohort	1970s; follow-up through 1987	United States	7,508 NHANES I, NHEFS	25–74	Yes	Yes
Kampert et al., 1988[11]	Matched case-control	1970–1977	San Francisco Bay area, California, United States	1,884 breast cancer, 3,442 controls matched by age, time, and hospital	25–89	No	Yes
Lee et al., 2003[12]	Retrospective cohort	1975–1981, 1987	Rhode Island, United States	1,307 with full-term pregnancies divided into four age groups identified from Vital Statistics Records	≥40	No	Yes

Rosner et al., 1994[13]	Cohort	Began in 1976	United States	91,523 nurses (Nurses' Health Study)	30–55	No	Yes
Ramon et al., 1996[14]	Matched case-control	Nov. 1989 to Feb. 1992	Barcelona, Spain	184 breast cancer, 184 matched hospitalized controls, 184 community controls	≥30	No	Yes
Hinkula et al., 2001[15]	Population-based cohort	1974–1997	Finland	86,978 grand multiparous from the Population Register of Finland		No	Yes
Lord et al., 2008[16]	Case-control		Australia	1,457 breast cancer cases and 1,455 controls	≥30	No	Yes
Cervical Cancer							
La Vecchia et al., 1993[21]	Case-control	1983–1985	Milan, Italy	742 cervical cancer, 5,619 nonmalignant controls	<75	Yes	No
Kvale et al., 1988[22]	Cohort	1956–1959	Norway (Nord-Trondelag, Aust-Agder, and Vestold)	62,079 (342 cases of squamous cell cervical carcinoma)	32–74	Yes	No
Mogren et al., 2001[23]	Retrospective cohort	1955–1995	Sweden (Vasterbotten and Vasternorrland)	40,951 pregnancies resulting in delivery	14–73	Yes	No

(continues)

Appendix IV *(continued)*

Study, Year, and Reference Number	Study Design	Study Period	Geographic Area	Population	Age in Years	Risk Associated With Early AFB	Risk Associated With Late AFB
Guo et al., 1994[24]	Correlation	1973–1975	65 rural counties in China	Cervical cancer mortality rates correlated with ecologic data on diet, lifestyle, and biochemical markers from a nutritional survey	<65	Yes	No
Bjorge and Kravdal, 1996[25]	Retrospective cohort	1935–1971; follow-up through 1991	Norway	2,879 cervical cancer	20–56	Yes	No
Biswas et al., 1997[26]	Case-control	1990–1992	Bankura, India	134 histologically confirmed squamous cell carcinoma of the cervix, 134 controls (relatives and neighbors)	25–70	Yes	No
Parazzini et al., 1992[27]	Case-control	1981–1990	Northern Italy	366 cervical cancer, 323 controls	18–59	Marginally insignificant	No

Endometrial Cancer

Lochen and Lund, 1997[28]	Cohort	1970–1985	Norway	431,604 married, 752 corpus uterine deaths	45–74	Yes	No
Parslov et al., 2000[29]	Matched case-control	1987–1994	Denmark	237 endometrial cancer, 538 population controls	25–49	Yes	No
Hinkula et al., 2001[30]	Population based cohort	1974–1997	Finland	86,978 grand multiparous, 419 cases of endometrial cancer		Yes	No
Parazzinni et al., 1991[31]	Case-control	1983–1988	Milan, Italy	568 histologically confirmed endometrial cancer, 1,925 non-malignant hospital controls	28–74	No	No
Mogren et al., 2001[23]	Retrospective cohort	1955–1995	Sweden (Vasterbotten and Vasternorrland)	40,951 pregnancies resulting in delivery	14–73	No	Yes
Lambe et al., 1999[32]	Nested case-control	Women born 1925–1974	Sweden	4,839 endometrial cancer cases with concomitant fertility information 24,183 controls (for each case, five age-matched controls were randomly selected from a population-based fertility register)		Yes	No

(continues)

Appendix IV (continued)

Study, Year, and Reference Number	Study Design	Study Period	Geographic Area	Population	Age in Years	Risk Associated With Early AFB	Risk Associated With Late AFB
Brinton et al., 1992[33]	Case-control	Jun. 1987 to May 1990	United States	405 endometrial cancer, 297 population controls	20–74	No	No
Ovarian Cancer							
Mogren et al., 2001[22]	Retrospective cohort	1955–1995	Sweden (Vasterbotten and Vasternorrland)	40,951 pregnancies resulting in delivery	14–73	No	Yes
Greggi et al., 2000[34]	Case-control study	Jan. 1988 to Dec. 1998	Rome, Italy	440 epithelial ovarian cancer admitted to hospital; 868 controls admitted to same hospital for acute nongynecological, nonhormonal, and nonneoplastic conditions	13–80	No	Yes

Study	Study type	Years	Location	Cases/controls	Age		
Adami et al., 1994[35]	Nested case-control	Women born 1925–1960; follow-up through 1984	Sweden	3,486 ovarian cancer, 19,980 controls (for each case, 5 individually, age-matched controls were selected from the fertility register)	15–59	Yes	No
Whiteman et al., 2003[36]	Population-based case-control	Diagnosed in the 1990s	Australia (Queensland, New South Wales, and Victoria)	620 parous women ovarian cancer, 723 age-matched parous controls	18–79	Yes	No
Whittemore et al., 1992[37]	12 U.S. case-control studies	1956–1986	United States	2,197 invasive epithelial ovarian cancer, 8,983 controls; Caucasian		No	No
Lund, 1991[38]	Cohort	Married w/ children in 1970; follow-up through 1985	Norway	800,814	25–74	No	No
Nandakumar et al., 1995[39]	Case-control	1982–1985	Bangalore, India	97 ovarian cancer who were ever-married,		No	No

(*continues*)

Appendix IV *(continued)*

Study, Year, and Reference Number	Study Design	Study Period	Geographic Area	Population	Age in Years	Risk Associated With Early AFB	Risk Associated With Late AFB
				194 age-matched, ever-married controls in the same residential area (for each case, two controls according to 5-year age groups			
Hankinson et al., 1995[40]	Prospective cohort	1976–1988	United States	121,700 female registered nurses, 260 confirmed epithelial cancer cases (Nurses' Health Study)	30–55	No	No
Riman et al., 2001[41]	Case-control	Oct. 1993 to Dec. 1995	Sweden	193 epithelial borderline ovarian tumors, 3,899 randomly selected controls from a continuously updated population register	50–74	No	No

Kvale et al., 1991[42]	Prospective cohort	1956–1959; follow-up 1961–1980	Norway (Vestfold, Aust-Agder, and Nord-Trondelag)	60,565 women (471 cases of ovarian cancer) participating in a cancer screening program	27–69	No	No
Colorectal Cancer							
Potter and McMichael, 1983[47]	Community-based case-control	1979–1980	Adelaide, Australia	155 cancer cases (99 colon cancer, 56 rectal cancer), 311 gender- and age-matched controls (for each case, two controls)	30–74	No	Yes
Howe et al., 1985[48]	Matched case-control	1976–1978	Toronto & Calgary, Canada	229 cancer cases (158 ever-married colon cancer cases, 71 rectal cancer cases) 499 gender and age matched controls, plus or minus 5 years (168 neighborhood controls matched to colon cancer cases, 74 neighborhood controls matched to rectum cancer cases, 257 non-malignant hospital controls)		No	Yes

(continues)

Appendix IV *(continued)*

Study, Year, and Reference Number	Study Design	Study Period	Geographic Area	Population	Age in Years	Risk Associated With Early AFB	Risk Associated With Late AFB
Kune et al., 1989[49]	Matched case-control	Cancer diagnosis Apr. 1980 to Apr. 1981	Melbourne, Australia	675 colorectal cancer, 720 age-gender frequency-matched controls	≥25	No	Yes
Kvale and Heuch, 1991[50]	Population-based cohort	1956–1959	Norway (Vestfold, Aust-Agder, and Nord-Trondelag)	63,090 (581 colon cancer cases, 250 rectal cancer cases) participating in a screening program	32–74	No	No
Troisi et al., 1997[51]	Cohort	1973–1980; follow-up through 1990	United States	57,529 women (154 pathologically confirmed cases of colon cancer and 49 cases of rectal cancer) participating in a screening program	31–90	No	No

Study	Study type	Time period	Location	Population			
Negri et al., 1989[52]	Case-control	1985–1988	Northern Italy	432 cancer cases (279 colon cancer cases, 153 rectal cancer cases), 386 controls admitted to hospital for a wide spectrum of acute, non-neoplastic, nondigestive disorders	32–74	No	No
Broeders et al., 1996[53]	Nested case-control	1960–1984	Netherlands	1,415 colon cancer, 7,073 age-matched controls 733 rectal cancer, 3,665 age-matched controls	<60	No	No
Chute et al., 1991[54]	Cohort	No history of cancer in 1976; follow-up through 1984	United States	118,404 female registered nurses (191 colon cancer cases and 49 rectal cancer cases)		No	No
Brain Cancer							
Cantor et al., 1993[61]	Case-control	1986–1989	United States	169 brain cancer patients		Yes	No
Hatch et al., 2005[62]	Case-control	1994–1998	Phoenix, AZ, Boston, MA, Pittsburgh, PA	212 glioma, 151 meningioma 436 frequency-matched controls		No	

(continues)

Appendix IV *(continued)*

Study, Year, and Reference Number	Study Design	Study Period	Geographic Area	Population	Age in Years	Risk Associated With Early AFB	Risk Associated With Late AFB
Thyroid Cancer							
Franceschi et al., 1990[63]	Case-control	1986	Italy (provinces of Pordenone, Padua, Milan, and Pisa)	165 thyroid cancer, 214 hospital controls with nonmalignant, nonhormonal, non-gynecologic conditions	13–75	No	Yes
Negri et al., 2002[64]	Pooled analysis of 14 case-control studies	1974–1992	Europe, North America, and Asia	43 female medullary thyroid cancer, 215 gender, age, and study center matched controls (for each case, five controls were matched)		No	Yes
Kravdal et al., 1991[65]	Cohort	Born 1935–1969	Norway	976 thyroid cancer	15–54	No	No
Pancreatic Cancer							
Ji et al., 1996[66] control	Population based case-control	Oct. 1990 to Jun. 1993	Urban Shanghai, China	451 pancreatic cancer, 1,552 controls randomly selected permanent Shanghai	30–74	Yes	No

Fernandez et al., 1995[67]	Case-control	1983–1992	Greater Milan area, Italy	residents frequency-matched by age (5-year category) and gender 133 pancreatic cancer, 377 hospital controls admitted to hospital for acute, nonneoplastic, nondigestive, nonhormone-related disorders	<75	No	Yes
Skinner et al., 2003[68]	Cohort	1976–1998	United States	115,474 female nurses (243 confirmed incident pancreatic cancer cases; Nurses' Health Study)	30–55	No	No
Bladder Cancer							
Cantor et al., 1992[69]	Case-control	1986–1989	Iowa, United States	317 bladder cancer, population-based controls (frequency-matched by 5-year age groups)	40–85	Yes	No

Please note that the references in Appendix IV correspond to the references in Chapter 13.

APPENDIX V

Answers to Chapter Questions

Chapter 1

1.1 How does epidemiology enable the fulfillment of the three core public health functions presented in the outset of this chapter?

    (i)   Assessment and monitoring of health of populations at risk and identifying health problems and priorities. Descriptive epidemiology provides useful surveillance and assessment methods for identifying sudden changes in the occurrence and distribution of health-related states or events, for following long-term trends and patterns in health-related states or events, for identifying changes in risk factors, for identifying changes in risk behaviors and exposures, and for providing clues as to the causes of disease. Several reproductive health indicators are used in surveillance and assessment (see Chapter 5, "Descriptive Reproductive Health Indicators").

    (ii)   Formulation of policies and priorities designed to solve identified health problems. A list of information provided through epidemiology that is useful for formulating policies and priorities was given in the chapter. Before solving an identified health problem and properly allocating scarce health resources, the following information is needed, which can be attained through epidemiology: knowledge of

the risk factors associated with the problem, knowledge of individuals and populations at greatest risk, knowledge of the critical window of vulnerability, knowledge of where the problem is greatest, knowledge of the urgency with which the problem needs to be addressed, and knowledge of the efficacy and effectiveness of prevention and treatment programs.

(iii) *Ensuring that all populations have access to appropriate and cost-effective care, including prevention, protection, and health promotion services. Cost-effective health care is considered by many to be a basic human right. Minimizing inequity and providing cost-effective health care is a primary aim of many nations. Health education should be readily available on family planning, contraceptive safety and efficacy, maternal morbidity and mortality, perinatal and infant health, and sexually transmitted disease.*

1.2 Describe the primary purpose of reproductive epidemiology.

To provide information useful for improving reproductive health. Such information plays a vital role in reducing poverty, increasing economic growth and female productivity, lowering infertility, and improving maternal health and child survival. Both public health and individual decision making relies on epidemiologic information for making informed choices.

1.3 In this chapter we noted that epidemiology uses the scientific method. Explain.

Like the scientific method, epidemiology involves a collection of data through observation or experiment. Health problems are identified through observational studies. Hypotheses are formulated in an attempt to identify whether an association exists between a possible risk factor and an adverse health outcome, and study designs and statistical methods are used to evaluate the hypotheses.

1.4 How does reproductive epidemiology contribute to public health?

First, public health is concerned with the overall health of a community. In Question 1.1, we explained how epidemiology may contribute to the core areas of public health. More specifically, reproductive epidemiologic studies contribute to public health by: (1) identifying risk factors, (2) identifying individuals and populations at greatest risk, (3) providing an understanding of the critical window of vulnerability, (4) identifying where the public health problem is greatest, (5) monitoring the extent of the public health problem, (6) identifying the urgency with which the problem needs to be addressed, (7) evaluating the efficacy and effectiveness of prevention and treatment programs, and (8) providing information useful in family planning and healthcare management.

Chapter 2

2.1 Identify and discuss routes of human exposure in the environment.

Harmful substances in the outer environment enter the body through various routes. Exposure may occur through breathing in (inhalation), swallowing (ingestion), contact with skin, and intravenous routes. A substance is considered outside the body until it crosses cellular barriers in the gastrointestinal tract or lungs.

2.2 Give an example of each of the following environments and how each can affect reproductive health outcomes: physical, chemical, biological, and psychosocial.

An example of a physical environment is ionizing radiation, which is associated with increased risk of spontaneous abortion, congenital defects, and reduced sperm count. An example of a chemical environment is lead, which is associated with increased risk of low birth weight, neural tube defects, and reduced sperm count. An example of a biological environment is rubella (German measles), which is associated with an increased risk of low birth weight and birth defects. An example of a psychosocial environment is stress, which is associated with increased risk of preterm birth and spontaneous abortion.

2.3 Discuss the difference between the inner environment and the outer environment.

Harmful substances in the outer environment enter the body through various routes. A substance is considered outside the body until it crosses cellular barriers in the gastrointestinal tract or lungs, which consists of the inner environment. After a toxicant passes the lining of the skin, lungs, or gastrointestinal tract, it enters fluid surrounding the cells of that organ (interstitial fluid). A toxicant in the interstitial fluid can enter cells of local tissue, enter blood capillaries and the body's circulatory system, or enter the lymphatic system.

2.4 Discuss the difference between a teratogen and a genetic factor. Why would it be important to know the difference?

A teratogen is any environmental exposure (e.g., ionizing radiation, infections, drugs, and environmental chemicals) that may cause disturbance of the growth and development of an embryo or fetus, causing birth defects. Genetic refers to familial traits, genetically transmitted features, occurring among members of a family usually by heredity.

2.5 Describe the difference between the personal and the ambient environment, and give examples of both.

Personal environment refers to the environment in which we have control, such as our daily level of physical activity. On the other hand, the ambient environment refers to what a person has little or no control over such as air pollution.

2.6 Identify some of the high-risk occupations for environmental exposures, and discuss some of the precautions that can be taken to reduce risk.

There are numerous high-risk occupations (e.g., http://www.ctdol.state .ct.us/wgwkstnd/highrisk.htm). Occupations associated with reproductive problems involve prolonged standing, frequent heavy lifting and heavy physical work (high energy expenditure), and irregular work hours for women, and stress, exposure to radiation, chemicals, and biological factors for men and women.

2.7 Define and discuss three reproductive problems and identify a risk factor for each.

Low birth weight—a woman's exposure to CMV, HBV, HIV, German measles, chicken pox, heavy physical work, prolonged standing, lead, noise (>90 dBA), and ionizing radiation.

Reduced sperm count—a man's exposure to ionizing radiation, extreme heat, lead, glycol ethers, dibromopropane, pesticides, carbon sulfide, specific types of welding, long-term smoking, alcohol, and obesity.

Spontaneous abortion (miscarriage)—a woman's exposure to ionizing radiation, noise (>90 dBA), mercury, organic solvents, tetrachloroethylene, glycol ethers, dibromopropane, ethylene oxide, anesthetic gases, antineoplastic drugs, irregular work hours, stress, heavy physical work, frequent heavy lifting, prolonged standing, human parvovirus B19, and toxoplasmosis.

Chapter 3

3.1 Define research and discuss the basic elements of research that help transform ideas into concrete research operations.

Research is a scientific or scholarly investigation that aims to advance human knowledge. Prior to an analytic study investigation, the researcher develops a statement of the research problem and identifies appropriate variables, data, and hypotheses. These basic elements of research help transform ideas into concrete research operations.

3.2 Describe what a reproductive health problem is and the importance of a standard case definition in analyzing the problem.

A reproductive health problem is a disruption to the normal reproductive process. The problem is established through observed or measured phenomena. A case definition is a set of standard clinical criteria to determine the presence of a particular health-related state or event. A standard set of clinical criteria is necessary to ensure that cases are consistently diagnosed, regardless of where or when they are identified and who diagnosis the case. Whatever the criteria, it should be applied consistently and without bias to all those under investigation.

3.3 Identify a reproductive health issue and draft a research problem, research question, and research hypothesis for the issue.

3.4 Describe each of the four types of data: nominal, ordinal, discrete, and continuous.

The type of graphs, statistics, and statistical tests employed will depend on the type of data one has (see Table 3.1). Nominal data consist of unordered categories. Ordinal data consist of ordered categories. Discrete data consist of integers (whole numbers) in which the ordering and magnitude is important, and continuous data consist of numerical information measured on a continuum.

3.5 Define public health surveillance and its functions in reproductive health epidemiology.

Public health surveillance is the systematic ongoing collection, analysis, interpretation, and dissemination of health data. We monitor health-related states or events (1) to detect sudden changes in occurrence and distribution of health-related states or events, (2) to follow long-term trends and patterns in health-related states or events, (3) to identify changes in risk factors, and (4) to detect changes in health behaviors.

3.6 What are three common ways morbidity (incidence) is presented in the epidemiologic literature?

As ratios (risk ratio, rate ratio), as proportions (point prevalence, attributable proportion), and as rates (incidence rate, person-time rate).

3.7 Which measures provided in Question 3.6 involve a comparison group and thus allow us to test hypotheses about associations between exposure and outcome variables?

Risk ratio, rate ratio.

Chapter 4

4.1 Describe the difference between medical surveillance and public health surveillance, and identify some of the health-related states or events public health surveillance monitors.

Medical surveillance involves close observation of individuals who had been exposed to a communicable disease so that early symptoms could be detected and prompt isolation and control measures imposed. Public health surveillance is the systematic collection, collation, analysis, interpretation, and dissemination of health data. It provides a means for monitoring communicable diseases, injuries, birth defects, chronic diseases, and health behaviors. Public health surveillance is also used to monitor changes in environmental risk factors (physical, biological, chemical, or psychosocial), evaluate prevention and control programs, monitor long-term trends, plan future resource needs for prevention, and suggest topics for future research.

4.2 Explain why it is important for a surveillance program to define clear objectives.

Clear objectives help focus attention, resources, priorities, and efforts on meaningful outcomes. Clear objectives can help simplify the process, minimize cost, and maximize the value of the surveillance program.

4.3 Identify the 10 operational aspects of a surveillance system. Choose two aspects, and explain why each is important to include.

(1) A case definition of the health-related state or event, (2) specification of the population under surveillance, (3) specification of the time period of data collection, (4) specification of the information that will be collected, (5) details on the reporting sources or data sources,

(6) description of how the data will be handled, (7) description of how the data will be analyzed, (8) identification of those who will interpret the results, (9) description of who should be provided the results (e.g., medical and public health communities and policy makers), and (10) description of how the information will be disseminated.

Example Answers

(1) A case definition of the health-related state or event—a clear case definition, consistently applied, is necessary to avoid bias in your investigation.

(2) Specification of the population under surveillance—specification of the population under surveillance is required to monitor health-related states or events over time effectively and efficiently and to make comparisons between/among populations.

4.4   Describe each of the four categories of surveillance methods: active, passive, sentinel, and special systems surveillance (include benefits and limitations in the use of each).

Active surveillance occurs when the health department takes the initiative to contact public authorities through regular telephone calls or visits to laboratories, hospitals, and providers. The benefits are these: less prone to nonreporting or underreporting; tends to promote closer personal ties between health department staff and medical providers; a reasonable method to document a suspected outbreak, to validate the representativeness of passive reports, to improve completeness, and for targeting and eliminating a given health problem. The limitations are these: relatively expensive and is usually limited to short-term intensive investigation and control activities or seasonal problems.

Passive surveillance is the most common form of surveillance, relying on data collected from disease observations on an ad hoc basis. The benefits are these: relatively less expensive, less burdensome to health officials, and may provide useful information for identifying trends or outbreaks. The limitation is this: prone to nonreporting or underreporting.

Sentinel surveillance is when case data are collected from only part of the population in order to obtain information about the overall population, such as disease pattern. The benefits are these: less expensive than collecting data from the total population; may be higher quality than obtained through passive surveillance as it is often more logistically feasible to obtain higher quality data from a smaller population. The limitation is this: it may be difficult to obtain a representative subset of the total population.

Special systems surveillance is a surveillance system designed to generate information that is not possible to acquire through active, passive, or sentinel surveillance (e.g., diagnostic testing required to confirm case). The benefit is this: it may be only way to obtain information. The limitation is this: population at risk limited to only those tested.

4.5　Discuss cluster investigations, present the four-stage process, and discuss management issues, data, and statistical challenges associated with cluster investigations.

Cluster investigations are characterized by clusters with definable health outcomes, either new or rare; a suspected environmental cause; an unusual situation confirmed by statistical testing; and a short-term public health impact that is immediate and self-evident. The four stages of a cluster investigation include: initial contact and response, assessment, major feasibility study, and etiologic investigation. During the investigation, the public should be informed of the potential health problem, possible risks, and progress made along the course of the investigation. Cluster investigations where quality surveillance data are lacking may cause delays in the investigation, prevent the identification of trends, inhibit identifying a true cluster, limit being able to investigate a purported cluster, and prevent communication of important information to those who need to know. Statistical challenges often arise with cluster investigations because hypotheses are typically post hoc rather than a priori, "boundary shrinkage," and small numbers.

Chapter 5

5.1 Calculate the ASFR.

Age of Women	Estimated Females	Births	ASFR	ASFR × 5
15–19	10,611	442	42	208.27
20–24	10,680	1,081	101	506.09
25–29	10,545	1,182	112	560.46
30–34	10,092	950	94	470.67
35–39	10,076	499	50	247.62
40–44	10,500	105	10	50.00
45–49	11,430	7	1	3.06

ASFR: age-specific fertility rates

5.2 Calculate the TFR.

The sum of the last column presented in number 1 divided by 1,000 equals 2.05.

5.3 Calculate the maternal mortality rate given the following fictional information: The small nation of Iritaniba, population 4,500,000, reported 1,300,000 women of childbearing age, 136,000 live births, and 200 maternal deaths in 2001.

$$MMR = 200/136,000 \times 100,000 = 147 \text{ per } 100,000$$

5.4 Refer to the Human Development Report for the United States (http://hdrstats.undp.org/countries/data_sheets/cty_ds_USA.html). Identify the statistics involving CP and births attended by skilled health personnel, and then refer to these statistics for other countries. What is the general relationship?

In the United States, the contraceptive prevalence proportion (% of married women aged 15–49) from 1997–2005 was 76%. Only 10 of 177 countries reporting contraceptive prevalence had higher estimates. Births attended by skilled health personnel (%) from 1997–2005 was 99%. 38 of 177 countries reported 100%. The majority of countries were well below 99%.

5.5 Refer to the paper by Stanley K. Henshaw, Susheela Singh, and Taylor Haas. (Recent trends in abortion rates worldwide. *International Family Planning Perspectives* 1999;25(1). Available at: http://www.guttmacher

.org/pubs/journals/2504499.html.) What do the authors predict will cause a rapid fall in abortion rates in developed countries? Do the authors believe that legalization of abortion and access to abortion services will lead to an increased reliance on abortion for fertility control over the long run?

Because a range of contraceptive methods is becoming more widely available and effectively used. No.

5.6 Why might a country with a fertility rate of less than 2.1 continue to have an increase in its population?

High rates of immigration and/or an unusually large number of women of childbearing age compared with the number of old people.

5.7 If the TFR is below the replacement rate and assuming migration remains constant, will the population eventually fall, even if there is currently a high percentage of the population in the childbearing ages?

Yes. In a few decades, the population in the United States may begin to fall, as is presently occurring in Russia and Italy.

5.8 According to the article by Sonya Norris (http://dsp-psd.pwgsc.gc.ca/Collection-R/LoPBdP/EB-e/prb0032-e.pdf), can reproductive infertility be reversed? What are some treatments for reproductive infertility?

Yes. Hormonal treatment to induce ovulation; surgery to reverse infertility due to blocked or damaged fallopian tubes; artificial insemination; in vitro fertilization; gamete intrafallopian transfer; and surgically extracted sperm used in intracytoplasmic sperm injection.

Chapter 6

6.1 Describe the difference between observational and experimental studies.

All descriptive and analytic studies are observational except for the analytic experimental study. Here an intervention is assigned to some or all of the individuals in the study. In observational studies, the investigator merely observes and assesses variables and associations between variables.

6.2 Compare and contrast cross-sectional surveys and ecologic studies.

Cross-sectional: all variables are measured at a point in time; there is no distinction between potential risk factors and outcomes. Ecologic: aggregate data involved (i.e., no information is available for specific individuals). Prevalence of a potential risk factor compared with the rate of an outcome condition.

6.3 Compare and contrast case-control and cohort studies. Discuss the strengths and weaknesses of each.

The case-control study is backward-looking, beginning with identification of cases and controls, and then explores exposure status. Multiple potential exposures can be investigated. This study design is effective for chronic conditions in which a long latency period exists and where the outcome is rare. Cohort studies are forward looking. They begin by determining exposure status and then following the cohort into the future to see if the level of exposure influences one or more outcomes of interest. This study design is best when the exposure is rare. Cohort studies are best suited for studying acute diseases and conditions. Several outcomes can be associated with a given exposure, more so with greater time of follow-up (see Table 6-2 for a complete list of strengths and weaknesses for these designs).

6.4 Discuss the general steps for constructing a cross-sectional study, case-control study, and cohort study.

Cross-sectional study: select the sample; measure the variables.

Case-control study: select a sample of cases; select a sample of controls; measure the predictor (exposure) variable.

Prospective cohort study: assemble the cohort; measure predictor variables and potential confounders; follow up the cohort and measure outcomes.

Retrospective cohort study: identify a suitable cohort; collect data about predictor variables; collect data about subsequent outcomes.

6.5 Match the following:

a	Yields prevalence	a. Cross-sectional study
b	Unit of analysis the population	b. Ecologic study
a	Potential bias from low response rate	c. Case study
a	Not feasible for rare outcomes	
c	In-depth description	
b	Takes advantage of preexisting data	

6.6 Match the following:

b	Useful for identifying a time sequence of events	a. Case-control study
		b. Cohort study

a   Relatively less expensive

b   Several outcomes can be studied

b   Not feasible for rare outcomes

b   Not feasible for long latency periods

a   Useful for studying rare outcomes

b   Bias may result from loss to follow-up

a   Yields odds ratio

b   Yields incidence (risk), relative risk, attributable risk

a   Potential bias in measuring exposure variables

a   Prone to recall and interviewer bias

6.7 In a case-control study conducted in South Africa, 89 women with a child having a birth defect were identified (cases), and 178 women with a child without a birth defect were identified (controls). Among the cases, 53 women used agricultural chemicals (pesticides) during pregnancy. Among controls, 22 had used pesticides during pregnancy. Calculate an appropriate measure of association between pesticide use and birth defect. How might bias influence your result?
OR = 10.4. Perhaps those who have a child with a birth defect would better recall whether they used pesticides during their pregnancy. This would result in an overestimation of the true association.

Chapter 7

7.1 What are some challenges in obtaining valid exposure measurements, and how can these be overcome?
The quality of exposure data determines a study's validity. If there are problems with collecting data or defining the exposure, bias may result.

For example, exposures at different times in gestation may result in different outcomes, or a given exposure may equally result in one of several outcomes. Another challenge is assessing an exposure that occurred in the distant past.

7.2 What is the ideal study design for attempting to determine causality, and what makes it effective?

The ideal study design is the randomized, blinded, experimental control trial because confounding and bias are controlled for by randomization and blinding, respectively.

7.3 Describe two models that are used to describe causation.

The epidemiology triangle illustrates infectious disease causation. It shows the interaction and interdependence between agent, host, environment, and time. The agent, host, and environment are each affected by time and interact with each other in complex ways to produce adverse health outcomes, and thus, all three components must be considered when determining causation.

Rothman's causal pies model describes the multifactorial nature of causation for many health outcomes when the epidemiology triangle cannot. The factors that are causing health problems are represented as pieces of a pie, with the whole pie making up a sufficient cause for the problem. There can be more than one sufficient cause, each composed of multiple component causes, such as the host, agent, and environment.

Chapter 8

8.1 The human body requires certain types of nutrients to function properly. List these and describe their function.

Proteins *are required for the structure, function, and regulation of the body's cells, tissues, and organs. They are essential components of muscles, skin, and bones. Examples of proteins are enzymes, hormones, and antibodies.*

Dietary fats *are present in food (e.g., meat, meat products, dairy products, nuts, seeds, and avocados). Fat supplies energy and transports nutrients.*

Carbohydrates (e.g., sugars, starches, celluloses, and gums) serve as a major energy source in the human diet.

Insoluble fiber is plant fiber that the human digestive system cannot process; it does not break down as it goes through the human digestive tract. A diet high in fiber speeds up the transit through the digestive system, and soluble fiber can lower blood cholesterol levels.

Vitamins are organic substances found in food that are used by the body to regulate metabolism and maintain normal growth and functioning.

Minerals are the building blocks that make up muscles, tissues, and bones and are important to life-supporting systems. The following minerals play an important role in the human biological processes: potassium, chloride, sodium, calcium, phosphorous, magnesium, zinc iron manganese, copper, iodine, selenium, and molybdenum. Information about these minerals (RDA and bodily function) can be found elsewhere (http://en.wikipedia .org/wiki/Dietary_mineral#cite_note-lipp-0).

Water makes up most of a person's weight (i.e., approximately 70%). Water helps transport nutrients to cells, regulates body temperature, and rids the body of waste material.

8.2 Describe the effects of overweight and obesity on the reproductive health of women.

Overweight and obese women are more prone to experience amenorrhea, pregnancy complications, miscarriages, and birth defects compared with women of normal weight. Obese women are more than two and a half times as likely to have infertility problems, and fertility treatments are less successful for them. Obese women are more susceptible to polycystic ovary syndrome and have a greater risk for miscarriage. Women who are obese during pregnancy are at increased risk for type II gestational diabetes and hypertension disorders.

8.3 Describe the effects of overweight and obesity on the reproductive health of men.

Obesity in men is related to altered spermatogenesis, reduced sperm count and erectile dysfunction. Erectile dysfunction has been particularly associated with infertility.

8.4 Why is iron deficiency a serious concern?

Iron deficiency is the most prevalent form of malnutrition in the world. In general, iron deficiency is associated with anemia. Eighteen percent of maternal morbidity is contributed to iron deficiency. Pregnant women have an increased need for iron because the developing fetus draws iron from the mother to last through the first 6 months after birth. Iron deficiency during pregnancy may also lead to morbidity and premature birth to low birth weight babies.

Chapter 9

9.1 Explain the different forms of female sterilization. Include the benefits and risks of each.

Transabdominal surgical sterilization is also known as tubal litigation. It involves cutting (irreversible) or crimping (reversible) the fallopian tubes so that released eggs get stuck and cannot fertilize. Sterilization implants (Essure system) require minor abdominal surgery to implant small springs in the fallopian tubes. These cause the growth of scar tissue that prevents fertilization there. Both methods of sterilization prevent pregnancy and are associated with decreased risk of ovarian cancer. Neither method protects against sexually transmitted infection; both methods are associated with increased risk of ectopic pregnancy.

9.2 Explain the patterns of contraception use in India.

Indian women know about modern forms of contraception, but most do not practice it because of limited access due to cultural and social influences. After marriage, women are pressured to bear children quickly, and the men choose how frequently this happens. The male dominates the home life in India, and he may beat his wife for using birth control if he had not given her permission to do so. When families decide to stop having children, most women choose to be sterilized.

9.3 What region of the world has the lowest rate of contraceptive use? Why?

Latin America has the lowest rate of birth control use compared to any other region in the world because it has so many factors discouraging or preventing it. These include tradition, religion, and wealth. In areas where women are considered inferior to men, women have little or no say if contraceptives are used at all. The Catholic Church has a heavy influence in almost all Latin American countries, and it strongly dis-courages using any form of birth control. Poorer individuals in Latin America have more limited access to resources.

9.4 Describe the benefits and risks of IUDs.

An IUD is an effective and reversible form of birth control because it can be removed at anytime. It lasts for 3 to 10 years when inserted by a trained professional. IUD risks include unexpected expulsion, menstrual irregularities, perforation of uterus, and increased risk of ectopic pregnancy, among other things. IUDs do not protect against sexually transmitted infections. They initially cost hundreds of dollars and are available only by prescription.

Chapter 10

10.1 Describe the effects that lead exposure has on male fertility and female reproduction ability.

Research has shown that lead exposure decreases male sperm count. The risks for spontaneous abortion, stillbirths, and premature births are increased with increased levels of occupational lead exposure in pregnant women.

10.2 What types of fish most commonly contain high levels of methylmercury? What is the risk posed to Americans by eating them?

Fish absorb the mercury that accumulates in bodies of water. Large, older fish, including whales, sharks, swordfish, and King Mackerels, tend to contain the highest levels of mercury. Studies have shown a link between pregnant women's fish consumption and neuropsychological problems for their children later in life, as well as harm to the developing fetus during the pregnancy. Consumers need to be aware of the health hazards posed by mercury-containing fish, because even though the Food and Drug Administration regulates imports of all fish, it cannot control individual consumption patterns.

10.3 Explain the risk that hormone disruptors have on human health.

Environmental estrogens (xenoestrogens) are hormone disruptors. They interfere with the normal functioning of the body's endocrine system by binding to its hormone receptor sites and causing unnatural reactions. These reactions may include increasing the levels of natural estrogen production or altering the way in which natural hormones are metabolized. Mothers can pass on these environmental estrogens through breast milk.

In males, xenoestrogen exposure can cause decreased sperm counts, and in females, the risk for ectopic pregnancies is increased.

10.4 What are PCBs, and how have they been shown to affect reproductive health?

***Polychlorinated biphenyls** (PCBs) are mixtures of up to 209 chlorinated compounds. There are no known natural sources of PCBs. PCBs can adversely affect reproduction and fertility, birth, or development. In utero exposure to environmental levels of PCBs is associated with lower birth weight and smaller head circumference. In utero exposure to environmental levels of PCBs has also been associated with poorer cognitive functioning in young children. Spontaneous abortion and pregnancy loss are also significantly associated with maternal exposure to PCBs. PCBs have not been shown to adversely affect male fertility or the female menstrual cycle.*

Chapter 11

11.1 Explain the four types of female genital cutting.

Type I involves the removal (total or partial) of the clitoris or prepuce. Type II is the partial or total removal of the clitoris and labia minora. Type III involves the narrowing and sealing of the vaginal opening by cutting and positioning the labia minora and/or the labia majora. Type IV includes all other harmful, nonmedical procedures that disfigure the female genitalia.

11.2 Explain the opposing viewpoints of supporters and critics of the 1973 *Roe vs. Wade* decision.

Those who support the Roe vs. Wade *decision believe in a woman's right to choose whether to abort her pregnancy. Proponents commonly believe that prohibiting abortion is an invasion of privacy and that abortion is necessary, in some instances, in order to protect the health of the mother.*

Critics of legalized abortion generally base their belief on moral and ethical considerations that the unborn child has a right to live, regardless of what the mother wants.

11.3 What factors have been shown to be elements of a woman's coping strategy when dealing with abortion?

The impact of abortion on a woman's physical and mental health is still being studied, but research suggests that certain nonquantifiable personality characteristics and qualities (i.e., self-esteem and optimism) play a key role in her ability to cope with social and mental stresses.

Possible future effects on the female's physical health and fertility may also contribute to her psychological stress.

11.4 What are the health effects of teenage pregnancy on the mother?

One study shows that pregnancy puts teen mothers at higher risk for developing anemia, preeclampsia, and maternal mortality. Pregnant teenagers also experience higher rates of depression. Pregnant teenagers have experienced lower rates of emergency and elective caesarean section compared with all other mothers.

11.5 Describe the evidence for the protective and selective effects of marriage on women's health.

Within the United States, some limited research suggests that being married leads to better overall health. Married women seem to have better overall health than unemployed, unmarried women. Married persons also have lower suicide rates than all others.

To a limited degree, women who are in better physical health have also been shown to marry more often than those with poorer health. Women who experience divorce or separation tend to have better health than those who never marry at all in the short-term. In the long-term, however, divorced and separated women experience similar health as those who never marry.

Chapter 12

12.1 Identify and discuss complications to both mother and infant due to a young age of a mother at first birth.

Maternal—greater risk or death during childbirth; higher numbers of complications such as anemia, pregnancy-induced hypertension, intrauterine growth retardation, premature rupture of the membranes, preeclampsia, and preterm labor, as compared with older mothers; increased maternal cervical and endometrial cancer risk has been associated with early maternal age at first birth.

Infant—developmental problems and long-term disability; low birth weight; death; less likely to be immunized or breast fed, receive regular medical care, and are more likely to be overfed or underfed.

12.2   Discuss the mental health complications to mother and others due to a young age at first birth.

Early age at first birth is associated with feelings of loneliness, isolation, and depression. Becoming a parent at an early age and leaving school erodes emotional well-being.

12.3   Identify factors associated with social health consequences of young age at first birth, and discuss the various implications of these factors.

Early age at first birth may result from lower educational attainment, but the lower education may also contribute to an early age at first birth. Education is directly associated with health. Isolation and loneliness that may result from an early age at first birth can adversely affect health. An early age at first birth can also adversely affect relationships and earning potential, which in turn adversely affects health.

12.4   Identify one example from within the chapter, and describe epidemiologically how we know that mothers who were young at first birth are at higher risk for that specific complication/consequence.

In a cohort study of 807 women conducted in New Zealand beginning in 1975, 8.2% of the women who had their first baby before the age of 21 years initially reported being separated from the father of the child compared with 6.4% of the women who had their first child after the age of 21 years.

12.5   Discuss some of the cultural differences associated with those at risk for being young at first birth (i.e., factors unique among Blacks, Hispanics, and Whites).

Early age at first birth among Blacks is associated with having more siblings, being raised by single parents, and having early menstruation. For Hispanic women, early age at first birth is also associated with being raised by single parents, whereas for Whites, early childbearing is associated with coming from a large family. Family background appears to play a more significant role among Blacks than Whites in determining age at first birth, whereas circumstances of poverty contribute to increased risk of adolescent pregnancy among all racial/ethnic groups.

Chapter 13

13.1 Discuss the various definitions for young age at first birth, why there are different definitions, and which one you would establish as a standard.

In general, there is a lack of consistency among public health organizations in defining "young" and "old" age at first birth. Some define early adolescent childbearing as all females giving birth at age 15 or younger. The basis of this definition stems from better birth outcomes when the maternal age was 16 and older. National vital statistics information categorizes maternal age into the following age groups: 10 to 14, 15 to 17, 18 to 19, 20 to 24, 25 to 29, 30 to 34, and 35 to 44. Studies focusing mainly on the risks of teenage childbearing typically define teenage mothers as females between the ages of 15 and 19 and may be broken down as ages 15 to 17 years and ages 18 to 19 years.

13.2 Discuss the connection between breast cancer and age at first birth.

The relationship between maternal age at first full-term birth and breast cancer risk is consistent across several studies. Research indicates that older age at first birth is directly related to increased breast cancer risk. Roughly 30% of breast cancer cases in U.S. women were attributed to later age at first birth and/or nulliparity. In one study, the only variable that discriminated breast cancer from benign breast disease was early age at first birth.

13.3 Select one of the two prominent hypotheses of the causal mechanisms of breast cancer, and discuss how maternal age at first birth could influence the mechanism.

One study believes that hormonal changes in early pregnancy result in molecular changes that stabilize p53, a tumor suppressor gene that promotes cell cycle arrest. With p53 stabilized, it remains functionally active longer to repair cumulative DNA damage and to prevent cellular proliferation induced by carcinogens.

13.4 Select one of the cancers discussed in the chapter (other than breast cancer). Discuss the association between the cancer and age at first birth. Interpret the findings from the literature, what the findings tell us, and how significant those findings are.

Research has indicated that high parity and delayed childbearing may reduce death associated with endometrial cancer. Some authors have suggested that childbirth provides a protective effect by promoting the mechanical shedding of cells in the endometrial lining that may have undergone a malignant transformation, where these cells tend to increase with age. Endometrial cancer is considered a hormone-dependent cancer. Long-term unopposed exposure to endogenous estrogen, decreased progesterone secretion, and anovulatory cycles are believed to result in malignant changes in the endometrium. Unopposed estrogen (estrogen exposure without progesterone) promotes an increased rate of endometrial cell division and potential carcinogenic changes. The endometrial layer of the uterus is continually exposed to high levels of estrogen. During pregnancy when progesterone production is high, it reduces the length of time that the endometrium is exposed to estrogen alone. This may explain the increased risk of endometrial cancer among nulliparous women. In addition, infertility contributes to an increased risk for endometrial cancer secondary to exposure to exogenous estrogen among women receiving hormone replacement therapy for either infertility or for premenopausal symptoms.

13.5 Select an article from the table presented in Appendix IV, and discuss the findings in context of age at first birth and cancer risk.

INDEX

Figures and tables are indicated by f and t following the page number.